RICH MAN,
POOR MAN

RICH MAN,
POOR MAN

HERMAN P. MILLER

THOMAS Y. CROWELL COMPANY

ESTABLISHED 1834   NEW YORK

Designed by Abigail Moseley
Manufactured in the United States of America
L.C. Card 75-127609
ISBN 0-690-70039-3

1 2 3 4 5 6 7 8 9 10

For
Elaine, June, and Judi

Contents

Preface

The first edition of this book was published early in 1964. That was not so long ago, yet so much has happened—the war in Vietnam and the domestic war on poverty, the peace movement, the riots in the cities, the student rebellions, and now the growing awareness that unless we change our ways, we will destroy the only world we will ever have. In seven short years many of the statistics in the first edition have become obsolete and many new types of statistics have become available. Only Chapter III and Appendix A could be used without change from the first edition. Most of the other chapters have been completely rewritten, and several new chapters have been added. I had originally planned to await the 1970 census results before undertaking a revision. The more I thought about the matter, however, the less important it seemed to wait. The chief virtue of the decennial census is that it provides local area data. We are concerned here with national problems and with national trends, which can be accurately measured by the monthly sample survey of 50,000 households conducted by the Bureau of the Census. So why wait, especially when the need for current information is so great?

In preparing the first edition, I assumed without question that "richer is better." Now I am not so sure. Many people today are asking, "Riches for what?" That question led to a new first chapter bearing that title, and a new concluding chapter which examines the relationships between population growth, rising incomes, and pollution. Chapter II has been updated and expanded, with a new section on who pays the taxes as well as estimates of the net gain or loss to each income class resulting from paying taxes to the government and deriving benefits from expenditures by the government.

Chapter V on the Negro, Chapter VII on poverty, and Chapter IX on the rich have been vastly expanded and bear little resemblance to the scanty materials on these subjects included in the first edition. Chapter VIII, "Help for the Poor," is entirely new.

New statistics on the annual and lifetime earnings of women in relation to education have been added to Chapter X as well as a considerable amount of new information on the characteristics of college students.

Chapter XI, "It's the Job That Counts," has been updated and supplemented with new figures on occupational mobility and occupational prestige. A statistical appendix has been added showing projections to 1985 of population, families, births, deaths, age distribution, school enrollment, income distribution, expenditure patterns, and miscellaneous other facts which may be useful for many purposes. Appendix B, "Tools of Income Distribution Analysis," explains the Pareto Curve, Lorenz Curve, and Gini Index of Concentration and describes the methods used to estimate aggregates, to compute the income shares received by each fifth of the total number of families, and to make projections, as well as other techniques employed in the analysis of income data. It is primarily intended for classroom use. The techniques are quite simple and the explanations provided may also be of interest to the general reader.

This book is the product of nearly a quarter of a century of work at the Census Bureau. I still remember the day I first applied for a job at the bureau back in February 1946. I was a young man then, still in my army uniform.

The bus approached Suitland, Maryland—a small suburb about twelve miles southeast of Washington, D.C. There, rising out of the rolling Maryland countryside like a cement shoebox, was Federal Office Building No. 3. That building, along with a temporary wartime housing project, spoiled the rural setting—small farms, a frame schoolhouse, a general store, several other small retail establishments, and lots of open space. I was to learn later that the government had great plans for Suitland. It was going to become a model place in which to work and play near the nation's capital—complete with golf course, swimming pool, tennis courts, and wooded areas for picnicking. It never happened. The once rural town of Suitland is now just an extension of the urban sprawl that surrounds so many American cities. It has more than its share of filling stations, hamburger stands, and shopping centers. The temporary housing project has been replaced by four permanent government buildings to house the Weather Bureau, the Navy Oceanographic Office, and a Federal Records Center. What little land is left is used for parking cars. And the inside of FOB No. 3 matches the outside. Thousands of dollars have been spent to beautify the place and make it more livable, but what can you really do with a building that was constructed as a warehouse for government records in 1942 and was hastily converted to house the Census Bureau staff that had mushroomed during World War II.

Despite the drabness, the Census Bureau is a truly remarkable place— a place where lively people come together every day to learn more about the society in which they live and to provide the leaders of government with the information they need. Some of the nation's leading statisticians, mathematicians, economists, and sociologists have worked here and some still do. Major advances in the application of scientific sampling to human populations were made here. UNIVAC I, the first computer ever designed for large-scale data processing, was installed here; it is now in the Smithsonian. The bureau is the acknowledged leader throughout the world in the art of census-taking; and thousands of statisticians in countries all over the world received their training here. The bureau has been a place of great intellectual ferment for many years—and the end is nowhere in sight.

Such is the world in which this book was nurtured. It is a good world—an honest world—and I hope it stays that way.

So many friends and colleagues have been of help over the years that it is hard to know where to start mentioning names and where to end. Conrad Taeuber has been more like an understanding uncle than a boss. He has always given me encouragement and freedom; he has said "no" only on those rare occasions when his experience and wisdom foresaw harm. Dick Hornseth has been a perennial sounding board for ideas. His magic touch with the computer has made it possible to launch many projects that would otherwise have been impossible. My luncheons with Joe Waksberg, Danny Levine, Meyer Zitter, and those other hardies who manage to survive the food in the "Executive Dining Room" have been a constant source of pleasure and information. I could not possibly omit my car pool in listing acknowledgments because all of my ideas were tried on them, if the idea had first survived my wife's

PREFACE

criticism. Members of my staff in the Population Division have also been most helpful. I cannot name them all, but I would be derelict if I did not thank Helen Collins, Mary Henson, Roger Herriot, Charles Johnson, Emmet Spiers, and Arno Winard.

My wise and good friend, Sar Levitan, read the entire manuscript. He helped me avoid some serious errors.

My wife, Elaine, as always, listened patiently and forced me to keep it simple and short. My daughter, Judi, who served as a proofreader for the first edition of this book, is now a college student and ranks as a full-fledged contributor to this edition. It was her influence that led to the new first chapter, "Riches for What?" and the general exploration of the interrelationship between population growth, pollution, and affluence.

Silver Spring, Maryland

RICH MAN,
POOR MAN

I

Riches for What?

For thirty years I have been trying to explain to people what an economic statistician does. Almost everyone is familiar with the work of doctors, dentists, lawyers, and accountants. In many circles, a mother referring to "my son, the doctor" immediately establishes her son—and herself—as a person to respect. But what is there to say about "my son, the economic statistician"? Nothing, because most people don't even know what that is.

After years of trying, I am beginning to make some headway. This progress has come generally from the subject matter of this book—income distribution.

Now there is a term to contend with! Income distribution. It means different things to different people. You can tell from the sound of the words that it deals with who gets what. Using the universal language of poetry, Carl Sandburg sums up one of the central problems of income distribution in *The People, Yes:*

"So, you want to divide all the money there is
and give every man his share?"
"That's it. Put it all in one big pile and split
it even for everybody."
"And the land, the gold, silver, oil, copper, you want
that divided up?"
"Sure—an even whack for all of us."
"Do you mean that to go for horses and cows?"
"Sure—why not?"

"And how about pigs?"

"Oh to hell with you—you know I got a couple of pigs."

No doubt Sandburg would have been willing to share his "pigs" with others, but he did not believe the rest of us felt that way—and we probably didn't at the time. But there is a new wind ablowin' across this land and many of us are feeling, thinking, and saying things we never did before. The Gallup Poll conducted in January 1969 showed that four out of every five Americans favored a proposal that would guarantee enough work to provide each family with an employable wage earner with an income of $3,200 a year.[1] Perhaps the best indication of the change in attitude is the fact that a Republican President has submitted to Congress a detailed plan for a guaranteed minimum income of $1,600 for a family of four.[2]

During the past few years the eradication of hunger and the alleviation of poverty has become *a* major issue in American politics and *the* major issue among our young. To want to eliminate poverty means to care about others—to be willing to share our "pigs" even when we have them.

One of the basic tenets of American life is that richer is better. We have long prided ourselves on our high gross national product (GNP) and the rapid rate at which it grows. But many people are now beginning to ask some embarrassing questions about the GNP—which is the total value of goods and services produced each year. Many are now asking, "riches for what?" Thus, for example, Professor Richard A. Falk of Princeton University stated at a Congressional hearing on the effects of population growth on natural resources and the environment that "we have tended to become [so] convinced that the health and progress of our society, and of world society for that matter, is directly and uncritically correlated with the expansion in the gross national product that we lose sight of the fact that such an index of 'development' may, after a certain level, serve more as a sign of societal deterioration than improvement."[3] He goes on to add that "if the United States were to double its GNP, I would think it would be a much less livable society than it is today."[4]

This feeling is understandable and even to be expected in an affluent society which has experienced steadily rising income per capita for a quarter of a century. As more and more of our primary wants for food, shelter, clothing, medical care, and steady employment are met, our thoughts turn to the gratification of secondary wants such as beauty, recreation, and "the quality of life" generally. Increasingly, we find that communities which were once economically poor and were anxious to attract industry have now become economically affluent and are beginning to complain about some of the undesirable consequences of industrialization. It is safe to say that if unemployment and lack of income once again became serious problems in these communities, they would soon forget about "the quality of life" and begin to seek ways in which to increase their income.

We cannot turn our backs on a high and rising GNP. Having once enjoyed the pleasures of affluence, we are not likely to give them up voluntarily. The goal must be to use our affluence in such a way as to minimize the harmful effects and improve the quality of our lives, not destroy it. It can be done if only we learn to pay the full price for the things we do and not just the market price. There is something wrong with an accounting system which does not count, as a cost of producing or using products, the destruction of the environment caused by such activity. The challenge of using affluence constructively in a dynamic economy has been summed up very well by Dr. Roger Revelle, director for the Center of Population Studies of Harvard University: "In the past our growing affluence has led to environmental destruction. In the future . . . our growing affluence can give us far greater opportunities to perceive and protect the quality of life and the diversity, beauty and wonder of our land. As long as we were preoccupied with the struggle for existence we could give little thought and less energy to cherishing our surroundings. Now the situation has radically changed. For the good of our own bodies and souls we need to assume new responsibilities. . . ."[5]

We seem to be getting richer and richer in the number of things we own and poorer and poorer in our ability to enjoy them. The increase in our private wealth is matched by the growth in public misery—crime, filth, pollution, and congestion. Several years ago the Harvard economist John Kenneth Galbraith raised a very pertinent question before a Congressional committee. What advantage, he asked, is there "in having a few more dollars to spend if the air is too dirty to breathe, the water is too polluted to drink, the commuters are losing the struggle to get in and out of our cities, the streets are filthy and the schools are so bad that the young, perhaps wisely, stay away, and hoodlums roll citizens for some of the dollars they saved in taxes." President Richard M. Nixon raised the same question in his first State of the Union message. He said:

> The decade of the sixties was also a period of great growth economically. But, in that same ten-year period we witnessed the greatest growth of crime, the greatest increase in inflation and the greatest social unrest in America in a hundred years. Never has a nation seemed to have had more and enjoyed it less.

That last sentence of the quotation from the President's State of the Union message is one that all Americans should take to heart—"Never has a nation seemed to have had more and enjoyed it less." Lord Carlisle noticed the same characteristic about Americans when he visited this country in 1841. He wrote then that the United States was "probably the country in which there was less misery and less happiness than in any other of the world."[6] Evidently, for many Americans, riches have not brought happiness.

There is no question that private riches are increasing and are likely to continue to rise. Incomes as measured in dollars of constant purchasing power will nearly double during the next fifteen years if they keep growing at the same rate as during the past fifteen years. By 1985 half the families will have incomes over $15,000 in terms of 1970 purchasing power; the proportion would be much larger if allowance were made for inflation. What will this income be used for? No one can say for sure, but it seems likely that we will continue the patterns of the past. The increased affluence will probably be used to buy more expensive homes and rent more luxurious apartments, all loaded with the latest gadgets. There will be many more swimming pools in backyards, heated where necessary, and homes with three and four cars will perhaps be as common as two cars today. Increased funds and more leisure time, resulting in part from the increase in the number of three-day weekends now being legislated in many states, will undoubtedly result in a vast rise in expenditures for travel and other types of recreation. All of these activities will undoubtedly bring a great deal of satisfaction to the individual families that partake of them, but they will also intensify many of the domestic problems we now have. Pollution, traffic jams, overcrowded colleges, and many other problems are associated in many minds with population growth and, to some extent, they are. But what many people fail to realize is that rising incomes also add to our woes, perhaps even more than population growth. This conclusion can be demonstrated with a simple numerical example.

In 1968 there were 64,300,000 families and unrelated individuals

(i.e., persons living alone), with an average income of $8,454. Aggregate income in that year was $544 billion. This amount is represented by box A in Table I-1. If the trends of recent years continue, there will be 85,900,000 families and unrelated individuals in 1985, with an average income of $14,865 as measured in dollars of constant purchasing power. Aggregate income in that year would be $1,277 billion, representing an increase of $733 billion since 1968. Three components of this increase can be separately identified. If there were no change in average income and only the number of families increased, aggregate income would grow by $183 billion, as shown in box B. If the number of families remained the same and only the average income per family increased, aggregate income would rise by $412 billion, as shown by box C. And finally, box D shows the expected growth in aggregate income ($139 billion) attributable to the fact that both the number of families and average income per family will be rising. On this basis, we could conclude that 56 percent of the increase is attributable to economic growth (the rise in average income per family), 25 percent to population growth, and 19 percent to the combined effects of the growth in population and the growth in income. The analysis can be carried one step further if we assume that box D can be distributed proportionately between boxes B and C. When this is done, we arrive at the conclusion that 69 percent of the expected increase in aggregate income is due to economic growth and 31 percent to population growth. It can be demonstrated, using the same technique, that by 1985 four-fifths of the expected increase in expenditures for housing and for personal and medical care, and two-thirds of the expected increase for transportation and for household operations and furnishings will be attributable to economic growth.

This analysis leads to the conclusion that the great bulk of the rise in expenditures for goods and services—and the concomitant increase in pollution, transportation, and other problems accompanying it—would take place even if our population stopped growing tomorrow but continued to increase its income and to spend its money in the same old way. But we do not have to continue in the same old way. There are alternatives. We can decide, through our elected officials, to use more of our income to meet more of our social needs. We cannot buy fresh air or pure water on our own. We cannot buy better jails on our own. They can be obtained only if we are willing to pay the cost of making the improvements. Some of the cost may come in the form of higher prices and some in the form of higher taxes. It is possible to reduce the smog

TABLE I-1

Components of Increase in
Aggregate Income: 1968-1985

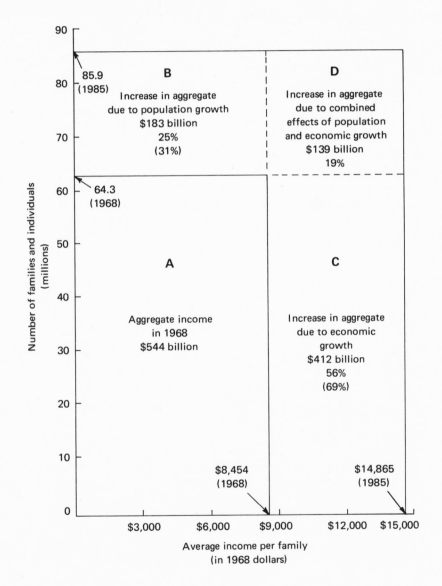

resulting from the exhausts of automobiles and jet planes. We can insist upon better methods of disposing of industrial waste. We know how to reduce some of the brutalizing aspects of prison life. We can provide more reasonable minimum incomes for all families and thereby reduce some of the social problems associated with poverty. We can do all of these things, but they will cost a great deal of money. According to experts at the Organization for Economic Cooperation and Development, it would take a continuing outlay of 2 percent of the gross national product—or about $20 billion in the United States in 1970—just to ensure that environmental deterioration were gradual rather than rapid. About 4 percent of the GNP would be required to hold the line; and actively cleaning up past pollution and preventing future pollution would cost three to four times as much.[7] The OECD experts expressed the fear that public support for anti-pollution programs would diminish, once "the high cost of remedial action and its controversial implications for economic growth" became known.

There can be little doubt that we will grow richer as a nation and that our incomes will be widely distributed. But no matter how rich we become, we do not have the resources to deal with the problems that are destroying the quality of our life unless we change our ways. Reducing fertility would help some, but it is only a partial answer. What we need is a national commitment to use our growing affluence to attack our domestic problems. Nothing less will do. The choice is ours. If we choose to spend our money on wars, our ability to deal with domestic problems will be seriously impaired. If we choose to invest in space exploration, we may solve all the mysteries of the universe and remain ignorant about man himself. If we choose to give ourselves tax cuts, we will spend the money on things we can buy—more material goods—which will intensify many of our problems. If we choose to spend more of our money for public services, we may buy pure air and water, cleaner and more efficient transportation systems, better schools, the elimination of hunger and reduction of poverty.

Which will we choose? There can be little doubt, based on past experience. Until conditions grow much worse than they are, we will probably move farther out into the suburbs where we will need more roads, more sewers, more expensive homes, more cars—and more vacations to get away from the headaches we will have made. In England, for example, the fight against air pollution began as a direct result of the disastrous smog that hit London in December 1952, lasting for three days and killing about 4,000 sufferers from bronchial and cardiac illness. This event led to the Clean Air Act of 1956, which brought the gradual creation of smoke-control areas across the United Kingdom. It will probably take a similar catastrophe to produce similar legislation in the United States. We are likely to opt for more private goods and services, while our social needs will continue to lag. Perhaps this view is unduly pessimistic, but there is little evidence to support any other conclusion.

Nearly everyone is opposed to higher taxes—the public, the administration, and the Congress. A study conducted by the Survey Research Center of the University of Michigan in November 1969 showed that 85 percent of the nation was opposed to any increase in income taxes and 80 percent felt that the government should spend less.[8] The reason for this feeling is not hard to find. Between 1965 and 1968, the gross average weekly earnings of production workers rose by $2.39. This figure is before taxes. After social security and federal income taxes are deducted, the weekly wage of a worker with three dependents went up by exactly eight cents during this period. Family incomes are going up because more wives and other family members are working; but insofar as the average worker is concerned, three years went by without a raise in take-home pay—and that during a period of peak employment. Preliminary figures for 1969 suggest that there was no improvement during that year.

Little wonder that what started out as the tax reform bill of 1969 became a tax cut in the hands of Congress. The "vast silent majority" of middle-class workers made their wishes known. As a result we got a new tax bill which placed a few more dollars into the pockets of nearly everyone but reduced by several billion dollars our ability to cope with domestic problems. Nearly everyone professes a desire to clean up the environment, reduce crime, diminish racial tensions, and correct other domestic problems, but few seem willing to make the necessary sacrifices to attain these goals. Factory workers claim, with some justification, that inflation and increased taxes have already cut deeply into their take-home pay and that further increases in taxes would necessitate reductions in levels of living. Businessmen can also undoubtedly find good reasons to claim hardship. If the money to achieve the professed goals does not come from new taxes, where will it come from? One source would be a major change in government expenditures—a transfer of funds from military to civilian spending. There is some hope in this direction, but at present it is just that—a hope.

TABLE I-2

Gross and Spendable
Average Weekly Earnings: 1960-1968*

Year	Gross average weekly earnings	Spendable average weekly earnings for worker with 3 dependents
1960	$78.24	$70.77
1961	79.27	71.48
1962	81.55	73.05
1963	82.91	73.63
1964	84.49	76.38
1965	86.50	78.53
1966	87.37	78.39
1967	87.57	78.13
1968	88.89	78.61

*In 1957-59 dollars. Data are production or nonsupervisory workers on private nonagricultural payrolls.

U.S. Department of Labor, *Monthly Labor Review,* December 1969, p. 99.

It is obvious that a lot of wishful, fuzzy thinking is going on at all levels of our society. If we are really serious in our desire to get more of the things we cannot buy for ourselves, we will have to change our attitudes. Perhaps there was a time when each of us could maximize his satisfaction by spending his hard-earned money as he saw fit, without taking the needs of others into account. If there ever was such a time, it no longer exists. Each of us can only maximize his own satisfaction today by taking the needs of others into account. Each time we land at an airport, the black jet stream we create spoils the air we ourselves breathe. Each time we dump raw sewage or industrial waste into a river or a lake, we pollute the water we ourselves drink and destroy the fish we might have eaten. Each untreated emotionally disturbed child is the man who may one day rob us on a city street or kill a President. It is no act of altruism today to favor more spending for the solution of domestic problems. It is merely a matter of each of us furthering his own self-interest.

At present, we are paying little more than lip service to the solution of these problems and this is one of the reasons for the difficulties we are having with the younger generation. They hear a great deal of pious talk about the need for change, but they see little change actually taking place. They hear constant griping about high taxes, but they see their parents growing more affluent and less concerned about social problems. The fact that the younger generation shares this affluence only adds to their sense of guilt.

Perhaps we can still pull ourselves together and do those things that must be done to correct the ills that plague us today. It seems doubtful at this writing. At one time we could attribute our woes to poverty. That is not the answer today. We have the money; we just lack the will. We do make social improvements, but never enough and nearly always reluctantly. By some strange magic there are always funds to do those things which destroy man and his environment and never enough to build a better world—to relieve suffering and fear, to create beauty. Better teachers and schools for our children can always wait another year; more adequate incomes and housing for the poor can be postponed for the future; better jails, hospitals, and care for institutional inmates can be put off for a while. But we must immediately have new weapons—no matter that those we now have can destroy the world ten times over; we must immediately have new cars that can go 120 miles per hour even though our highways are hazardous at 70 miles per hour; we must immediately have a man on the moon and when that is achieved a man on Mars, anti-ballistic missiles, monstrous new jets, etc., etc.

There is hope for the future. It is not in ourselves, but in our children. Nearly half of the families that will be in existence in 1985 have not yet been formed. These families will be headed by children who are now throwing stones at their teachers or are watching their older brothers and sisters mock the establishment. In 1985 it will be their society, not ours. They will be the affluent majority and it will be interesting to see whether they will put the lie to John Gardner's prediction that we will "get richer and richer in filthier communities until we reach a final state of affluent misery—Croesus on a garbage heap."[9]

This discussion gets us deep into the consideration of the social and economic aspects of income distribution. Before going any further with the analysis, however, it might be best to back up a bit and take a broad look at the income picture.

II

Where Do You Fit
in the Income Picture?

The amount of income that is produced by a given country pre-
scribes the levels of living that are possible for its inhabitants. A given
amount of income may be widely distributed throughout the population
and provide adequate levels of living for all, or it may be concentrated in
the hands of a few persons and provide pyramids and palaces for princes
and kings and nothing but hovels and hunger for everyone else. It is for
this reason that statistics on income distribution are needed in addition
to those on gross national product, particularly in a wealthy country like
the United States.

India, with an annual income of only $80 or $90 per person, can do
little to alleviate the poverty of its teeming masses by taxing the rich
more and giving it to the poor. If the total income produced in India
each year were more equally divided, it might prevent thousands of people from starving to death, but at best a redistribution of income in India
would not provide more than a bare subsistence level of living.

In the United States, however, where the average income per person
is over $4,000 per year, it is very important that we know how in-
comes are distributed, for if there are large numbers of people with
incomes too low to maintain a minimum level of living for this country
it is possible to do something about it. Increases can be made in social
security payments to the aged, in unemployment compensation for
those unable to find work, and in public assistance to mothers with dependent children. There is even a proposal now to provide a guaranteed
income for all the poor, regardless of where they live or with whom they

live. It is also possible to help the poor by providing more and better services, such as low-cost public housing, training programs, and better schools and medical facilities.

Even in a very wealthy country like the United States, there are limits to the amount that the middle class and the well-to-do can be taxed without destroying their incentives to work, save, and invest which are the ultimate sources of our fabulous wealth. We do not know what these limits are. There is some evidence that they may be quite great and that it may be possible to tax ourselves more than we do without any serious reduction of incentives to work. One recent study of the economic behavior of rich people showed that seven-eighths of high-income respondents do not curtail their work at all because of the income tax and that income taxes do not appear to have any significant effect either on the timing of retirement or on the employment of wives.[1] At least we can agree that although there are limits to taxation, there is a surplus among higher-income American families at present which could be used to alleviate the extremes of poverty, if such action were deemed necessary or desirable.

Statistics on income distribution are used for many different purposes. Their most important use, perhaps, was in revealing the existence of millions of poor people in the United States and thereby calling attention to the need for an attack on poverty early in the 1960's. These statistics were not only instrumental in starting that "war," they were also the single most important measure of year-to-year progress in that war—and they showed that we made progress.

Like all numbers that are widely used, the income statistics are also often misused. For example, in the widely distributed book *The Population Bomb* (2 million copies have been printed), Paul Ehrlich tells his disciples how to "sell" population control to a friend or associate who is an "extreme liberal." He advises them to "emphasize that the rich are getting richer and the poor poorer, both in the United States and in the world as a whole. Declare that as long as population continues to grow, this disparity will worsen."[2] As we shall demonstrate subsequently, there is no evidence that this statement is true for the United States.

Below are figures showing the spread of income in the United States. They come from a study conducted by the U.S. Bureau of the Census in March 1969. You may be interested in finding out where you fit in the income picture. Since only seven different income groups are shown, these figures give an unrealistic view of the actual spread of income. It is really much greater than most people imagine. The noted economist Paul Samuelson has described income distribution in the following terms: "If we made an income pyramid out of a child's blocks, with each layer portraying $1,000 of income, the peak would be far higher than the Eiffel Tower, but almost all of us would be within a yard of the ground."[3] This statement gives you some idea of the diversity that is compressed within these seven groupings.

TABLE II-1

Families by Income Level: 1968

Income level	Number of families	Percentage Families	Income
All families	50.5 million	100%	100%
Under $3,000	5.2 million	10	2
Between $3,000 and $7,000	13.4 million	27	14
Between $7,000 and $10,000	11.8 million	23	20
Between $10,000 and $15,000	12.6 million	25	31
Between $15,000 and $25,000	6.1 million	12	23
Between $25,000 and $50,000	1.2 million	2	7
$50,000 and over	150,000	0.3	2
Median income	$8,600		
Average (mean) income	$9,700		

Note: Sums of tabulated figures in this chapter may not equal totals because of rounding.

Derived from U.S. Bureau of the Census, *Current Population Reports,* Series P-60, No. 66.

About 5 million families received less than $3,000 in 1968. They represented about one-tenth of all families and received one-fiftieth (2 percent) of the income. Some lived on farms where their cash incomes were supplemented by food and lodging that they did not have to purchase. But even if this income were added to the total, the figures would not change much.

At the top income level were about 150,000 families with incomes of $50,000 and over. They represented 3/10 of 1 percent of all families and received 2 percent of all the income.

Another way to view these figures is to examine the share of income received by each fifth of the families, ranked from lowest to highest by income. Table II-2 shows that in 1968, the poorest fifth of the families had incomes under $4,600; they received 6 percent of the total. In that same year, the highest fifth of the families had incomes over $13,500; they received 41 percent of the total.

Who sits at the top of the heap? The figures show that until you get to the very top the incomes are not so high. The top 5 percent of the families had incomes over $23,000. They received 14 percent of all the income. Families with incomes over $42,500 were in the top 1 percent and they received 5 percent of the total.

TABLE II-2

Share of Income Received by Each Fifth of Families and by Top 5 Percent and Top 1 Percent: 1968

Families ranked from lowest to highest	Income range	Percentage of income received
Lowest fifth	Under $4,600	6%
Second fifth	Between $4,600 and $7,400	12
Middle fifth	Between $7,400 and $10,000	18
Fourth fifth	Between $10,000 and $13,500	24
Highest fifth	$13,500 and over	41
Top 5%	$23,000 and over	14
Top 1%	$42,500 and over	5

Derived from U.S. Bureau of the Census, *Current Population Reports,* Series P-60, No. 66.

The figures in Table II-2 show the distribution of income before taxes. Since families in the higher income groups pay a larger share of the taxes, their share of income should be smaller on an after-tax basis. It is, but not by as much as you might think. Table II-3 shows the figures both ways for 1966, using data collected by the Survey Research Center of the University of Michigan. This table shows that the share of income received by the top fifth of the families and individuals is reduced by only two percentage points when taxes are taken into account. The reason taxes have such little impact is that our tax structure is not very progressive. In fact, in 1965, families at each income level between $2,000 and $15,000 paid the same proportion of their income in taxes (see Table II-4). There is some progressivity in the federal tax structure. Families in the $2,000 to $4,000 income class pay 16 percent of their income in federal taxes whereas those in the $15,000 and over class turn over 32 percent of their income to the federal treasury. State and local taxes, however, are regressive from beginning to end. Families with incomes under $2,000 pay one-fourth of their income in state and local taxes (mostly sales taxes at the bottom income class), whereas families in the top income class pay only 7 percent of their income in taxes to state and local governments.

The government not only takes money away from people, it also gives it back to some in the form of transfer payments like social security, unemployment compensation, public assistance, etc. When transfer payments are taken into account, a large measure of progressivity is added to the tax structure. Families at the very lowest income levels receive more in transfer payments than they pay in taxes to the federal,

---

TABLE II-3

Share of Income Received by Each Fifth of Families and Individuals, Before and After Taxes: 1966

Families and individuals, ranked from lowest to highest	Percentage of aggregate income received	
	Before taxes	After taxes
Lowest fifth	5%	5%
Second fifth	11	11
Middle fifth	18	17
Fourth fifth	23	25
Highest fifth	43	41

Derived from University of Michigan, Survey Research Center, *Survey of Consumer Finances: 1967.*

TABLE II-4

Taxes and Transfers as a Percentage of
Income: 1965

	Taxes			Transfer payments	Taxes less transfers
Income class	Federal	State and local	Total		
Under $2,000	19%	25%	44%	126%	−83%*
$2,000-$4,000	16	11	27	11	16
$4,000-$6,000	17	10	27	5	21
$6,000-$8,000	17	9	26	3	23
$8,000-$10,000	18	9	27	2	25
$10,000-$15,000	19	9	27	2	25
$15,000 and over	32	7	38	1	37
Total	22	9	31	14	24

*The minus sign indicates that families and individuals in this class received more from federal, state, and local governments than they, as a group, paid to these governments in taxes.

Joseph A. Pechman, "The Rich, the Poor and the Taxes They Pay," *The Public Interest,* November 1969. The data are from the *Economic Report of the President,* 1969, p. 161.

state, and local governments. The share of income paid in taxes, less transfer payments, does rise with income level.

One writer stated recently, in commenting on the impact of fiscal policy on the distribution of income, that from "reading conservative popular writers, one would assume that the federal government, in particular, did little else than redistribute income from those who work hard to those who do not. Reading the radical press would probably lead one to conclude that redistribution is indeed taking place but that it is from the poor to the wealthy, further concentrating and distorting the original distribution by the economic system."[4] Hard facts are difficult to come by in this area. Conservatives and radicals can undoubtedly interpret such information as is available as a confirmation of their views. The figures shown in Table II-4 take into account taxes and transfer payments only; they make no allowance for benefits accruing to each income class as a result of government expenditures for public schools, roads, national defense, and similar activities. It takes some very heroic assumptions to get at the net impact of *all* public expenditures on the distribution of income. Such a study was made several years ago, initially as a doctoral dissertation submitted to Johns Hopkins University and later as an article in a book of essays on fiscal policy published by The Brookings Institution.[5] In this article, the author, Irwin Gillespie, first distributed the tax burden by income class, using the following assumptions:

> With regard to federal taxes, it is assumed that: the individual income tax is borne entirely by the individual; the estate and gift taxes fall entirely on those in the highest income bracket; two-thirds of the corporate profits tax is borne by the owners (and therefore is allocated by a distribution of dividends received), and one-third is shifted forward to consumers; excise and customs are shifted forward to consumers of the products taxed; social security contributions fall on wage earners (the employee's share and half the employer's share) and total consumption (half of the employer's share).
>
> State and local taxes, including the individual income tax, estate and gift taxes, and the corporate profits tax are treated in the same way as their federal counterparts. In addition, it is assumed that: excise taxes are shifted to total consumption goods, while sales taxes are shifted to consumption goods less food product purchases; property taxes are borne equally by homeowners (and renters) and consumers; social security contributions are borne entirely by wage and salary earners.[6]

Gillespie then attempts to estimate the benefits received from government expenditures by income class. The procedure is quite complex and is not summarized as neatly as the distribution of the tax burden. In the case of highways, for example, 75 percent of the expenditures was distributed as a benefit to highway users and 25 percent as a benefit to nonusers (i.e., as a benefit to property owners whose sites were increased in value); expenditures on education were distributed as a benefit to families with children in elementary and secondary schools and in colleges; expenditures on public health were assumed to be consumed equally by all families, etc. The one critical assumption which had to be made involved general expenditures, which includes national defense among other things, and accounted for $50 billion out of a total of $83 billion of government expenditures in 1960. Gillespie used four different assumptions to distribute the benefits of general expenditures. The one he regards as the standard case, and the one that is reported here, assumes that general expenditures are distributed proportionately to income and are therefore allocated according to the distribution of families by income levels.

Table II-5 shows how families at each income level are affected when the joint net impact of the burden of tax payments and the benefits of government expenditures are taken into account. The incomes of families at the lowest level (under $2,000) are increased by 55 percent and those at the $2,000–$3,000 level are increased by 44 percent. The incomes of families at the $10,000 and over level are reduced by 13 percent. Within the $4,000 to $10,000 there is very little change. It does appear, therefore, when all factors are taken into account, that the poor do benefit appreciably as a result of the government's efforts to redistribute income.

TABLE II-5

Percentage Change in Income, by Income Class, After Tax Payments and the Benefits of Government Expenditures: 1960

Income class	Percentage change in income
Under $2,000	55%
$2,000 to $2,999	44
$3,000 to $3,999	19
$4,000 to $4,999	−1
$5,000 to $7,499	−3
$7,500 to $9,999	2
$10,000 and over	−13

Article by W. Irwin Gillespie, "Effect of Public Expenditures on the Distribution of Income" in Richard A. Musgrave, *Essays in Fiscal Federalism*. Washington, D.C.: The Brookings Institution, 1965, p. 162.

Are U.S. incomes too unequally distributed?

There is no objective answer to this question. It all depends on how equally you think incomes should be distributed.

Around the turn of the century, the French poet and philosopher Charles Péguy wrote: "When all men are provided with the necessities, the real necessities, with bread and books, what do we care about the distribution of luxury?"[7] This point of view went out of style with spats and high-button shoes. There is an intense interest in the distribution of luxury in the modern world.

Since we all cannot have as many material things as we should like, many people are of the opinion that those who are more productive should get more both as a reward for past performance and as an incentive to greater output in the future. This seems like a reasonable view, consistent with the realities of the world. Lincoln said: "That some should be rich shows that others may become rich and hence is just encouragement to industry and enterprise."[8] The fact is that all modern industrial societies, whatever their political or social philosophies, have had to resort to some forms of incentives to get the most work out of their people.

Despite its reasonableness, this view has its critics. Some have argued that a man endowed with a good mind, drive, imagination, and creativity, and blessed with a wholesome environment in which these attributes could be nurtured, has already been amply rewarded. To give him material advantages over his less fortunate fellows would only aggravate the situation. The British historian R. H. Tawney wrote in his book *Equality*: ". . . some men are inferior to others in respect to their intellectual endowments. . . . It does not, however, follow from this fact that such individuals or classes should receive less consideration than others or should be treated as inferior in respect to such matters as legal status or health, or economic arrangements, which are within the control of the community."[9]

Since there is no objective answer to the question as it has been formulated, it may be fruitful to set it aside and turn to the comparison of income in the United States and other major countries for which such data are available.

Anyone who doubts that real incomes—purchasing power—are higher in the United States than in all other major countries just hasn't been around. But how much higher? That is hard to say. How do you compare dollars, pounds, rubles, and francs? Official exchange rates are often very poor guides. Differences in prices, quality of goods, and living standards add to the complexity. In view of these problems, international comparisons are sometimes made in terms of the purchasing power of wages. But even this measure has serious limitations. What constitutes a representative market basket in different countries, and how does one compare the market basket in one country with another? For example,

Italians may like fish, which is relatively cheap, whereas Americans may prefer beef, which is quite expensive. How then would one compare the cost of a "typical" meal for families in the two countries? Because of this kind of problem, and many others, international comparisons of levels of living must be made with great caution. One study that casts some light on the subject was published in 1959 by the National Industrial Conference Board. It shows the amount of work it would take to buy the following meal for a family of four in several different countries. The items were selected from an annual survey of retail prices conducted by the International Labor Office:

Beef, sirloin	150 grams
Potatoes	150 grams
Cabbage	200 grams
Bread, white	50 grams
Butter	10 grams
Milk	0.25 liter
Apples	150 grams

The results are shown in Table II-6. The industrial worker in the United States had to work one hour to buy the meal above. The Canadian worker, whose level of living is not far behind that of his American cou-

TABLE II-6

Work Time Needed to Buy a Meal: 1958

Country	Minutes of work
United States	60
Canada	69
Denmark	88
West Germany	131
United Kingdom	138
Belgium	200
Austria	244
France	277
Italy	298

Zoe Campbell, "Food Costs in Work Time Here and Abroad," *Conference Board Business Record*, December 1959.

sin, had to work nine minutes more to buy the same meal. In Europe, the Danes came closest to the American standard, but even in Denmark the average worker had to toil one-half hour longer to feed his family. In West Germany and Great Britain it took more than two hours of work to buy the same meal and in Italy it took five hours. These and many other figures of a similar nature show that American workers are paid more in real terms than the workers of any other major country.

A rough comparison of the gross national product per capita in several different countries in 1967 is shown in Table II-7. These estimates were compiled by the United Nations, which converted the official figures for each country to U.S. dollars at prevailing dollar exchange rates. For reasons already cited, these numbers should be regarded as only very rough approximations of the amounts of income produced in each nation. The conclusions based on these data are much the same as those based on the work time required to buy a meal previously discussed. GNP per capita is far higher in the United States than in any other country.

TABLE II-7

Per Capita Gross National Product of Different Countries: 1967

United States	$4,037	United Kingdom	$1,977
Sweden	3,041	Israel	1,491
Canada	2,805	Italy	1,279
Switzerland	2,597	Japan	1,158
Denmark	2,497	Mexico	528
France	2,324	India	88
Australia	2,260		

Statistical Abstract of the United States, 1969, pp. 832-3.

If international comparisons of levels of income are difficult, comparisons of the distribution of income are virtually impossible. There are many opinions on the subject, but few of them are solidly based. Aldous Huxley, for example, believed that incomes are more unequally distributed in England than in France because "the highest government servants in England are paid forty or fifty times as much as the lowest."[10] Following a similar line of reasoning, Max Eastman found inequality greater in Russia than in the U.S. because the managing director of an American mining firm receives about forty times as much as one of his miners, whereas a man in the same position in Russia may earn up to eighty times as much as a miner.[11] This type of evidence might satisfy a literary man. The statistician is harder to please.

The United Nations, which has done some work in this field, cautions that "despite the intense interest in international comparisons of the degree of inequality in the distribution of income . . . surprisingly little incontrovertible evidence has been amassed. The margins of error of the available statistics . . . combined with differences in the underlying definitions . . . make it extremely hazardous to draw conclusions involving any but possibly a very few countries."[12] No reputable scholar would deny the wisdom of these remarks. Yet judgments must be made and some figures, if they are carefully considered and properly qualified, are better than none. Even the world's leading authority on income distribution, Professor Simon Kuznets of Harvard University, agrees that international comparisons of income distribution, despite their serious limitations, have value because they are based on "a variety of data . . . rather than irresponsible notions stemming from preconceived and unchecked views on the subject."[13]

Do the rich get a larger share of income in the United States than they do in other countries? According to the available evidence this is not the case. The United States has about the same income distribution as Denmark, Sweden, and Great Britain and a much more equal distribution than most of the other countries for which data are shown.

The figures in Table II-8 classify the top 5 percent as "rich." This is a rather low point on the income scale. In the United States it would include all families receiving more than $23,000 a year. A more interesting comparison would be the share of income received by the top 1 percent ($42,500 or more per year) or perhaps an even higher income group. Such information, however, is not available for most other countries.

A comprehensive study of international comparisons of income was made in 1960 by Professor Irving Kravis of the University of Pennsylvania. He summarized the income distribution among the countries for which data are available in the following way:

More nearly equal distribution than U.S.
    Denmark
    Netherlands
    Israel (Jewish population only)

WHERE DO YOU FIT IN THE INCOME PICTURE?

About the same distribution as U.S.
    Great Britain
    Japan
    Canada
More unequal distribution than U.S.
    Italy
    Puerto Rico
    Ceylon
    El Salvador

TABLE II-8

Percentage of Income Received by Top 5 Percent of Families in Selected Countries

Country		Income percentage
United States	(1950)	20%*
Sweden	(1948)	20
Denmark	(1952)	20
Great Britain	(1951-52)	21
Barbados	(1951-52)	22
Puerto Rico	(1953)	23
India	(1955-56)	24
West Germany	(1950)	24
Italy	(1948)	24
Netherlands	(1950)	25
Ceylon	(1952-53)	31
Guatemala	(1947-48)	35
El Salvador	(1946)	36
Mexico	(1957)	37
Colombia	(1953)	42
Northern Rhodesia	(1946)	45
Kenya	(1949)	51
Southern Rhodesia	(1946)	65

*The numbers represent total income before taxes received by families or spending units.

Simon Kuznets, "Quantitative Aspects of the Economic Growth of Nations," *Economic Development and Cultural Change,* Vol. XI, No. 2 (January 1963), Table 3.

It is of particular interest to compare the earnings of workers in the United States with those of workers in socialist countries where, in theory at least, the ravages of the marketplace have been eliminated and the goal is to pay workers in accordance with their need rather than their ability to produce. Such comparisons must be restricted to wage earners for whom comparable data are available in both places. The results may therefore differ significantly from figures which cover the entire population, particularly in the United States, where many people receive non-wage income from a business in which they are self-employed or from interest, dividends, and other sources. Nevertheless, it is useful to make the comparison. There is a difference between the United States and several socialist countries, but it is not very great. In the United States the highest-paid (top 5 percent) manual workers in nonfarm industries earn about 78 percent more than the average worker in these industries. In socialist Czechoslovakia and Hungary the differential is somewhat less

TABLE II-9

Dispersion of Wages in Various Countries

Country	Percentage by which wages of top 5% of workers exceeds average
West Germany	54%
Belgium	58
Sweden	60
Netherlands	62
United Kingdom	69
United States	78
Canada	85
France	100
Czechoslovakia	70%
Hungary	73
Poland	104
Yugoslavia	107

Harold Lydall, *The Structure of Earnings.* Oxford, Clarendon Press, 1968, p. 142. Most of the figures shown cover the wage or salary income of full-period, manual wage or salary workers in nonfarm industries. In some cases the figures represent all workers of this type rather than just full-period workers.

(70 and 73 percent), and in Poland and Yugoslavia it is somewhat greater (104 and 107 percent). In Canada and France the differential between the high-paid and average worker appears to be somewhat greater than in the United States, but in most western European countries it is somewhat less. Wage incomes appear to be appreciably more equally distributed in West Germany, Belgium, Sweden, the Netherlands, and the United Kingdom than in the United States. It must be remembered in all of these comparisons that the average level is much higher in the United States than in the other countries. It is only the spread of wages that is under consideration here.

III

Not Everyone Lies
to the Census Man

At this point you probably want to know how much confidence you can place in these figures. A great deal. The income figures are surprisingly accurate and complete. The methods used to compile them are sound—the techniques have repeatedly demonstrated their worth for similar tasks. The results are double and triple checked—they match figures obtained from completely different, independent sources.

Most of the numbers quoted in this book were gathered by asking people to report how much money they make. Even though you know that the questionnaires used to collect these data were prepared, tested, and vouched for by the United States Bureau of the Census, you may still view the results with justified skepticism. Are the right people asked, in the right way? Do they really answer these kinds of questions, and, if so, do they tell the truth? Or was steelman Clarence Randall, in *The Folklore of Management*, correct when he judged that "the American people are getting annoyed at having their privacy invaded so incessantly by the little men and women who ask questions. At first they were intrigued and amused. Now they are bored and petulant. They solemnly give phony answers, and have a hearty laugh after they have closed the front door on the survey taker."[1]

The first thing you must recognize is that the difficulty of collecting income data is highly exaggerated. This is true despite the secrecy that generally surrounds private finances. Many persons who make party talk with intimate details of their sex habits are as reticent as Victorian ladies when it comes to the amounts of their paychecks—to their friends and neighbors, that is. To a professional interviewer who can guarantee the anonymity of their replies, they nearly always spill everything. Sex life, education, religion, family history, financial affairs—nothing seems too personal to be put into an anonymous statistical record. The census taker, backed by the prestigious power of the federal government and an unblemished record of secrecy spanning nearly two centuries, probably faces less resistance than other fact gatherers.

The great majority of people who are asked income questions in the census provide complete and accurate reports. (Each one seems to think that his neighbors are not so honest or so foolish.) Detailed records were kept in the 1960 census. They showed that 94 percent of the people who were asked the income questions answered them. The remaining 6 percent who did not answer were not all uncooperative. Some were temporarily away from home or they were in hospitals, jails, old-age homes, and similar places where the income information was not known by those who completed the census form for them. Some were home, but were sick and could not be interviewed. Others just did not know how much they made and refused to guess. On the basis of past experience, it seems unlikely that more than 1 percent refused to answer the income questions.[2]

Today income information is regarded as one of the key facts collected in the census. Indeed, many people would not think of taking a census now without collecting information about income. But that was not the case thirty years ago.

"Wake up, America, before it is too late"

There is a long history of the collection of financial information in the population census. In 1850, census takers obtained information on the value of real estate owned by each individual. In 1860 and 1870 questions on bonds, stocks, mortgages, etc., were added. Yet, when it was proposed that information on personal income be collected for the first time in the 1940 census, the press and the Congress exploded. Newspaper editorials and cartoons lambasted the Census Bureau for asking such questions. The census taker was depicted as a sharp-nosed Uncle Sam called "Paul Pry." Senator Charles Tobey took to the airwaves with a nationwide address. "Wake up, America," he said, "before it is too late. Eternal vigilance is still the price of liberty. Stand up and fight. . . . These census questions demanding you to divulge your income manifestly violate your constitutional rights."[3] He further attacked the questions as unwarranted prying which made available personal information to local people who were politically appointed as enumerators.

Fortunately, the income questions were not dropped in the 1940 census and a very useful body of information emerged. Very few people objected to the questions or refused to answer them, and so they were added again in the 1950 census. This time, Representative Clarence Brown of Ohio took up the cudgels. He charged the Truman Administration with "police state" methods in instructing census takers to ask individuals their income. He cited the inclusion of income questions in the census as "a perfect example of socialism in action. You have no right as an individual. You tell all to Washington. You knuckle under to the Government or go to jail."[4]

It is surprising now how many people attacked the income questions in 1950. Arthur Krock of *The New York Times* wrote several learned pieces on the subject. George Sokolsky was vitriolic and misinformed. Even Herbert Hoover criticized the questions. Finally, the Congress Heights Citizens Association in Washington, D.C., after announcing that prizes of $10, $5, and $3 would be awarded for the best-decorated homes in its territory during Christmas, passed a resolution opposing the income questions in the 1950 census as "an infringement of the rights and freedom of citizens."

The income questions were asked in the 1950 census anyway, and the information was provided with very little objection. By 1960 there was no organized opposition to the inclusion of income questions in the census, and what has emerged is one of the most useful bodies of income statistics ever assembled.

But how good are the figures?

The decennial census of population in the United States is an actual nose count. An attempt is made to count every single human being in the country. In the 1940 census, every person in the country was asked to report wages and salaries (in addition to the other items included in the census). In 1950 the income survey was changed to a sampling basis. Every fifth person in the general census was questioned about his total income (not just wages and salaries). This technique was also followed in 1960, but the size of the sample was expanded to include every fourth family.

Many people who accept 100 percent nose counts as accurate are relatively dubious about sample surveys. Their suspicion has been aroused—and rightly—by flagrant misuses of this method, particularly among advertisers.

It is easy to see, however, that samples can be useful—you don't have to drink the whole pot of soup to tell how it tastes; a couple of spoonfuls are enough. The technique gives honest, accurate results if two requirements are rigorously observed:

1. The soup must be well mixed. That is, the sample must be chosen so that it is faithfully representative of the whole and so that every person stands a known chance of being selected. Since the census asks income of every fourth family in every city, hamlet, and farm area in the entire country, this requirement is more than adequately fulfilled.

2. You must not taste the soup with a salt-laden spoon. That is, the test has to be fair. Questions must not be phrased in such a way that they will favor one kind of reply over another. The simplicity of the census questions and the care taken in their composition eliminate this sort of bias.

Even with these precautions duly observed, one other fact about sample surveys should be faced. The answers they give must be considered not as absolutes, but in terms of a range. For example, the average (median) income of all families in the 1960 census was $5,660. More properly this should be stated: the chances are two out of three that the average income that would be obtained in a complete census would differ from $5,660 by less than a dollar. This "statistical error" becomes more important when you try to slice up the raw data to draw conclusions about small groups. If you want to know the average income of professional men in the Chicago metropolitan area as based on the census, you have to take an answer like this: the chances are two out of three that a complete census of professional men in Chicago would have produced a median that would differ from $7,385 by less than $40 (see Appendix A, Table A-1).

These qualifications are not serious. Even a 100 percent nose count is subject to errors (though of a different kind). The purely statistical errors in the census figures on income are small enough to be ignored. They are more than outweighed by other factors. The big question is: how can you tell if the answers that people give the census taker are correct? Maybe they lie. Maybe they just don't know.

The demonstration of truth

Income data are not like a crossword puzzle. You can't check them by looking up the answer in the next day's newspaper. What you can do is match one set of figures, obtained from one source, with related figures from other sources. The Census Bureau spent over a million dollars in 1950, and more than that in 1960, checking the accuracy of the census results.

The Office of Business Economics of the U.S. Department of Commerce provides one standard against which the census income figures can be checked. Each year this office prepares the figures on gross national product. Compiled from such reliable data as the wage records of business firms and governmental agencies, they are regarded as among the most accurate of all figures prepared in Washington. The OBE estimated that the American people received $351 billion in cash income in 1959; the census measure of total income was $332 billion, a difference of 6 percent (see Appendix A, Table A-2). The OBE figure is higher mainly because people forgot (accidentally? on purpose? who knows?) to tell the census man about much of their *extra* income beyond ordinary earnings. The figures on wages and salaries and self-employment income match almost exactly. If the 6 percent difference were applied to family income, the median would be raised to $6,000 (the census figure is $5,660).

A closer comparison can be made between the census and the Current Population Survey (CPS), which asks the income of a large nationwide sample every March. (See Appendix A for a detailed description of CPS.) In census years, many of the families covered in CPS are asked the same questions twice—once for CPS and once for the regular census. You may not be surprised to learn that a large proportion of them give different answers. But the differences tend to balance out, and the overall averages are remarkably similar (see Table III-1).

A still closer check is provided by the Reinterview Surveys. The

Census Bureau sends specially trained enumerators back to selected homes to ask the census questions—which had already been answered once—all over again. The main result of this test has been to turn up a large number of persons with very small incomes which they did not report the first time around. The probing of an expert interviewer often reveals some "forgotten" information.

TABLE III-1

Comparison of Income Reported for 1959 and 1949 in Current Population Survey and Census by Persons Aged 14 and Over

Sex, color, and residence	1959			1949		
	CPS	Census	Difference	CPS	Census	Difference
Males						
Overall	$3,996	$4,103	$107	$2,346	$2,434	$88
White	4,208	4,319	111	2,471	2,573	102
Nonwhite	1,977	2,273	296	1,196	1,361	165
Nonfarm						
Overall	$4,230	$4,254	$24	$2,563	$2,613	$50
White	4,425	4,474	49	2,669	2,741	72
Nonwhite	2,347	2,409	62	1,476	1,571	95
Farm						
Overall	$1,696	$2,098	$402	$1,054	$1,339	$285
White	2,003	2,283	280	1,194	1,489	295
Nonwhite	664	778	114	488	577	89
Females						
Overall	$1,222	$1,357	$135	$960	$1,029	$69
White	1,313	1,441	128	1,070	1,138	68
Nonwhite	809	909	100	495	590	95
Nonfarm						
Overall	$1,290	$1,397	$107	$1,049	$1,104	$55
White	1,361	$1,478	117	1,158	1,200	42
Nonwhite	928	948	20	614	672	58

TABLE III-1—Continued

Sex, color, and residence	1959			1949		
	CPS	Census	Differ-ence	CPS	Census	Differ-ence
Farm						
Overall	$480	$731	$251	$392	$458	$66
White	665	826	161	433	533	100
Nonwhite	311	367	56	290	311	21

Data for 1959 from *U.S. Census of Population: 1960, General Social and Economic Characteristics, United States Summary,* Table 97; data for 1949 from *U.S. Census of Population: 1950, Characteristics of the Population, United States Summary,* Vol. II, Part I, Table 138; CPS data from *Current Population Reports—Consumer Income,* Series P-60, Nos. 7 and 35, Tables 16 and 22 and underlying tabulations.

It's dangerous to lie to the income tax man

The professional economist might be willing to accept the above comparisons as an assessment of census income statistics. The man in the street, however, is likely to be more hard-nosed. His idea of a valid check would be a comparison with income tax returns, much along the lines suggested by King Gama in Gilbert and Sullivan's *Princess Ida*:

I know everybody's income and what everybody earns;
And I carefully compare it with the income tax returns.

After all, tax returns are sworn statements. Some people may lie about their deductions; but the great majority report their income accurately, especially if taxes are withheld at the source. Why not compare a sample of census reports with income tax returns?

A very good idea, and that is exactly what is done. In 1960, the census schedules were located for a sample of 3,100 tax returns, after elaborate precautions were taken to guarantee that the confidentiality of the data would be maintained. The income information reported in both places was then compared. The results of this study were summarized in a report prepared by the Bureau of the Census.[5] They show that there is no significant difference overall between the incomes reported on tax returns and those reported in the census. Of course, not everybody reported the same income in both places. Far from it. In some cases the tax returns were higher and in others the census reports were higher. Overall, however, the differences balanced out and the distribution was about the same. The discrepancy of $149 between the averages is not significant (see Table III-2).

TABLE III-2

Comparison of Income Reported in 1960 Census and to Internal Revenue Service*

Family income	Percentage reporting this income in census	Percentage reporting this income on tax returns
None	2.4%	—
Loss rather than income	0.1	0.9%
$1 to $599	1.2	1.5
$600 to $999	1.0	1.9
$1,000 to $1,999	4.4	7.1
$2,000 to $2,999	7.0	8.3
$3,000 to $3,999	9.9	9.7
$4,000 to $4,999	12.2	12.9
$5,000 to $5,999	12.7	11.6
$6,000 to $6,999	13.2	10.9
$7,000 to $7,999	8.2	8.4
$8,000 to $8,999	6.1	6.2
$9,000 to $9,999	5.3	5.2
$10,000 to $14,999	11.3	10.9
$15,000 to $19,999	2.7	2.6
$20,000 to $24,999	0.9	0.4
$25,000 and over	1.4	1.4
Average (mean) income	$6,812	$6,663

*Data based on fully matched families.

U.S. Bureau of the Census, *Evaluation and Research Program of the U.S. Census of Population and Housing*, Series ER-60, No. 8, p. 3.

Studies like those described above show that the income figures collected in the census cannot be far wrong. Still skeptical? You will find a more detailed and more technical evaluation of income statistics in Appendix A.

IV

The Pie Gets Bigger,
the Critics Louder

Growth in average family income: 1929-1968

The year 1929 is a landmark in U.S. history. It was the year of the stock market crash. It is also the first year for which reliable statistics are available showing the distribution of families by income level. There are good figures showing changes in *average* income back to the turn of the century, but we have little more than rough approximations of the *distribution* of families by income level before 1929. We might therefore begin by asking what has happened to average family income since the onset of the great depression.

It is important to be very careful about dollars here because prices have risen and a dollar buys much less today than it did in 1929. Therefore, all figures will have to be expressed in dollars of constant purchasing power: 1968 dollars have been used for that purpose. Moreover, taxes have gone up as well as prices. In order to get a reasonable approximation of change in purchasing power, the income should be measured after federal income taxes are deducted. The figures below satisfy both conditions. In view of the recent rise in social security taxes and the growing importance of state and local taxes, it would be desirable if these taxes were also deducted, in order to obtain an estimate of the disposable income available to consumers for personal spending or saving. The necessary data, however, are not readily available, and so we will have to be satisfied with family income less federal income taxes.

There are some very important lessons to be learned from this set of numbers. In the first place, you can see that there is nothing magical about economic growth. Nothing is built into the economic system to guarantee that purchasing power—levels of living—will automatically go up each year. Indeed these few figures show that a decline began in 1929, lasted for about a decade, and was not fully recovered until World War II broke out.

During the war years there was a tremendous growth in real income. This resulted in a huge growth in savings, since there were few consumer goods around to be purchased. Factories were working at full steam and prices were controlled. As a result, real incomes rose by $800 in five years, or about $160 per year.

The end of World War II did not bring the mass unemployment that so many economists had forecast, but the removal of price controls and the huge backlog of consumer demand backed by fat bank accounts forced prices up. The reduction in hours of work also reduced family income. Consequently there was a slight drop in purchasing power throughout most of the Truman Administration. Real family incomes were lower in 1952, when Truman left office, than they were in 1945, when he entered it.

The Eisenhower Administration concentrated heavily on the control of inflation. The figures show that this policy was quite successful in terms of producing increases in family purchasing power. During the eight years of the Eisenhower Administration real family income rose by nearly $1,000, or a little more than $100 a year.

Incomes continued to grow regularly during the Kennedy and Johnson years. Between 1961 and 1963 incomes rose by about $500, or by about $250 per year. During the five years of the Johnson Administration (1963-1968) incomes rose by $1,200, or by about $250 per year. Largely because of the sharp rise in prices in 1967 and 1968, the rate of growth in real income was distinctly lower in those years than it had been earlier in the decade.

The rising income levels between 1950 and 1970 suggest that a new type of individual is now appearing on the American scene, one who has never had firsthand experience with severe economic depression. People born in 1942 are reaching maturity. Most of them have completed their education. Many are already married and having families. These youngsters have been reared in a period in which there has been no major economic depression. There have been recessions, to be sure, but these are minor economic ripples compared with the national depressions each

Average Income of Families and Individuals

THE PIE GETS BIGGER, THE CRITICS LOUDER

39

previous generation of Americans experienced. Some of these young people live in depressed areas where jobs are scarce, but these are the exceptions rather than the rule. Never in the postwar era has the whole country suffered the bleak despair of the economic famines that formerly came again and again—in 1837, 1857, 1893, 1907, 1921, and 1929.

The growth in income, as shown in Table IV-1, can be traced back much further than 1929. Since 1890, our national income, adjusted for price changes, has grown at the average rate of more than 3 percent per year compounded.[1] It has doubled every twenty years. Even when allowance is made for population growth, income per person today is four times what it was in 1890. That growth was no accident. A better understanding of why it occurred in the past is the best guarantee that it will continue in the future. Our geographic location plays a very important role. While we have an abundance of good land, water, mineral resources, and timber, the importance of these factors should not be overemphasized. It has been pointed out that "at the time our Constitution was drawn up other countries had equally fertile soil, other countries had more abundant labor, larger amounts of capital, better educational institutions, better roads and other means of communication, and natural resources more adequate for the agrarian economies of those times."[2] What we had in addition was a form of government and a general outlook which accepted and encouraged change. "Change and attempted improvement have been in the very genes of the millions of immigrants who have come to our land over the centuries. Many came seeking freedom in a very wide sense—freedom from government domination; freedom from church domination; freedom from class rigidity. An urge toward 'progress' has been part and parcel of our thinking, of our social environment, from the days of the earliest settlers. Our people, no matter whence they came, tended quickly to throw off the old and seek the new."[3] Our wealth did not arise out of thin air. It is attributable to the fact that we were blessed with abundance of resources and that we have a set of values which encouraged the development of our physical and human resources.

The social critic is always most interesting when he is cautioning that we are going "to the dogs," that the nation is losing its moral fiber and that the younger generation no longer hold cherished values. Certainly it is difficult for anyone over 30 to look at our long-haired kids, with their strange dress and even stranger ways, and imagine that any good will

TABLE IV-1

Average Income of Families and Individuals, After Taxes (in 1968 Dollars)

Year	Average income
1929	$4,706
1935-36	4,055
1941	4,988
1944	6,344
1946	6,381
1947	5,794
1948	5,803
1949	5,635
1950	5,890
1951	5,917
1952	5,990
1953	6,255
1954	6,269
1955	6,610
1956	6,889
1957	6,885
1958	6,799
1959	7,061
]960	7,133
1961	7,174
1962	7,437
1963	7,648
1964	8,004
1965	8,324
1966	8,660
1967	8,781
1968	8,900

1948 to 1968, derived from unpublished data of Office of Business Economics; 1929 and 1947, from "Size Distribution of Income in 1963," *Survey of Current Business,* April 1964. Figures for 1935-36, 1941, 1944, and 1946 derived from Herman P. Miller, *Income Distribution in the United States,* Government Printing Office, 1966, p. 9.

come of it. The physical violence on the campuses, the demonstrations, marches, and sit-ins, are frightening. But seen in their broadest perspective these actions are expressions of the values that are responsible for our greatness—freedom and change. They are attempts to give contemporary meaning to traditional values. The intense concern in the United States today with social issues points in this direction. In a recent article, Zbigniew Brzezinski, director of Columbia University's Research Institute on Communist Affairs and a former member of the State Department Policy Planning Council, summarized the matter in these terms: ". . . contemporary America is demonstrating today its flexibility and adaptability, not rigidity and stagnation. Change is always too rapid for some and too slow for others. Yet, in such areas as poverty, race relations, education and social mores, the reality of the last decade has been that of positive change and that change is continuing."[4]

Changes in the distribution by income level: 1929-1968

Averages can be very misleading. All that an average tells you is the amount that each one would get if the total were equally divided. The total is not equally divided and it makes a big difference just how unequally divided it is.

The increase in income since the depression of the thirties has been widespread throughout the population and has resulted in a general movement of families up the income scale. There have, of course, been many exceptions. The aged, uneducated, and unskilled have not moved ahead as fast as the others, but even for many of these groups the sharp edge of poverty has been blunted.

The typical picture, particularly since the end of World War II, has been one of gradually rising family incomes, due not only to the full-time employment of chief breadwinners but also to the rising tendency for wives to supplement family income. These factors, in combination with the increasing productivity of American industry, have caused a persistent drop in the number and proportion of families at the lower income levels and a corresponding increase in the middle- and upper-income brackets. The extent of the increase in family income can be seen most clearly in the tables below. Here again, all the numbers are expressed in terms of constant purchasing power, so that the effects of inflation are eliminated. There is a technical problem that must be mentioned here. There are no figures which are entirely comparable for the complete period since 1929. The only figures available are those prepared by the Office of Business Economics covering family *personal* income for 1929-1962 and those prepared by the Bureau of the Census covering family *money* income for 1947-1968. The difference between the two series is that the OBE data include nonmoney income and are adjusted for underreporting of income, which is characteristic of all income data collected in household surveys. In contrast, the census data cover money income only and are not adjusted for underreporting. During the years in which the two series overlap (1947-1962), they show remarkably similar trends.

In 1959 Robert Heilbroner, in *The Future as History,* wrote: "In the economic folklore of our country we still look back to 1929 not only as a year of great business prosperity but as a year of widespread and fundamental well-being. But when we examine the economy of 1929 critically, we find that the facade of business prosperity concealed an inner structure of widespread economic frailty."[5]

TABLE IV-2

Distribution of Families and Individuals by Personal Income (in 1968 Dollars)

Income level	1913	1929	1947	1962
Under $3,000	61%	50%	24%	17%
Between $3,000 and $6,000	27	32	36	34
Between $6,000 and $8,000	6	8	18	9
Between $8,000 and $10,000	2	4	8	13
$10,000 and over	4	6	14	27

Figures for 1929, 1947, and 1962 derived from "Size Distribution of Income in 1963," *Survey of Current Business,* April 1964, Table 4. Figures for 1913 are very rough approximations. They were estimated by assuming that the Lorenz Curve did not change between 1913 and 1929 and that during this period the average income per family increased by 1.6 percent per year compounded. The assumption regarding the constant Lorenz Curve is based, first, on the fact that IRS data for 1913-1929 show no change in the share of income received by the top 1 percent and the top 5 percent of the population (see Table IV-4); and, second, on the fact that the share of income received by the bottom 20 percent of the families had not changed for nearly forty years (see Tables IV-5 and IV-6).

TABLE IV-3

Distribution of Families and Unrelated Individuals by Money Income (in 1968 Dollars)

Total money income	1947	1957	1962	1968
Number of families (thousands)	45,402	54,131	58,011	64,313
Median income	$4,183	$5,397	$6,044	$7,434
Under $3,000	34%	28%	26%	19%
$3,000 to $5,999	37	28	24	21
$6,000 to $7,999	13	19	17	15
$8,000 to $9,999	7	12	12	13
$10,000 and over	9	13	21	33

Derived from *Current Population Reports,* Series P-60, No. 66, Table 5.

This conclusion is clearly supported by the figures. If $3,000 is used as the poverty line, it can be noted that in 1913 about three-fifths of the families and individuals had incomes that would be regarded as substandard today. By the end of World War II this proportion was reduced to one-third and by 1968 it was further reduced to one-fifth.

The figures at the other end of the income scale show why ours is called an affluent society. In 1968 about one family out of every three had an income over $10,000. In many cases this high an income was achieved only because the wife and the husband were both working; but the income is there nonetheless and it is available for air conditioners, dishwashers, second cars, and prestige schools. In 1929, an income over $10,000 was achieved by only one family out of twenty.

Looking back, there is good reason to wonder why the 1920's were ever regarded as a golden age. Incomes fell during the depression, to be sure, but they didn't fall from any great heights. By modern standards, life in 1929, the apex of the "golden age," would be very trying, to say the least. Take for example a simple matter like electric power. Today electricity in the home is taken for granted as a more or less inalienable right of every American. Practically every home—on the farm as well as in the city—is electrified. Even on southern farms, ninety-eight out of every hundred homes have electricity. In 1930, nine out of every ten farm homes were without this "necessity." And the country was much more rural then than it is now.[6]

A more striking example is provided by the presence of a toilet in the home. Figures are not available for 1930, but the information was collected ten years later in the census. As recently as 1940, about 10 percent of city homes and 90 percent of farms lacked toilet facilities within the structure.[7] This is not Russia or China that is being described, but these United States only thirty years ago.

It was generally believed during the depression that the basic economic problem facing the United States was overproduction. More goods were being produced than could be consumed. This feeling was expressed by the most advanced thinkers of the age and by the top political leaders. President Roosevelt stated in a talk before the Commonwealth Club of San Francisco on September 23, 1932: "Our industrial plant is built; the problem just now is whether under existing conditions it is not overbuilt."[8] It is easy to see, with the benefit of forty years of hindsight, that there were vast unfilled needs in 1929. By modern standards it was anything but a golden age.

Long-term changes in income shares

The political aspects of income distribution come to the fore when statistics on income inequality are considered. Critics of the system regard it as unfair that a small proportion of the families receive a large share of the income (e.g., the top 1 percent of families receive 5 percent of the aggregate income). They rarely specify how much inequality would be consistent with their concept of fairness and they generally overlook the fact that under a system of complete equality—each family receiving the same amount of income—conditions might be more unfair than they are at present. Defenders of the system, on the other hand, are quick to point to any diminution of inequality as a sign of progress. Thus, for example, Arthur F. Burns, chairman of the Federal Reserve Board, stated in 1951 that "the transformation in the distribution of our national income . . . may already be counted as one of the great social revolutions of history."[9] Paul Samuelson, one of the nation's leading economists, stated in 1961 that "the American income pyramid is becoming less unequal."[10] Several major stories on this subject have appeared in *The New York Times,* and the editors of *Fortune* magazine announced in 1955: "Though not a head has been raised aloft on a pikestaff, nor a railway station seized, the U.S. has been for some time now in a revolution."[11]

Why all this interest in income inequality? Despite the existence of much poverty in the United States, there is general agreement that real levels of living are much higher than they were only ten years ago and that the prospects for future increases are very good. Since conditions are improving, you may wonder why it is important to consider the gap between the rich and the poor. Isn't it enough that the *amount* of income received by the poor has gone up substantially? Why be concerned about their share? Many who have thought about this problem seriously regard the *share* as the critical factor. When Karl Marx, for example, spoke about the inevitability of increasing misery among workers under capitalism, he had a very special definition of misery in mind. Sumner Slichter, in summarizing the Marxian position on this point, states: "Marx held that wages depend upon the customary wants of the laboring class. Wages, so determined, might rise in the long run. Hence, Marx conceded that real wages *might* rise, but not the relative share of labor. Even if real wages rose, misery would grow, according to Marx, since workers would be worse off relative to capitalists."[12]

Arnold Toynbee has approached the problem of income shares in still another way. He notes that minimum standards of living have been raised considerably and will continue to be raised in the future, but he observes that this rise has not stopped us from "demanding social justice; and the unequal distribution of the world's goods between a privileged minority and an underprivileged majority has been transformed from an unavoidable evil to an intolerable injustice."[13]

In other words, "needs" stem not so much from what we lack as from what our neighbors have. Veblen called this trait our "pecuniary standard of living" and modern economists refer to it as the "relative income hypothesis,"[14] but it all comes back to the same thing. Except for those rare souls who have hitched their wagons to thoughts rather than things, there is no end to "needs." So long as there are people who have more, others will "need" more. If this is indeed the basis for human behavior, then obviously the gap between the rich and the poor cannot be ignored, however high the *minimum* levels of living may be raised.

Reasonably reliable statistics on the share of total income received by the top income groups in the United States date back to 1913, the year the Federal Income Tax Law was enacted. Ever since that time, the Internal Revenue Service has published annual figures showing the number of tax returns filed by income class. These figures do not permit the calculation of income shares for the entire distribution because, for many years, only the higher-income groups were required to file tax returns. However, it is possible to estimate the share of total income that was received by the top 1 percent and the top 5 percent back to 1913. This work was done by Professor Simon Kuznets, who calculated the amount of income per tax return and the population represented by the tax returns for each income class. He then computed the per capita income for each income class and ranked the income classes from highest to lowest by level of per capita income. The cumulative totals of population and income recorded on the tax returns were then converted to percentages of the total population and of the aggregate income received. The share of the top 1 percent and the top 5 percent were then estimated by interpolation.

Table IV-4 shows that there was no change in the share of income received by the top 1 percent or the top 5 percent of the population between 1913 and 1930. In 1914, at the outbreak of war in Europe, the top 1 percent received about 13 percent of the income. This range prevailed in all but two years during the twenties and showed some tendency to rise during the latter part of the period. There was a slight drop in the share of income received by the top groups during the thirties, a marked drop during World War II, and relative stability during the early postwar years.

TABLE IV-4

Percentage Share of Total Income* Received by Top 1 Percent and Top 5 Percent of Population: 1913 to 1948

Year	Top 1 percent	Top 5 percent
1948	8	18
1947	8	17
1946	9	18
1945	9	17
1944	9	17

TABLE IV-4—Continued

Year	Top 1 percent	Top 5 percent
1943	9	18
1942	10	19
1941	11	22
1940	12	23
1939	12	23
1938	11	23
1937	13	24
1936	13	24
1935	12	24
1934	12	25
1933	12	25
1932	13	27
1931	13	26
1930	14	26
1929	15	26
1928	15	27
1927	14	26
1926	14	25
1925	14	25
1924	13	24
1923	12	23
1922	13	25
1921	14	25
1920	12	22
1919	13	23
1918	13	23
1917	14	25
1916	16	(NA)
1915	14	(NA)
1914	13	(NA)
1913	15	(NA)

NA = not available

*Total income is defined here as the sum of employee compensation, entrepreneurial income, rent, interest, and dividends.

U.S. Bureau of the Census, *Historical Statistics of the United States: Colonial Times to 1957*, p. 167.

Changes in income distribution covering all income classes and not just the top groups can be measured only since 1929. For reasons previously cited, changes in the distribution of personal income can be measured from the figures prepared by the Office of Business Economics for 1929 to 1962 and changes in the distribution of money income can be measured from the census data for 1947 to 1968. The figures from both sources are shown in Tables IV-5 and IV-6.

TABLE IV-5

Percentage of Personal Income Received by Each Fifth of Families and Individuals and by Top 5 Percent

Families and individuals ranked from lowest to highest	1929	1935	1941	1944	1962
Total	100%	100%	100%	100%	100%
Lowest fifth }	13	{ 4	4	5	5
Second fifth }		{ 9	10	11	11
Middle fifth	14	14	15	16	16
Fourth fifth	19	21	22	22	23
Highest fifth	54	52	49	46	46
Top 5%	30	27	24	21	20

Note: Sums of tabulated figures in this chapter may not equal totals because of rounding.

U.S. Bureau of the Census, *Historical Statistics of the United States, Colonial Times to 1957,* p. 166; and Department of Health, Education and Welfare, *Toward a Social Report,* p. 44.

During the thirties there was a distinct drop in the share of the income received by the upper-income groups. In 1929, the last year of the prosperous twenties, the top 5 percent of the families and individuals received nearly one-third of the income. Their share dropped during the depression and amounted to about one-fourth of the income at the out-

TABLE IV-6

Percentage of Money Income Received by Each Fifth
of Families and Individuals and by Top 5 Percent

Families and individuals ranked from lowest to highest	1947	1957	1962	1967	1968
Total	100%	100%	100%	100%	100%
Lowest fifth	4	4	3	4	4
Second fifth	11	11	11	11	11
Middle fifth	17	18	17	17	17
Fourth fifth	24	25	25	24	25
Highest fifth	46	43	44	44	44
Top 5%	19	17	17	16	15

Herman P. Miller, *Income Distribution in the United States,* Government Printing Office, 1966, page 21; and unpublished data.

break of World War II. During the war years there was a further decline and their share dropped to 21 percent in 1944. Since that time there has been a further slight reduction in the percent of income received by the wealthiest group. The census data show that the share of income received by the top 5 percent of the families and individuals dropped gradually from 19 percent in 1947 to about 15 percent in 1968.

The trend described for the top twentieth applies to the top fifth as well. But now let's look at the bottom groups. In 1935, the poorest fifth of the families and individuals received only 4 percent of the income. Their share rose to 5 percent in 1944 and has remained at about that level since. The stability since 1944 of the shares received by each of the other quintiles is equally striking.

Although the figures show no appreciable change in income shares for twenty years, the problem is complex and there is much that the statistics cannot show. It is conceivable, for example, that a proportional increase in everybody's real income means more to the poor than to the rich. The gap in "living levels" may have closed more than the gap in incomes. Even if exact comparisons are not possible, many believe that by satisfying the most urgent and basic needs of the poor, there has been some "leveling up" in the comforts of life.

Other examples of a similar nature can be cited. The extension of government services benefits low-income families more than those who have higher incomes—by providing better housing, more adequate medical care, and improved educational facilities. The increase in paid vacations has surely brought a more equal distribution of leisure time—a good that is almost as precious as money. Finally, improved working conditions—air conditioning, better light, mechanization of routine work—has undoubtedly reduced the painfulness of earning a living more for manual workers than for those who are in higher paid and more responsible positions.

When allowance is made for all of these factors, and for many others not mentioned, it may well be that some progress has been made during recent years in diminishing the inequality of levels of living. But it is hard to know how much allowance to make, and our judgments could be wrong. Most opinions regarding changes in inequality, including those held by professional economists, are based on statistical measures of income rather than on philosophical concepts. With all their limitations, the income figures may well serve as a first approximation of changes in welfare. These figures show that the share of income received by the lower-income groups has not changed for twenty years.

An entirely different view of trends in income distribution is presented by Gabriel Kolko in his book *Wealth and Power in America.*[15] Kolko concludes: "A radically unequal distribution of income has been characteristic of the American social structure since at least 1910, and despite minor year-to-year fluctuations in the shares of the income-tenths, no significant trend toward income equality has appeared."[16] This conclusion is based on data for 1910 to 1937 prepared by the National Industrial Conference Board and for 1941 to 1959 by the Survey Research Center of the University of Michigan. Kolko states that the NICB data are the best material on income distribution by tenths for the period prior to 1941. This statement is very questionable. The NICB data were considered so poor by a panel of experts, including Selma F. Goldsmith and Simon Kuznets, that these figures were excluded from U.S. Bureau of the Census, *Historical Statistics of the United States: Colonial Times to 1957,* even though they had appeared in the earlier version of that book, *Historical Statistics of the United States, 1789-*

1945. The figures for 1929 and 1935 shown in Table IV-5 are considered by experts to be much more reliable than those used by Kolko.

An examination of the figures used by Kolko shows that the share of income received by the highest tenth of income recipients was 38 percent in 1921, 39 percent in 1929, 34 percent in 1937, and 29 percent in 1959.[17] He dismisses the figures for 1921 and 1929, without further explanation, as representing exceptional years. He then concludes that the difference between the prewar and postwar figures can be eliminated when the latter are "corrected to allow for their exclusion of all forms of income in kind and the very substantial understatement of income by the wealthy." The figures in Table IV-5 include many types of income in kind and they have also been adjusted for underreporting of income. They do not include various items that accrue primarily to the wealthy which Kolko thinks should be added, notably expense accounts and undistributed profits. Also excluded from the concept and not mentioned by Kolko are various types of fringe benefits, such as life insurance, medical care, health insurance, and pension plans, as well as government services, which have been increasing rapidly in recent years and are widely distributed throughout the population. A study published in 1954 by Selma F. Goldsmith and her colleagues showed that incomes were more equally distributed in the postwar period than in 1929, even when allowance is made for undistributed corporate profits.[18] A more recent study shows that the addition of capital gains to the distribution increases the share received by the wealthiest 5 percent by only a fraction of a percentage point.[19] Gillespie's figures presented in Chapter II suggest that there is a considerable redistribution of income in favor of the poor when the benefits of government activity as well as taxes are taken into account.

V

Let My People Go

The plight of the Negro in America is well known. Thousands of surveys have established that Negroes lag behind whites in health, education, employment, income, housing, and most other aspects of life. It has also been established that these conditions are getting worse, not better, in the poorest slum areas.

These facts, grim and foreboding, have been widely publicized throughout the world. There is, however, another aspect of Negro life which has received much less attention, but which shows great progress and hope for the future. A close examination of recent statistical evidence shows that despite the deterioration of social and economic conditions of Negroes in the very worst slums, the Negro population has experienced a marked improvement in many important aspects of life in recent years. Today for the first time Negroes are moving into the middle- and upper-income groups in substantial numbers.

This complicated pattern of progress mixed with retrogression makes it hazardous to generalize about the social and economic conditions of Negroes in America. Large numbers of Negroes are leaving depressed rural areas and the worst city slums and moving into better environments in which to raise their children. By coming to the city they have better jobs, greater freedoms, and wider horizons. Once in their new homes, many have taken advantage of improved facilities for education and training. Yet others remain trapped in the worst areas. They constitute a hard core—numbering in the millions—whose conditions have not improved and have even grown worse relative to the others. These people never get out of urban or rural slums or they drift from one slum to the next. They reside in areas where living conditions are deteriorating in the face of vast improvements taking place elsewhere. In part, the deterioration in the poorest Negro neighborhoods in our large cities reflects the fact that these areas are constantly losing their most talented and successful people to better neighborhoods, leaving behind the most impoverished and disadvantaged. These areas are also handicapped because they attract rural newcomers who come with the hope—as did immigrants of previous generations—of improving their level of living. The kaleidoscopic pattern begins to make sense only if we stop thinking of Negroes as a homogeneous, undifferentiated group and begin to think of them as individuals who differ widely in their backgrounds, interests, abilities, training, and opportunities.

Statistics are required if we are to go beyond impressionistic judgment. Many people find statistics dull; but they are necessary, particularly in the charged atmosphere which exists in the field of race relations in the United States. Census data are often inadequate and sometimes misleading, because they do not penetrate very deeply into the subjects covered. They do, however, have the advantage of being collected by a uniform set of procedures over a long period of time by an organization which has high scientific standards and a reputation for objectivity. For this reason they are extremely useful as guidelines for making judgments about how the Negro is faring in this country. Statistics cannot present the complete picture because they are necessarily limited to those aspects of life which can be measured. Many important social and economic indicators cannot be measured accurately; yet there is much that can be learned from careful examination of the factual evidence we have in hand. There will undoubtedly be differences of opinion regarding the conclusions and the policy implications that can be derived from the data. The presence of hard facts, however, does limit the realm of speculation.

The figures are also important as an antidote to much of the propaganda that is circulated on the subject. Some of this misinformation comes from very respectable sources. Thus, for example, Elliot Liebow in his very fine book *Talley's Corner* states that "the number of the poor and their problems have grown steadily since World War II."[1] The first part of that statement, which is verifiable, is not supported by the facts. On the contrary, there has been a very marked drop in poverty since the end of World War II. Similarly, James Farmer, the civil rights leader who later joined the Republican establishment, stated in a lecture in 1967 at Temple University that "unemployment among Negroes has been increasing, while unemployment among whites has been decreasing."[2] This statement was also not supported by the facts at the time it was made. Unemployment for both groups dropped steadily between 1961 and 1967.

Much more important than the well-meaning people who are misinformed about the facts are the radical and revolutionary groups who have little interest in the facts. Their goal is to win power and they will use any methods that may be necessary to achieve that goal. At present they are thought to be small in number, but they are making a serious bid for control in the ghettos. Much of what men like Eldridge Cleaver, Malcolm X, and Stokely Carmichael have said is true. Many of the conditions they describe are deplorable. But there is also much that they leave out. They try to make it appear as though conditions are becoming steadily worse for the Negro and there is no hope for improvement short of a revolutionary overthrow of the present system. The improvements in income, employment, housing, and education during the latter part of the sixties do not support this very pessimistic outlook. The changes have perhaps been too slow and too small for some tastes; but they are there, they are significant, and they offer some hope.

Negro population growth

During the first two decades of this century, the white population grew more rapidly than the Negro population primarily because of the high rate of immigration from Europe. As a result, Negroes dropped from 12 percent of the total population in 1900 to 10 percent in 1920. With the severe restriction of immigration after the first world war, the higher birthrate of Negro women began to show its effect. For several decades, the Negro fraction of the total population edged up slightly and reached 11 percent in 1960.

People have strange ideas as to how fertility differentials between Blacks and whites may affect the future composition of the U.S. population. One high government official called the Census Bureau several years ago and wanted to know when Negroes would constitute a majority in the United States. An official of a top Negro organization stated publicly that he was opposed to family planning programs because they were a plot to reduce the size of the Negro family and thereby diminish the political power of Negroes. An article in *Life* magazine early in 1970 stated that "blacks, who are 11 percent of the population today, will be 17 percent by 1980." [3] And Gabriel Kolko, in his widely read book *Wealth and Power in America*, wrote, "In the 1950's, the rate of growth of the Negro population was two-thirds greater than that of the white population. Thus the proportionate number of Negroes is rising." [4] This is true, but what Kolko fails to say is that if past differentials in fertility remain unchanged, this proportion will rise by only one percentage point in the next fifteen years.

TABLE V-1

Total Population and Negro Population: 1900-1985*

Year	Total (millions)	Negro (millions)	Percentage Negro
1900	76.0	8.8	12%
1910	92.0	9.8	11
1920	105.7	10.5	10
1930	122.8	11.9	10
1940	131.7	12.9	10
1950	150.5	15.0	10
1960	178.5	18.8	11
1969	199.8	22.3	11
1985	249.3	31.0	12

*Data exclude armed forces overseas. Data for 1960 and later years include Alaska and Hawaii; data for 1950 and later years also exclude armed forces in the U.S. living in barracks.

U.S. Bureau of the Census, *Current Population Reports,* Series P-23, No. 29. Except where otherwise noted, all tables in this chapter are from this source. The figures for 1985 in the above table are estimated from *Current Population Reports,* Series P-25, No. 388.

The birthrate for Negro women is about 40 percent higher than that for white women. Much of this difference is due to the fact that Negro

LET MY PEOPLE GO

women generally have a lower socioeconomic status and they are more likely to come from a southern rural background, where birthrates for both Blacks and whites tend to be high. The birthrates for all women have dropped sharply from their postwar peaks in 1957. The relative decline was slightly greater for white women than for nonwhites; but the differentials by and large have remained the same. Both Negro and white women in all socioeconomic groups have more children than are required for replacement. In a few of the categories, the fertility of Negro women is high enough to double the population in a generation.

Among Negroes, the highest fertility is in the South, where a substantial portion of the Negro population still lives in rural areas. Among both white and Negro women, those who are more educated tend to have fewer children. This pattern, however, is more pronounced among Negroes.

Negro women with fewer than four years of high school have more children than white women at the same educational level. The figures are about even for high school graduates. Negro college women have fewer children than white women with the same amount of schooling.

TABLE V-2

Births per 1,000 Women 15 to 44 Years Old: 1955-1967

Year	Nonwhite	White
1955	155	114
1956	161	116
1957	163	118
1958	161	115
1959	162	114
1960	154	113
1961	154	112
1962	149	108
1963	145	104
1964	142	100
1965	134	91
1966	126	86
1967	120	83

See Table V-1 for source.

Since the educational attainment of Negro women is rising rapidly, there is a good possibility that the difference between white and Negro fertility rates will decline in the future. Similarly, the fertility differentials between white and Negro women are greatest in the nonmetropolitan areas and they are smallest in the central cities; they are very great in the South and quite small in the other regions. The fact that the proportion of Negro women living in central cities outside of the South has been increasing in recent years provides further reason to believe that fertility differentials between white and Negro women will decline in the future.

Statistics on babies born out of wedlock—illegitimacy—are perhaps the most controversial of all data pertaining to the Negro. The figures are not very good. In the first place, the national data are estimated on the basis of reports prepared by thirty-four states and the District of Columbia, where legitimacy is shown on birth certificates. The following states do not report legitimacy: Arizona, Arkansas, California, Colorado, Connecticut, Georgia, Idaho, Maryland, Massachusetts, Montana, Nebraska, New Hampshire, New Mexico, New York, Oklahoma, and Vermont. The illegitimacy figures for these states are estimated from the data reported by other states in nine geographic divisions. The figures are also deficient because they make no allowance for misstatements on birth records or for the failure to report births. These and other factors probably result in a proportionately greater understatement of illegitimacy among whites than among Blacks.

Despite their shortcomings, however, the figures do strongly suggest that since World War II there has been an increase in the proportion of Negro children born out of wedlock. Professor Jessie Bernard in her book *Marriage and Family Among Negroes* states that "postwar data clearly reveal a downward trend in the proportion of nonwhite infants borne in wedlock. No longer do we have to ask if this is a statistical illusion formed by migration, improved record-keeping procedures, reduced sterility and reduced fetal mortality. . . ."[5] She also concludes that the increase in illegitimacy among Negroes "involved nonconformity to both the institutional norms imposed by society: life-long commitment between the two partners and their support and protection until maturity of children borne in the union."[6]

The data in Table V-4 show that in 1967, nearly three of every ten nonwhite infants were born out of wedlock. One decade earlier only two out of ten were born out of wedlock and the number was consider-

TABLE V-3

Children Ever Born to All Women* 35 to 44 Years Old, by Specified Characteristics of Women: 1969

	Negro		White	
	Children ever born per woman	Replacement index†	Children ever born per woman	Replacement index†
United States	3.6	175	2.9	142
Region				
North and West	3.3	160	3.0	143
South	4.0	191	2.9	138
Residence				
Metropolitan	3.3	162	2.8	137
In central cities	3.3	159	2.7	131
Outside central cities	3.6	172	2.9	140
Nonmetropolitan	4.5	216	3.1	151
Education				
Elementary school	4.5	215	3.5	172
High school	3.5	167	2.9	139
College (1 year or more)	2.3	113	2.6	128

*Married or unmarried.

†Index of 100 denotes a stable population: one in which women will produce by age 45 exactly the number of female children needed for their own replacement. Negro women 35 to 44 years old have completed approximately 96 percent of their eventual lifetime childbearing, and white women of this age group have completed approximately 97 percent of their eventual lifetime childbearing.

See Table V-1 for source.

ably below that level in 1940. The rate of illegitimacy among white women has grown more rapidly than among nonwhites; however, the nonwhite rate in 1967 was six times the white rate. Although only about one-tenth of the women of childbearing age are nonwhite, they accounted for well over half of all the children born out of wedlock in 1967.

TABLE V-4

Illegitimate Births: 1940-1967

Year	Number (thousands)		Percentage of all live births	
	Nonwhite	White	Nonwhite	White
1940	49	40	16.8%	2.0%
1945	61	56	17.9	2.4
1950	88	54	18.0	1.8
1955	119	64	20.2	1.9
1960	142	83	21.6	2.3
1965	168	124	26.3	4.0
1966	170	133	27.7	4.4
1967	176	142	29.4	4.9

See Table V-1 for source.

The reasons for illegitimacy, particularly among Negro women, are numerous and complicated. Some psychiatrists stress deep-rooted psychological factors. Thus, for example, Hertha Riese, in *Heal the Hurt Child,* states that a large proportion of women who have babies out of wedlock may be identifying "with their unmarried grandmother and mother. . . . They hang on to their children as they did to their two mothers, because as mothers they still remain the dependent and helpless child."[7] Dr. Riese also attributes some illegitimacy to "a spiteful relationship to the father and a love against which both, father and daughter, defended themselves by hostility."[8] Since most unwed mothers are poor young women, illegitimacy is often attributed to promiscuity—a failure on the part of low-income people to adopt the standards of acceptable sexual behavior. In many cases that is undoubtedly true. But psychologist Kenneth Clark argues that "the consistently higher illegitimacy rate among Negroes is not a reflection of less virtue or greater promiscuity, but rather of the fact that the middle-class teen-agers are taught to use contraceptives and learn how to protect themselves from the hazards of premarital and illicit sexual contacts. The middle-class girl is able to resort to abortions, or she gives birth secretly, surrendering the child for adoption. In the case of marginal young people, or the up-

wardly mobile Negro, what contraceptive ideas he has are unreliable. . . .
Illegitimacy among these groups, therefore, is a consequence in large
part of poverty and ignorance." [9]

In 1968, a study of unwed mothers was made by Dr. Patricia Schiller
at the Webster School in Washington, D.C. She made a detailed individual psychological examination of 400 pregnant school-age girls and
found that they had a "desperate need for a reciprocal love relationship
. . . the self-image of a vast majority was inadequate. Many felt anxious
about their personalities, appearances and a chance for success in marriage. To many a close physical showing meant love, caring and belong-
ing." [10] These findings, according to Dr. Schiller, corroborate the impressions of Dr. Clark Vincent in his book *Unmarried Mothers,* in which
he reported that most unwed mothers described either a love relationship or a close friendship with the men who fathered their children.

Further doubt on the promiscuity thesis is provided in the Child
Rearing Study of Low-Income Families conducted in the District of Columbia several years ago under a grant from the National Institutes of
Health. This study reports that "low income families know the standards
of acceptable behavior, even though statistics, such as those for illegitimacy, may suggest that they more often fall short of achieving those
standards." [11] The report also points out that "the sexuality of poor
families is not generally spontaneous, natural and free of inhibitions,
and that poor families do attach a stigma to illegitimacy." There also
seems to be a considerable amount of misinformation about sex among
the poor, and prudish attitudes and other inhibitions often preclude adequate communication between parents and children. Here, for example,
in her own words, is the statement by a mother of twelve children, all
legitimate, about her own sex education: [12]

> . . . I didn't know anything about sex or intercourse until I married. My
> mother and father never told us anything about sex or even about menstrua-
> tion. . . . After I started menstruating I told my sisters about it. I was the
> "teacher" for my sisters.
> . . . My mother used to sit down with all of us girls and tell us not to kiss
> boys. She also told us not to answer questions which the boys asked. She said,
> "If the boys you go to parties with and who come here to see you ask any
> questions, tell the boys to come and ask me and your father. . . ."
> We used to ask mother when she was carrying a baby how did she get that
> way. . . . She would just say, "It is mother nature." One of my sisters said she
> was going to slip out and find out what mother was talking about. This sister
> turned and slipped out and had a baby before she was married. . . .

I got married rather than slip up. I didn't say anything to my parents about getting married. I just went off and got married when I was 18 years old. No, mother didn't want me to get married and she told me absolutely nothing about marriage.

Migration from the South

The constantly growing concentration of Negroes in the central cities of metropolitan areas is one of the most important population trends in the United States. This change is closely related to the migration of Negroes from the South in recent years. Until the first decade of this century, about nine-tenths of all Negroes lived in the South. Although Negro birthrates in this region have remained high, the proportion of Negroes living in the South has dropped regularly. The reason for the decline is migration. In 1969, slightly more than half of all Negroes lived in the South. The mainspring of the growth of the Negro population in the northern and western cities has been migration from the South, supplemented, to be sure, by the high birthrate of those already living in large cities.

There was relatively little movement of Negroes from the South until the outbreak of World War I. In fact, the net migration of Negroes

TABLE V-5

Percentage Distribution of Negro Population by Region

Region	1940*	1950*	1960	1966	1969
United States	100%	100%	100%	100%	100%
South	77	68	60	55	52
North	22	28	34	37	41
Northeast	11	13	16	17	19
North Central	11	15	18	20	21
West	1	4	6	8	7

*Data exclude Alaska and Hawaii.

See Table V-1 for source.

TABLE V-6

Negroes as a Percentage of Total Population by Region

Region	1940*	1950*	1960	1969
United States	10%	10%	11%	11%
South	24	22	21	19
North	4	5	7	9
Northeast	4	5	7	9
North Central	4	5	7	8
West	1	3	4	5

*Data exclude Alaska and Hawaii.

See Table V-1 for source.

from the South during the entire period 1870–1910 was less than the net movement during the 1910–1920 decade, when an average of 45,000 Negroes left the South each year. Despite the great need for unskilled labor in the industrial economy that emerged after the Civil War, there was relatively little hiring of Negroes. Most of these jobs were filled by European immigrants who flocked to this country at the rate of about one million per year around the turn of the century. Nearly all Negroes who were employed in the North worked in "certain occupational niches such as domestic service, pullman car porters, and some construction and slaughter house jobs."[13] It was only after the flow of immigrants stopped with the outbreak of World War I and the pressure for workers increased in the booming war industries that the northern labor market was opened to Negro workers. During the decade 1910–1920 about one-half million Negroes left the South. Once the foothold in northern cities was established, the Negro migration stream nearly doubled during the prosperous twenties. During the depression the migration diminished due to the scarcity of jobs, but it reached the very high rate of 160,000 per year during the forties and was reduced only slightly during the fifties. During the sixties, the net migration of Negroes from the South dropped sharply. In the late sixties, the annual rate of net migration was about 80,000 per year, about half of the peak rate attained during the forties. One reason for the drop in recent years is the availability of job opportunities in southern cities. It is also likely that there has been some disenchantment with life in the big cities of the North.

TABLE V-7

Negro Population in the South and Estimated Net Migration of Nonwhites from the South: 1940-1969

	1940	1950	1960	1969
Negro population in the South (thousands)	9,905	10,222	11,312	11,630*

	1940-50	1950-60	1960-69
Average annual net migration of nonwhites from the South (thousands)	159.7	145.7	88.3

*Excludes armed forces living in barracks.

See Table V-1 for source.

At first Negroes moved into the older sections of the northern cities. That was where low-cost housing was available and where their friends and relatives lived. Once they gained a foothold in these new communities, the more successful families moved to adjacent areas where they formed the nucleus of an expanding Negro community within the central city. Although large numbers of these families attained incomes, jobs, and education that equaled or surpassed those of whites, they remained within predominantly Negro neighborhoods, primarily because they were excluded from white residential areas.

Concentration of Negroes in cities

People throughout the world have long shown a decided preference for city life. In the United States, two persons out of every three live in metropolitan areas. Since 1900, the nation's population has more than doubled. In that same time, the number of people in metropolitan areas has increased much faster (about three and one-half times).

Both Negroes and whites show a preference for metropolitan areas. The Negroes in metropolitan areas are concentrated in the central cities, where 56 percent of all Negroes now live. Whites live predominantly in the suburbs of metropolitan areas or in small cities. Only about one-fourth of the white population lives in central cities.

TABLE V-8

Percentage Distribution of Population Inside and Outside Metropolitan Areas

Location	Negro			White		
	1950	1960	1969	1950	1960	1969
United States	100%	100%	100%	100%	100%	100%
Metropolitan areas	56	65	70	60	63	64
Central cities	43	51	55	34	30	26
Suburbs	13	13	15	26	33	38
Outside metropolitan areas	44	35	30	40	37	36

See Table V-1 for source.

In recent years practically all of the growth in the metropolitan areas has been in the suburbs. Since 1960, the central cities as a whole have grown by only about 1 percent; the suburbs by 28 percent. In 1960, the suburbs had slightly fewer people than the central cities. Since then the balance has shifted. Today more than half the people in metropolitan areas live outside the central cities. There is every indication that this fraction is likely to grow.

Central cities are steadily becoming more Negro while the suburbs remain almost entirely white. As a group, the central cities gained about one-half million persons between 1960 and 1969. This net change was the result of an increase of 2.6 million in the Negro population and a decline of 2.1 million in the white population. About three-fourths of the growth in the Negro population since 1960 has occurred in the central cities.

TABLE V-9

Population of United States, by Race and Location

	Number (thousands)			Average annual percentage change	
	1960	1964	1969	1950-60	1960-69
Negro	18,793	20,514	22,331	2.3%	2.0%
Metropolitan areas	12,168	13,970	15,594	3.8	2.8
In central cities	9,687	11,282	12,317	4.1	2.7
Outside central cities	2,481	2,688	3,278	2.7	3.2
Nonmetropolitan areas	6,625	6,541	6,736	–	0.2
White	158,051	167,146	175,311	1.6	1.2
Metropolitan areas	99,740	106,406	111,736	2.2	1.3
In central cities	47,463	47,632	45,348	0.5	−0.5
Outside central cities	52,277	58,774	66,387	4.0	2.7
Nonmetropolitan areas	58,311	60,735	63,577	0.7	1.0

See Table V-1 for source.

Negroes in 1969 were 21 percent of the total population of central cities in metropolitan areas, compared with 12 percent in 1950. The larger the city, the faster the Negro population is growing and the greater the percentage of Negroes. Negroes are 26 percent of the population in cities of metropolitan areas with 1 million or more people, compared with 13 percent in 1950. Only 5 percent of the suburban population is Negro.

If past trends continue, nearly half of our population will be living in the suburban parts of our metropolitan areas in 1985 and only one-fourth will be living in central cities. Virtually all of the white growth is expected to take place in the suburban ring, whereas the nonwhite growth is expected to occur primarily in the central cities. One-third of the central city residents are expected to be Black in 1985 as compared with one-fifth at present.

TABLE V-10

Negroes as a Percentage of Total Population by Location

Location	1950	1960	1969
United States	10%	11%	11%
Metropolitan areas	9	11	12
Central cities	12	17	21
Central cities in metropolitan areas of:			
1 million or more	13	19	26
250,000 to 1 million	12	15	18
Under 250,000	12	12	12
Suburbs	5	5	5
Outside metropolitan areas	11	10	9

See Table V-1 for source.

These population trends permit us to see the financial problems of cities in somewhat better perspective. The increase in the size of the dependent population, as well as the higher standards of public service that are demanded generally, accounts for much of the rise in expenditures for welfare, education, police protection, and other public services in cities.

But that is not the full story. Another important aspect is the loss of people generally, rather than replacement of the middle class by the poor. Between 1960 and 1968, the population in central cities rose slightly, whereas the suburban population rose by 15 million. Since the volume of business generally depends on the size of the population, there has been a great movement of retail trade to suburban shopping areas. Manufacturing establishments have also found it advantageous to leave the city and most of the new home construction in recent years has been in the suburbs. As a result, an important part of the city tax base has been eroded. Even if city residents had the same income distribution as suburbanites, the city coffers would be in trouble.

It is not fashionable today among Black militants to talk about integration as a social goal, but there still are some Black leaders who attach great importance to this objective. In 1968, for example, Kenneth Clark wrote that "if we really mean to stabilize our cities, our suburbs, and our society as a whole, plans have to be developed with the clear goal of reducing present ghettos and preventing the establishment of future ones."[14] According to the available evidence not much progress was made in this direction during the sixties. Whites continue to leave the central cities in large numbers and are being replaced to a large extent by Blacks. This differential migration is causing the Negro population of central cities to become proportionately greater with the passage of time.

In choosing places in which to live, the more favored groups in terms of occupation, education, or income have selected suburban areas rather than central cities. This preference has not bridged the color line to any significant extent. White professional men live in suburban areas to a greater extent than the white population as a whole, but Negro professional men are more likely to be living in central cities. Similarly, white clerical or sales workers have shown some preference for suburban living, but Negro clerical or sales workers tend to live within the central cities. Among the white population, persons who have had only a grade school education are more likely to be found in the central cities, and those with high school and college education are disproportionately found in the suburbs. Among the Negro population, those at any given level of education are more likely to be living in the central cities than in the suburbs.

Unemployment

Unemployment is a sensitive indicator of economic change. As a rule of thumb, the unemployment rate of Negroes is about twice that of whites, regardless of the age or sex of the group that is compared or the general economic climate at the time of the comparison. The 2:1 ratio is particularly stable for adult men and women. Among teen-agers, however, there has been a growing disparity between the rates for whites and Negroes since the recession of 1957-1958. In 1969, nearly one-fourth of Negro teen-agers were unemployed, as compared with about 11 percent for the whites.

The fact that unemployment rates have dropped sharply—and that they have dropped proportionately as much for Negroes as for whites

TABLE V-11

Unemployment Rates*: 1949-1969

Year	Annual average		Ratio of nonwhite to white
	Nonwhite	White	
1949	8.9%	5.6%	1.6
1950	9.0	4.9	1.8
1951	5.3	3.1	1.7
1952	5.4	2.8	1.9
1953	4.5	2.7	1.7
1954	9.9	5.0	2.0
1955	8.7	3.9	2.2
1956	8.3	3.6	2.3
1957	7.9	3.8	2.1
1958	12.6	6.1	2.1
1959	10.7	4.8	2.2
1960	10.2	4.9	2.1
1961	12.4	6.0	2.1
1962	10.9	4.9	2.2
1963	10.8	5.0	2.2
1964	9.6	4.6	2.1
1965	8.1	4.1	2.0
1966	7.3	3.3	2.2
1967	7.4	3.4	2.2
1968	6.7	3.2	2.1
1969	6.5†	3.2†	2.0

*The unemployment rate is the percentage of unemployed in the civilian labor force.

†1969 figures are an average of January-November.

See Table V-1 for source.

during the economic expansion of the sixties—is a sign of progress. It must also be noted, however, that the unemployment rate for Negroes at the height of prosperity is greater than the rate for whites during any of the past three recessions. The high rate of youth unemployment is particularly distressing not only because of the immediate frustrations and hardships it causes for the youngsters and their families, but also because

TABLE V-12

Unemployment Rates by Sex and Age: 1957-1969*

	Nonwhite			White		
	1957	1968	1969	1957	1968	1969
Total	7.9%	6.7%	6.5%	3.8%	3.2%	3.2%
Adult men	7.6	3.9	3.7	3.2	2.0	1.9
Adult women	6.4	6.3	6.0	3.8	3.4	3.4
Teen-agers†	19.1	25.0	24.4	10.6	11.0	10.8

*Data for 1957 and 1968 are annual averages; 1969 figures are an average of January-November.
†Persons 16 to 19 years old.

See Table V-1 for source; also Bureau of Labor Statistics, *Employment and Earnings,* February 1969.

it undermines training programs and the attempts to prevent school dropouts. If one-fourth of Negro youths are still unable to find jobs after nine years of continuous prosperity, they have a right to join the chorus when Bayard Rustin asks: "What is this foolishness about training? You can't train any segment of the population unless there's a demand for their work."

In contrast to the favorable trends in the data for the nation, the census conducted in Watts shortly after the riots of 1965 showed that in this ghetto unemployment rates in that peak year were nearly as high as they had been in the recession year of 1960.

Equally significant as the high unemployment rate in Watts was the sharp rise in the proportion of men who had dropped out of the labor force (stopped working or looking for work). In 1960 about 70 percent of the men in Watts were in the labor force, as compared with only 58 percent in 1965. (Nationally, about three-fourths of the Negro men are in the labor force.) This change largely reflects a rise in hidden unemployment among men who have simply stopped looking for jobs.

During 1969, when national unemployment rates were at their lowest level since the Korean war, unemployment rates for Negroes in the poverty areas of large cities were still quite high. At that time, the national unemployment rate for nonwhites was 6.5 percent; the nonwhite unemployment rate was 15.2 percent in the poverty areas in Los Angeles, 13.5 percent in Detroit, and over 9 percent in Houston and Atlanta.

TABLE V-13

Unemployment Rates for Nonwhite Persons 16 and Over in Poverty Areas of Six Large Cities: July 1968–June 1969

Total U.S.	6.5%
Poverty areas of	
Atlanta	9.4
Chicago	8.8
Detroit	13.5
Houston	9.5
Los Angeles	15.2
New York City	6.7

See Table V-1 for source.

Occupational change

There were some rather striking changes in the occupational distribution of nonwhite men and women between 1960 and 1968. Among men, the most significant change was a drop in the proportion employed as farm workers (from 14 to 7 percent) and as laborers (from 23 to 18 percent). At the same time, the proportion employed as professional workers and as craftsmen increased rather sharply. The increase in professional and technical employment among nonwhite men translates into about 200,000 additional Negro families that have their feet firmly on the bottom rung of the middle-class ladder. These are the families that can make the break from Harlem to Long Island and from the District of Columbia to Bethesda. These are the new faces now appearing as TV announcers, government officials, and business executives.

It was not so very long ago that Negroes graduating from college could look forward to careers as preachers, teachers, or social workers, and little more. That situation now seems to have changed. Negroes are now being admitted to the better white colleges in growing numbers and white employers seem to be willing and even anxious to hire qualified Negro professional workers. Many personnel managers claim that the demand for Negro professionals far exceeds the qualified supply. If this is so, the numbers employed in the better-paid professional jobs might be expected to increase more rapidly in the future as more young Negro men complete college.

Despite the signs of progress, the most striking fact about the occupational distribution of nonwhite men remains their very heavy concentration in low-paid jobs. Nearly 40 percent of Negro men still work as laborers, janitors, porters, busboys, and in similar service jobs.

The progress for women has been much more striking than that for men. Cleaning up white people's homes is still a common type of job among Negro women. About 20 percent do this kind of work. Although the proportion has dropped sharply since 1960, it is still very high, especially when one considers that an additional 10 percent do the same kind of work as domestics (chambermaids, charwomen, janitors, etc.) but are employed by hotels, restaurants, hospitals, and similar service establishments rather than by housewives. Thus, in 1969, after several years of progress, conservatively 30 percent of the Negro women are doing unskilled and menial housework in one form or another.

Yet there has been a sharp increase in the number of Negro women employed in white-collar jobs. The proportion has risen from 19 to 34 percent for the three job categories—professional, clerical, and sales.

When the figures on occupational change are examined in terms of absolutes rather than percentages, the increase in the number of well-paying jobs among nonwhites becomes even more apparent. Between 1960 and 1969, there was a net increase of about 440,000 nonwhite professional and managerial workers, 637,000 clerical and sales workers, and 290,000 craftsmen—a total increase, in other words, of about 1½ million nonwhite workers in jobs that tend to have good pay or status.

Blacks hold poorer jobs than whites for a variety of reasons. Discrimination in employment is undoubtedly a major factor, but part of the difference is also due to the poorer family background, training, and educational attainment of Blacks. An attempt is made in Table V-16 to quantify some of the factors which account for the difference. If a numerical score ranging from 0 to 96 is assigned to each occupation, we can see from this table that white men had an average score of 43.5 in 1962 as compared with an average of 19.7 for Negro men. Only about

TABLE V-14

Percentage Distribution of Employment by Occupation: 1960 and 1969*

Occupation	Nonwhite				White			
	Male		Female		Male		Female	
	1960	1969	1960	1969	1960	1969	1960	1969
Total employed (thousands)	4,148	4,768	2,779	3,601	39,755	44,075	19,095	25,377
Professional, technical, and managerial	7%	11%	8%	12%	26%	29%	19%	19%
Clerical and sales	7	9	11	22	14	13	42	44
Craftsmen and foremen	10	14	1	1	20	21	1	1
Operatives	24	28	14	18	19	19	15	15
Service workers, except household	15	13	22	25	6	6	14	15
Private household workers			35	20			5	3
Nonfarm laborers	23	18	1	1	6	6	–	–
Farmers and farm workers	14	7	9	2	9	6	4	2

Note: Sums of tabulated figures in this chapter may not equal totals because of rounding.

*1960 figures are annual averages; 1969 data are an average of January–November.

Derived from Table V-1; also Bureau of Labor Statistics, *Employment and Earnings*, December 1969.

TABLE V-15

Employment by Occupation, and Net Change: 1960-1969*

Occupation	Employed, 1969 (thousands)		Change, 1960 to 1969			
			Number (thousands)		Percentage	
	Non-white	White	Non-white	White	Non-white	White
Total	8,369	69,452	1,442	10,602	21%	18%
Professional and technical	692	10,031	361	2,893	109	41
Managers, officials, and proprietors	254	7,721	76	832	43	12
Clerical	1,078	12,282	575	3,023	114	33
Sales	163	4,488	62	365	61	9
Craftsmen and foremen	704	9,485	289	1,346	70	17
Operatives	1,998	12,379	584	1,843	41	17
Service workers, except private household	1,525	6,371	311	1,535	26	32
Private household workers	712	900	−270	−91	−28	−9
Nonfarm laborers	876	2,809	−75	207	−8	8
Farmers and farm workers	366	2,986	−475	−1,349	−56	−31

*Annual averages for 1960; January-November averages for 1969.

See Table V-1 for source.

half of the difference of 23.8 points can be accounted for by family background and education; the remainder is due to all other causes, among which discrimination would be very important.

Similar findings were obtained in a study made for the Equal Employment Opportunity Commission in 1966. This study was based on 43,000 employees covering 26 million workers. In reporting the results, Charles B. Markham, former research director for the Commission, stated that lower educational level "accounts for only about one-third of the difference in occupational ranking between Negro men and majority group men; the inevitable conclusion is that the other two-thirds must be attributed to discrimination, deliberate or inadvertent."[15]

TABLE V-16

Factors Accounting for Differences
in Occupational Status of White and Negro Men: 1962*

	Mean occupation score	Difference in score	Factors accounting for difference†
White:	43.5		
		6.6	Family (A)
	36.9		
		0.6	Siblings (B)
	36.3		
		4.8	Education (C)
	31.5		
		11.8	Occupation (D)
Negro:	19.7		
		23.8	Total (T)

*Data are for native white and Negro men 25 to 64 years old, with nonfarm background and in the experienced civilian labor force in March 1962. The mean occupation score is based on a numerical rating from 0 to 96 assigned to each occupation.

†Difference due to:

Family (A)—socioeconomic level of family of origin (head's education and occupation).

Siblings (B)—number of siblings (net of family origin level).

Education (C)—education (net of siblings and family origin level).

Occupation (D)—occupation (net of education, siblings, and family origin level).

Total (T)—total difference (sum of components A through D).

Department of Health, Education and Welfare, *Towards a Social Report*. Government Printing Office, 1969, p. 25.

Income

Income is an important measure of success in our society. Although Negro family income remains low in comparison with the rest of the population, the income of both Negroes and whites is at an all-time high and the gap between the two groups has narrowed. In 1968 Negro family income was only 60 percent of white income; yet, three years earlier it was 54 percent and a decade earlier (1958) it was only about 50 percent.

TABLE V-17

Median Income of Nonwhite Families
as a Percentage of White Family Income: 1950-1968

Year	All nonwhite	Negro
1950	54%	NA
1951	53	NA
1952	57	NA
1953	56	NA
1954	56	NA
1955	55	NA
1956	53	NA
1957	54	NA
1958	51	NA
1959	52	NA
1960	55	NA
1961	53	NA
1962	53	NA
1963	53	NA
1964	56	54%
1965	55	54
1966	60	58
1967	62	59
1968	63	60

NA = not available

See Table V-1 for source.

One reason for the large difference between white and Negro family income is that most Negroes live in the South where incomes are far below the national average and where job opportunities for Negroes are more restricted than elsewhere. Table V-18 shows that in the North and West the Negro average income was nearly three-fourths of the white average. Although the income differential between the races has not changed much in the North and West since 1959, the overall Negro average has risen from 51 percent in 1959 to 60 percent in 1968 largely because more Negroes are living in the northern and western states.

Another reason why Negro incomes are lower than those of whites is that proportionately more Negro families are headed by women,

TABLE V-18

Median Income of Negro Families
as a Percentage of White Income: 1959 and 1968

Age of Head	1959			1968		
	United States	North and West	South	United States	North and West	South
All families						
Total	51%	71%	46%	60%	73%	54%
14 to 24	54	57	62	67	73	66
25 to 34	55	69	48	62	72	55
35 to 44	54	69	45	59	69	51
45 to 54	49	68	44	62	74	53
55 to 64	49	74	47	57	73	52
65 and over	52	75	58	65	83	69
Husband-wife families						
Total	57%	76%	50%	72%	85%	60%
14 to 24	61	75	64	88	99	79
25 to 34	64	78	54	78	87	66
35 to 44	60	74	50	72	84	61
45 to 54	55	70	48	70	84	56
55 to 64	51	75	49	59	81	53
65 and over	57	82	63	64	79	65

U.S. Bureau of the Census.

whose earnings are low because they are often burdened with family responsibilities and they generally lack the skills to command a decent wage in the labor market. For the country as a whole, the average income of Negro husband-wife families was 72 percent of the white average in 1968, and in the North and West it was 85 percent of the white average. Particularly significant is the fact that the incomes of young Negro families in the North and West are nearly the same as those of young white families. This represents a marked change from the situation a decade ago, when the income gap between young Negro families and white families outside of the South was 25 percent. The clear implication of these figures is that the incomes of young Negro couples in the northern and western states are responding favorably to the efforts that have been made in recent years to improve their education, training, and job opportunities. These are the groups that would be most likely to show the greatest improvement because many of them have recently completed their education or training at improved schools and are better prepared to compete for jobs.

The figures shown above pertain to the relative income gap, which has narrowed. But what about the absolute gap—the dollar gap? This gap between whites and nonwhites has widened since 1947. In that year, white families averaged $4,900 and nonwhites $2,500. The whites made $2,400 more. By 1968, the incomes of both groups had risen markedly, but so had the dollar gap. Family income in 1968 averaged $8,900 for whites and $5,600 for nonwhites. The whites made $3,300 more. Thus we find that although nonwhites gained *relatively* more income than whites between 1947 and 1968, the absolute gains were greater for whites.

Perhaps as significant as the gap between the incomes of the two groups is the actual amount of income received by nonwhite families. In 1968, one-fifth of the nonwhite families received more than $10,000 a

TABLE V-19

Distribution of Families
by Income Level (in 1968 Dollars): 1947, 1960, and 1968

	Nonwhite			White		
	1947	1960	1968	1947	1960	1968
Number of families (thousands)	3,117	4,333	5,075	34,120	41,123	45,440
Under $3,000	60%	41%	23%	23%	16%	9%
$3,000 to $4,999	23	23	22	28	16	11
$5,000 to $6,999	9	16	17	23	21	14
$7,000 to $9,999	5	13	18	15	26	24
$10,000 to $14,999	3 }	6	15	11 }	17	26
$15,000 and over		2	6		7	16
Median income	$2,514	$3,794	$5,590	$4,916	$6,857	$8,937

See Table V-1 for source.

year—more than double the proportion with incomes that high just eight years earlier, taking into account the changes in the cost of living. Conversely, the proportion of nonwhite families with incomes under $3,000 was cut by 50 percent from 1960 to 1968.

The working wife has been a significant factor in the rise of family incomes among both whites and nonwhites. At the middle-income levels, about two-thirds of the nonwhite women and one-half of the white women are employed. In both groups, the husbands are the chief providers and the women are merely supplementary earners. The earnings of working wives account for only one-fourth of the total Negro family income. The image that many people have of the Negro woman as the economic bulwark of the typical Negro family is not supported by the facts.

How much of the difference in income between white and Negro men is attributable to specific factors such as family background, years of school completed, and occupation? Table V-20 shows that, on the average, white men received $3,790 more than Negro men in 1961. Family background and family size accounted for $1,010 of this difference, lower educational attainment accounted for $520, and lower occupational status accounted for $830. But even after all of these factors are taken into account, there is still a gap of $1,430 (over one-third of the total difference) not accounted for, suggesting that Negro men earn less than white men with comparable family background, educational attainment, and occupational level. These figures suggest that in 1961 roughly one-third of the income differential between white and Negro men was attributable to market discrimination.

Education

Increases in educational attainment in recent years, as measured by years of school completed, have been made by both whites and Negroes, with the increases made by young adult Negro men being especially dramatic. In 1966, only half of Negro men 25 to 29 years old were high school graduates, but in 1969, 60 percent of the Negro men of this age had at least completed high school. The percentage of Negro men who have completed college has also increased in the recent past. In 1966, only 5 percent of Negro men 25 to 34 years old had completed college, as compared with 8 percent of the Negro men of this age in 1969.

TABLE V-20

Factors Accounting for Differences in Income of White and Negro Men: 1961*

	Mean income	Difference in income	Factors accounting for difference†
White:	$7,070		
		$940	Family (A)
	6,130		
		70	Siblings (B)
	6,060		
		520	Education (C)
	5,540		
		830	Occupation (D)
	4,710		
		1,430	Income (E)
Negro:	3,280		
		$3,790	Total (T)

*Data are for native white and Negro men 25 to 64 years old, with nonfarm background and in the experienced civilian labor force in March 1962.
†Difference due to:
   Family (A)—socioeconomic level of family of origin (head's education and occupation).
   Siblings (B)—number of siblings (net of family origin level).
   Education (C)—education (net of siblings and family origin level).
   Occupation (D)—occupation (net of education, siblings, and family origin level).
   Income (E)—income (net of occupation, education, siblings, and family origin level).
   Total (T)—total difference (sum of components A through E).

Department of Health, Education and Welfare, *Towards a Social Report*. Government Printing Office, 1969, p. 25.

The figures in Tables V-21 and V-22, however, show that even with these gains in educational attainment by young Negro men, there is still a large gap between the level of education of these men as compared with that of white men of the same age. Although 60 percent of the Negro men 25 to 29 years old have completed at least four years of high school, 78 percent of the white men of this age are at least high school

TABLE V-21

Percentage of Population 25 to 29 Years Old
Having Completed Four Years or More of High School:
1960, and 1966 to 1969

Year	Male		Female	
	Negro	White	Negro	White
1960	37%	63%	39%	65%
1966	49	73	47	74
1967	52	74	55	75
1968	58	76	54	75
1969	60	78	52	77

See Table V-1 for source.

graduates. And 20 percent of white men 25 to 34 years old have completed four years of college or more, as compared with 8 percent of the Negro men of this age.

In the past few years, there have been significant increases in the school enrollment of Negroes at the noncompulsory attendance ages.

TABLE V-22

Percentage of Population 25 to 34 Years Old
Having Completed Four Years or More of College:
1960, 1966, and 1969

Year	Negro			White		
	Total	Male	Female	Total	Male	Female
1960	4.3%	3.9%	4.6%	11.7%	15.7%	7.8%
1966	5.7	5.2	6.1	14.6	18.9	10.4
1969	6.6	7.6	5.6	16.2	20.2	12.3

See Table V-1 for source.

Among those below the compulsory attendance age—children 3 and 4 years old—the percentage enrolled in nursery school and kindergarten increased from 10 percent in 1964 to 19 percent in 1968. In fact, Negro children 3 and 4 years old are more likely to be enrolled in school than are the white children of this age. This early enrollment in preprimary education of young Negro children holds promise of a further narrowing of the gap in educational attainment between Negroes and whites. The Head Start projects with their nursery school and kindergarten programs of preprimary education, which began in 1965, must be given credit for a part of this increase in the enrollment of 3- and 4-year-olds.

Among those over the compulsory attendance age, there have also been substantial gains in the percentage enrolled in school. The percentage of 18- and 19-year-old Negroes enrolled in school increased from 36 percent in 1964 to 45 percent in 1968, and the percentage of 20- to 24-year-old Negroes enrolled increased from 8 percent to 12 percent during the same period.

The number of Negroes in college has also increased rapidly, as Table V-23 shows. In 1968, there were 434,000 Negroes enrolled in college— 6 percent of total college enrollment—an increase of 85 percent over the 234,000 Negroes enrolled in college in 1964. The Negroes enrolled in college are not as likely to be enrolled in predominantly Negro colleges (many of which have relatively low academic standards) now as they were in the past. In 1968, only a little over one-third of the Negroes in college were in predominantly Negro colleges, but in 1964 one-half of the Negroes in college were in Negro colleges.

Increase in "broken" families

One of the most controversial government reports produced during the decade of the sixties is the Labor Department study *The Negro Family,* popularly known as the Moynihan Report.[16] The fundamental thesis of this report is that much of the gap between whites and Negroes is attributable to a deteriorating family structure among Negroes. The report states categorically: "The Negro family in the urban ghettos is crumbling. A middle-class group has managed to save itself, but for vast numbers of the unskilled, poorly educated city working class, the fabric of conventional social relationships has all but disintegrated."[17] The re-

TABLE V-23

Negro College Students: 1964 and 1968*

	Year†		Increase, 1964-68	
	1964	1968	Number	Percentage
Total enrollment (all races)	4,643	6,801	2,158	46%
Total Negro enrollment	234	434	200	85
Percentage of total enrollment	5%	6%	NA	NA
Enrollment in predominantly Negro colleges	120	156	36	30
Percentage of all Negroes in college	51%	36%	NA	NA
Enrollment in other colleges	114	278	164	144
Percentage of all Negroes in college	49%	64%	NA	NA

NA = not applicable
*Enrollment figures in thousands.
†Fall term.

See Table V-1 for source.

port goes on to note that "the white family has achieved a high degree of stability and is maintaining that stability. By contrast, the family structure of lower class Negroes is highly unstable."[18]

One measure of family instability is the proportion of families headed by women. This is admittedly a very crude measure. Some women have family responsibilities thrust upon them because of widowhood and others have husbands who are away in the armed forces or are otherwise away from home involuntarily. Nevertheless, a very important reason why women head families is because of divorce or separation, and a sharp increase over time in the proportion of female-headed families may be regarded as symptomatic of a family problem. The figures below suggest that family instability has increased among nonwhites during the years 1950-1969. There has been no change in the proportion of white families headed by women since 1950. In contrast, the proportion of nonwhite families headed by women has increased from 18 percent in 1950 to 27 percent in 1969. Despite the rise in family income in recent years and the improvement in the occupational distribution of nonwhite men, there is no evidence of a corresponding improvement in family stability.

TABLE V-24

Percentage of Families Headed by Women: 1950-1969

Year	Nonwhite	White
1950	18%	9%
1955	21	9
1960	22	9
1966	24	9
1967	24	9
1968	26	9
1969	27	9

See Table V-1 for source.

Deterioration in the worst slum areas

Although the Negro ghetto goes by different names in different places—Harlem, Watts, Cardozo in Washington, Hough in Cleveland—it is basically the same everywhere: a decaying part of the central city that has been largely deserted by white residents and by those Negroes who could get out. These ghettos have no walls as in medieval European cities and the inhabitants wear no special uniform. Most of them, however, are just as surely locked in as were the Jews in Central and Eastern Europe a century ago. The important point, with respect to poverty, is that nearly half of the poor in the big cities of the United States live in these ghettos. Whereas the white poor in the big cities are dispersed, and a large proportion are aged, the Negro poor are concentrated and young— nearly 60 percent are under 21. According to Kenneth Clark, "Pathology is rampant in northern urban ghettos." [19] He points out that "the homicide rate and the delinquency rate in Negro ghettos . . . have not decreased. The ugliness of the ghetto has not been abolished. The overcrowding has increased. . . . Ghetto business continues to be unstable, inefficient, and for the most part controlled by absentee owners. Unemployment and underemployment remain high, particularly among males. The welfare system continues to reinforce family instability. . . . The educational system of the ghetto has decayed even further."[20]

If statistics are needed to document these points they can be found in the results of the test census that was taken in Cleveland several years ago. Outside of the poorest neighborhoods in Cleveland, Negro families made major gains between 1960 and 1965. Average incomes rose, the incidence of poverty was cut nearly in half, and the number of broken families was sharply reduced. But in the poorest neighborhoods, all of these social indicators showed deterioration. In Hough, one of the worst of the poor neighborhoods, the incidence of poverty increased, the proportion of broken homes increased, and the male unemployment rate remained virtually unchanged. A similar study made in various neighbor-

---

TABLE V-25

Changes in Conditions of Negroes in Cleveland: 1960 to 1965

	Poverty areas				Remainder of Cleveland	
	Total		Hough			
	1960	1965	1960	1965	1960	1965
Population (thousands)	203	202	53	52	48	75
Percentage population change	–	*	–	–2%	–	+55%
Percentage of families below poverty level	29%	31%	31%	39%	15%	13%
Percentage of families with female head	22%	27%	23%	32%	13%	12%
Median family income†	$4,756	$4,772	$4,732	$3,966	$6,199	$6,929
Male unemployment rate	13.8%	12.1%	15.7%	14.3%	8.8%	7.5%

*Less than ½%.

†1960 figures are for income in 1959, adjusted for price changes to 1964 dollars. 1965 figures are for income in 1964.

U.S. Bureau of the Census, *Current Population Reports,* Series P-23, No. 24, p. 95.

TABLE V-26

Changes in Conditions of Negroes
in Watts Area of Los Angeles: 1960 to 1965

	1960	1965
Number of families	6,180	5,300
Percentage population change	–	–14%
Percentage of families below poverty level	44%	43%
Percentage of families with female head	36%	39%
Median family income	$3,632*	$3,771†
Male unemployment rate	16%	14%
Percentage of deteriorating housing units	14%	21%
Percentage of dilapidated housing units	2%	4%
Median gross rent	$63	$73

*Income in 1959, adjusted for price changes to 1964 dollars.
†Income in 1964.

U.S. Bureau of the Census, *Current Population Reports,* Series P-23, No. 24, p. 96.

hoods in South Los Angeles after the riot in Watts several years ago showed much the same pattern.

There can be little question that despite the general improvement in the conditions of life for Negroes nationally, conditions have grown worse in places like Hough and Watts. As Negro families succeed, they tend to move out of these economically and socially depressed areas to better neighborhoods where they and their children have the opportunity to lead a better life. They leave behind the least educated and the most deprived—unwed mothers, deserted wives, the physically and mentally handicapped, and the aged. As a result there is a concentration of misery in the very hearts of our largest cities. It is precisely in such places that riots take place and it is here that more action is needed in massive doses to accelerate a narrowing of the gap in social and economic status between whites and Negroes.

VI

Puerto Ricans, Mexicans, and Other Minorities

Although Negroes constitute the largest racial minority in the United States, there are many other important racial, ethnic, and religious minorities in the nation. These groups include, among others, Mexican-Americans, Puerto Ricans, Cubans, American Indians, Japanese-Americans, Chinese-Americans, and Jews. Each is of interest because it is different and reflects the diversity of American life. Some, however, are also very important because they have more than their fair share of poverty, sickness discrimination, and other problems. Each group is small relative to the national total. In many places, however, these minorities represent a large fraction of the population and are viewed with great interest. The governor of South Dakota, for example, may care little about what Jews think or how they feel; the governor of New York can do so only at great peril to his political career. The mayor of Biloxi, Mississippi, may never think about his Chinese constituents, if he has any; the mayor of San Francisco must think about them all the time. There are many other cities, such as Miami, Los Angeles, and San Antonio, where ethnic minorities play a very important role.

Most statistics of the federal government are designed to deal with national problems involving economic growth, unemployment, poverty, and similar matters. For this purpose, a relatively small national sample of 50,000 households is adequate to provide reliable social and economic information each year for the total population and for Blacks and whites. We have such a sample and that is the reason the data are available for those groups. Much larger and more specialized samples, however, would be required to provide similar data for the other ethnic groups. Such samples are not now available, and for that reason the data for these groups are inadequate.

Most of our recent knowledge concerning the income, education, and occupational status of the nation's minorities comes from the 1960 census, in which racial and ethnic groups were identified through questions asked about race, language, and place of birth of each person and his parents. Similar information is being collected in the 1970 census. At this writing the 1960 census data are the most recent available and it is these figures that will be presented and discussed in this chapter.

Puerto Ricans

Puerto Ricans represent one of the newer minority groups in the United States. There were about 856,000 Puerto Ricans living in this country at the time of the 1960 census. Nearly three out of every four lived in New York City, for the most part in Manhattan, the Bronx, and Brooklyn. It is reasonable to turn to the census results for New York City for a cross section of their economic status.

Income

The Department of Labor estimated in 1959 that a family of four living in New York City and its suburbs needed an income of about $6,000 to maintain a "modest but adequate" level of living.[1] About 60 percent of the Puerto Rican families in New York City have four or more persons. How many achieve this $6,000 figure?

Half the Puerto Rican families in New York City had incomes under $3,800 in 1959. The median for nonwhites (99 percent Negro) in the city was $4,400, $600 greater, while the median for whites was $6,400. Four out of every five Puerto Rican families had incomes under $6,000 in 1959 (see Table VI-1). Keeping in mind the fact that many of these families are quite large and that they pay exorbitant rents for substandard homes, you can begin to appreciate their plight.

TABLE VI-1

**Percentage Distribution of Income
for White, Nonwhite, and Puerto Rican
Families in New York City: 1959**

Income level	White	Nonwhite	Puerto Rican
Under $2,000	8%	15%	16%
$2,000 to $4,000	14	29	37
$4,000 to $6,000	24	27	27
$6,000 to $8,000	21	15	12
Over $8,000	33	14	8

U.S. Censuses of Population and Housing: 1960, Census Tract Report for New York City.

Education

Without education the opportunity to rise above the lowest levels is slim indeed. Perhaps because many Puerto Ricans are recent immigrants to this country, their educational attainment is far below that of the whites and even below that of Negroes in New York City. The average Puerto Rican in the city had only 7½ years of schooling as compared with 9½ years for Negroes and nearly 10½ years for whites. One out of every two adult Puerto Ricans in New York City had not gone beyond the seventh grade and nearly three out of every four had no formal education beyond the eighth grade. What chance do people with this little schooling have to make a decent living in a society where one-third of the salesmen and one-fourth of the office clerks have college training? You can see the transmission belt of poverty operating at full steam. The children will suffer because there is generally a very close association between an individual's own educational attainment and his plans to educate his children.

Housing

The poverty of Puerto Rican families in New York City is reflected in the poor quality of their housing. Only 60 percent of the Puerto

89

Ricans in New York live in sound units, whereas 40 percent live in units that are either deteriorating or dilapidated. Evidently Puerto Ricans who live in the Bronx have higher economic status than those who live in Manhattan or Brooklyn. This pattern is reminiscent of that followed by the Jewish immigrants to New York in the early part of this century. The first sign of having "arrived" in the new world was a move away from the Lower East Side to the Bronx.

TABLE VI-2

Puerto Rican Housing Conditions
in New York City: 1960

Condition of housing	Total New York City	Manhattan	Brooklyn	Bronx
Sound	60%	52%	55%	72%
Deteriorating	30	35	33	22
Dilapidated	10	13	13	6

Note: Sums of tabulated figures in this chapter may not equal totals because of rounding.

U.S. Censuses of Population and Housing: 1960, Census Tract Report for New York City.

The higher economic status of Bronx residents is reflected in the figures on educational attainment and family income. Median years of school completed were about one-half year greater in the Bronx (8.0) than in Manhattan. Moreover, family incomes were also somewhat higher in that borough. One-half of the Puerto Rican families in the Bronx had incomes over $4,100 in 1959. The median in Brooklyn was $200 lower ($3,900) and in Manhattan it was $600 lower ($3,500).

You might think there would be a substantial rent differential for the inferior housing, but that was not the case at all. The average rent paid by all Puerto Rican families in the city was $62 a month. Those living in sound units paid $64. In deteriorating units the average monthly rent was $59 and in dilapidated units it was $56. In each case, this rental amounted to about one-fifth of the annual income received by the average family.[2] However, one Puerto Rican family out of every five in the city paid a third of their income for rent; in a large proportion of the cases it was rent for a substandard unit.

In New York City, Puerto Rican housing is inferior to that of non-whites. Both are far inferior to that of whites. Indeed, Negroes and Puerto Ricans occupy about one-half of all the dilapidated units in the city even though they account for only about one-fifth of all households.

Was there any improvement between 1950 and 1960 in the economic status of Puerto Ricans relative to nonwhites (Negroes) in New York City? The tentative answer is no.

According to the census results, the Negro increased his schooling by one full year on the average, whereas there was a drop of one-half year in the average years of schooling for Puerto Ricans (due undoubtedly to the low educational attainment of recent immigrants). In 1950, the average income of Negro men and women was $100 more than that received by Puerto Ricans. In 1960, the differential, on a family basis, rose to $400 in favor of the Negro. Conceivably the figures for Puerto Ricans are depressed by immigrants who must go through the process of Americanization.

Were they better off in Puerto Rico?

A report issued several years ago by the Bureau of Applied Social Research at Columbia University argued that the average Puerto Rican "would prefer living on his island if he were able to find there the kind of economic opportunity which exists in New York." It does seem that Puerto Ricans come to New York primarily because of anticipated economic gain. They leave their island voluntarily, and in numbers that accelerate when times are good in the States and jobs are plentiful. To what extent are their expectations realized?[3]

There are many opinions on the subject, but few objective answers. Christopher Rand in *The Puerto Ricans* reports: "One often hears that Puerto Ricans can earn twice as much in New York as on their island, and that living costs in the two places differ little except for the items of fuel and warm clothes in the New York winter."[4] He recognizes this as a probable exaggeration but concludes that "by and large more can be made in New York (in good times)—and more can be saved, too, or

TABLE VI-3

Comparison of Housing Conditions in New York City: 1960

Condition of housing	White	Nonwhite	Puerto Rican
Sound	87%	67%	60%
Deteriorating	11	25	30
Dilapidated	2	8	10

U.S. Censuses of Population and Housing: 1960, Census Tract Report for New York City.

spent on TV sets or washing machines." This judgment is not supported by the census results. The census was taken in Puerto Rico at the same time as in the States, using roughly the same definitions and procedures. This provides a comparison between Puerto Ricans living in New York City and those living in San Juan, the largest city on the island.

It turns out that family income is higher in New York by 60 percent: $3,800 against $2,300 (see Table VI-4). But rents are also much higher—70 percent—and the quality of housing is much worse. On this basis it seems unlikely that *real* incomes—money incomes adjusted for differences in the cost of living—actually are higher in New York.

Housing is not only a major item in the cost of living, but also an excellent indicator of levels of living. It also happens to be one of the few items for which objective comparisons can be made between New York and San Juan. Therefore it may prove worthwhile to examine the results carefully. All but a handful of Puerto Ricans living in New York reside in rented units and 40 percent of these units have one or more major defects. In San Juan, only about half of the families live in rented units and an equal number either own their homes or are in the process of buying them. These homes, incidentally, are not shacks by any means. The great majority of them are in sound condition and contain complete plumbing facilities. Even if home ownership is ignored and only the total picture is examined, it appears that Puerto Ricans in San Juan have better housing than those in New York. About the same proportion in both places live in dilapidated homes; but nearly three-fourths of the San Juan residents live in sound structures as compared with only 60 percent of the New Yorkers.

TABLE VI-4

Puerto Rican Family Incomes,
New York City and San Juan: 1959

Income level	New York	San Juan
Under $2,000	16%	43%
Between $2,000 and $4,000	38	28
Between $4,000 and $6,000	27	13
$6,000 and over	20	15
Median income	$3,800	$2,300

U.S. Census of Population: 1960, Census Tract Report for New York City; and Detailed Characteristics, Puerto Rico, Table 119.

The census findings are confirmed by impressions of on-the-spot observers. Christopher Rand reports: "New stucco or cement dwellings can be seen everywhere, and public-housing projects galore can be seen in the towns—San Juan, with its suburbs, is sometimes called the world's best-endowed city now in regard to public housing."[5]

Those who rent get a better deal in San Juan. The overall average is $36 per month, against $62 in New York. And San Juan rents are more responsive to the quality of the housing, covering a wide range: $48 for sound housing, $26 for deteriorating units, $18 for dilapidated units. In New York, Puerto Ricans paid high rentals for all grades of housing; the comparable figures were $64, $59, and $56.

Other costs of living may also be higher in New York. Clothing requirements are undoubtedly greater, and the expense of establishing a foothold in a new environment must be counted.

These comparisons seem to downgrade the economic explanation for Puerto Rican immigration. There appears to be no great immediate advantage in moving from San Juan to New York. The figures don't tell the complete story, however.

93

TABLE VI-5

Puerto Rican Family Housing, New York City and San Juan: 1960

Condition of housing	New York	San Juan			
		Total	Owner occupancy		Renter occupancy
			Land and building	Building only	
Number of units	156,000	96,000	29,000	18,000	49,000
Sound	60%	72%	91%	45%	70%
Deteriorating	30	18	7	32	19
Dilapidated	10	10	2	23	11

U.S. *Censuses of Population and Housing: 1960*, Census Tract Report for New York City; and U.S. *Census of Housing: 1960, Advance Reports,* Puerto Rico, HC (A2)—53, Table I.

Only *average* real income seems to be about the same in both places. Many families are below the average. These may be the ones who migrate. To the extent that this is true, New York is getting selected immigrants—people who could not make the grade in their own home towns.

Another fact to remember is that San Juan has a population of about 600,000 out of nearly 2½ million on the island. About half the people live in rural areas where incomes are very low. A substantial portion of the migrants undoubtedly come from these rural areas. They may move to New York rather than to San Juan because they have only unskilled services to offer and New York may provide a better market for those services.

Thus, while real income levels may be the same, *on the average,* in both places, the income levels among prospective migrants may be substantially worse on the island. To test this theory, much more information—and more comparable information—about conditions in Puerto Rico and New York would be needed.

Spanish-Americans[6]

Those of us who live on the Eastern Seaboard—and this still includes about one out of every three Americans—know very little about the three and a half million people who are identified by the Census Bureau as "persons with Spanish surname." These people live in the southwestern part of the United States and in 1960 were distributed as follows: Arizona 194,000; California 1,400,000; Colorado 157,000; New Mexico 269,000; and Texas 1,400,000.

Early in the sixteenth century, the Spaniards conquered the territory that is now the American Southwest. The largest and earliest settlements were in New Mexico, but there were also others in California and Texas. This group, sometimes identified as Spanish-American or Hispano, lived in the territory that came under the American flag by the annexation of Texas, the Treaty of Guadalupe Hidalgo, and the Gadsden Purchase. Beginning about 1910, a second major group, consisting of immigrants from Mexico and their children, was added. Direct immigration from other Spanish-speaking countries has been negligible.

Ethnically, the population of Spanish-American and Mexican descent ranges from Indians to those of unmixed Spanish ancestry. Indians and the part-Spanish, part-Indian Mestizos are particularly frequent among the recent immigrant generation, the Mexican-Americans.

Special recognition of the interest in the Spanish-American and Mexican-American population of the United States was first given in the collection and publication of data on "Mexicans" in the 1930 census. These figures were collected largely because of the heavy immigration from Mexico during the twenties. Somewhat related data were collected in the 1940 census. In 1950 and 1960 white persons of Spanish-American and Mexican-American origin were identified on the basis of their Spanish surname. This procedure was limited to the five southwestern states referred to earlier.

Not so well off as whites

Unlike the Puerto Ricans, who have a common origin and are concentrated in New York City, the Spanish-Americans are widely scattered and have diverse backgrounds. Over four-fifths of them are native

Americans and more than half have mothers and fathers who are both native American. Thus, to a very large extent, this is an indigenous population rather than recent immigrants.

Unlike other parts of the country, nonwhites in the five southwestern states are not always predominantly Negro. In New Mexico, for example, three-fourths of the nonwhites are Indians, and in Arizona nearly two-thirds are Indians. In Texas, nonwhites are almost entirely Negro; but even in California and Colorado only three-fourths of the nonwhites are Negro. Table VI-6 has been arranged so that the incomes

TABLE VI-6

Comparison of Median Incomes, by State: 1959

Color	Arizona	California	Colorado	New Mexico	Texas
White	$2,996	$3,583	$2,876	$2,961	$2,632
Negro	1,622	2,528	2,289	1,751	1,167
Other nonwhite	1,034	3,014	2,361	1,378	1,943
Spanish-American	1,944	2,835	1,929	1,912	1,536

U.S. Census of Population: 1960, Detailed Characteristics, report for each state, Table 133; and Vol. II, *Persons of Spanish Surname.*

of Spanish-Americans can be compared separately with whites, Negroes, and other racial groups in each state. The "other" groups are predominantly Chinese and Japanese in California, American Indians in New Mexico and Arizona, and about equal numbers of American Indians and Orientals in Colorado and Texas.

The incomes of Spanish-Americans are far below those of whites in all states. In 1959, they fared poorest in Texas, where their median ($1,500) was only 58 percent of the white median, and best in California, where they had 79 percent of the white median. In the other three states their median was about 65 percent of that received by whites. The relationships in 1959 were not much different from those which prevailed ten years earlier. Although the situation was not static, no major changes appear to have taken place. During the fifties there was a slight increase in the income of Spanish-Americans relative to whites in California and Colorado and a slight decrease in Arizona.

Four-fifths of the Spanish-Americans live in California and Texas. Their relative economic position appears to be far better in California than in Texas. What factors account for the difference? Part of it is accounted for by the fact that a larger proportion in California live in urban areas where job opportunities are better and wages are higher. The "typical" Easterner thinks of Spanish-Americans as migrant farm workers. This may have been the case at one time, but it was far from true in 1960. Spanish-Americans in California and Texas are predominantly urbanites—85 percent in California and 79 percent in Texas live in urban areas.

Another factor that helps account for the higher incomes in California is the greater opportunity for employment in industry. This is particularly true for women. In California, 61 percent of the employed Spanish-American women worked in offices or in factories. In Texas, only 38 percent worked in these kinds of jobs. A much larger proportion of the women in Texas worked in the low-paying service trades. Many of them were domestics. The occupational distribution of the male labor force was much the same in both states; but it is likely that there was less discrimination in pay in California because a large proportion of the work in that state is done under government contract.

The lower incomes of Spanish-Americans in Texas may also be due to their low educational attainment in that state. Table VI-7 shows that Spanish-Americans were four and a half years behind whites in years of

TABLE VI-7

Comparison of Median Number of Years of Education, by State: 1960

Color	Arizona	California	Colorado	New Mexico	Texas
White	11.3	12.0	11.9	11.1	10.7
Nonwhite	7.7	10.8	11.2	7.9	8.7
Spanish-American	8.0	9.0	8.6	8.4	6.2

U.S. Census of Population: 1960, Detailed Characteristics, report for each state, Table 103; and Vol. II, Persons of Spanish Surname.

school completed in Texas, but only three years behind in California. Their lack of education in Texas, combined with language difficulties, may have made them ineligible for some of the better paying jobs.

Better off than nonwhites

Spanish-Americans are poorer than whites. That is a well-known fact. They are also better off than most nonwhites. That is also a fact, but it is not so well known. Spanish-Americans have generally had a very good press in the eastern part of the country. Their plight has been well publicized and considerable sympathy—well deserved—has been engendered. In the process, unfortunately, the impression has been created that their plight is worse than that of Negroes and other minority groups on the West Coast. Lyle Saunders states: "Not all Spanish-speaking are poor, but in general more of them are poor than is true for any other group. . . . While not all Spanish-speaking people live in slums . . . more of them do proportionately than any other population group."[7] These statements were not true in 1949 when they were written, nor were they true in 1960.

What are the facts as revealed in the 1960 census? They can be summarized as follows. Although Spanish-Americans are not so well off as whites, they are better off than Negroes (except in Colorado, where both are few in number) and Indians, and nearly as well off as Japanese and Chinese. These relationships not only existed in 1960 but they were also much the same ten years earlier.

In California, the median income of Spanish-Americans ($2,800) was about $300 above the Negro median even though Spanish-Americans were about two years behind in their schooling. In Texas, the other state with a large concentration of Negroes, the Spanish-Americans were $400 ahead of the Negro in median income—a differential of 32 percent. Here again the economic advantage of the Spanish-American was maintained despite a two-and-a-half-year disadvantage in schooling.

The difference between the incomes of Spanish-Americans and Indians is even greater than that cited above. Despite a doubling in the average income of Indians in Arizona during the fifties, the Spanish-American was still $900 ahead in 1959. In New Mexico the average income of Indians also doubled during the fifties, but the Spanish-American was still $500 ahead in 1959.

Orientals were the only large minority group on the West Coast that had higher incomes than Spanish-Americans. But the difference was not very great. The median for Japanese and Chinese in California was $3,000; for Spanish-Americans it was $2,800.

Quality of housing

The low economic status of Spanish-Americans and nonwhites in the western states is reflected in the poor quality of their housing. Conditions were best in California, which is considered one of the most progressive states with respect to social services. Yet even in this state two out of every ten Spanish-American and nonwhite families were living in homes that were either badly run down or dilapidated. Only one out of ten whites in the state resided in homes this bad. Conditions were much worse in Texas. There four out of every ten families in these minority groups lived in substandard homes.

Living conditions for Spanish-Americans and nonwhites were somewhat better in Colorado and New Mexico than in Texas; but the housing in Arizona was far worse than in any of the other states shown. Five out of every ten Indian families in this state lived in deteriorating or dilapidated homes. This was over three times the rate shown for white families. The low incomes and poor housing of the Indians in Arizona suggest that the opening sentence of the Meriam Report was as valid in 1960 as it was thirty-five years earlier, when it was written: "An overwhelming majority of the Indians are poor, even extremely poor, and they are not adjusted to the economic and social system of the dominant white civilization."[8]

There are no national data showing how the Spanish-American population has fared since 1960. Some more recent figures are available for one city—Los Angeles—as the result of a census taken in parts of that city after the riots in the summer of 1965. Despite the fact that these figures pertain to a single city, they are of interest because this is one of the largest cities in the nation, it contains a Spanish-American population, and it contains a large Negro population with which comparisons can be made.

In East Los Angeles, the median income of Spanish-American families (adjusted for price changes) dropped by 8 percent from $5,500 in 1959 to $5,100 in 1965. During this same period, the median income of Negro families in South Los Angeles dropped 4 percent from $4,900

TABLE VI-8

Comparison of Housing, by State: 1960

Condition of housing	Arizona	California	Colorado	New Mexico	Texas
White					
Sound	86%	91%	87%	87%	83%
Deteriorating	10	7	10	9	12
Dilapidated	4	2	2	4	4
Nonwhite					
Sound	49%	80%	69%	68%	61%
Deteriorating	26	15	27	18	27
Dilapidated	25	5	4	14	12
Spanish-American					
Sound	62%	78%	66%	71%	61%
Deteriorating	24	16	26	18	26
Dilapidated	14	6	8	11	13

U.S. Census of Population: 1960, Summary of census tract reports for standard metropolitan statistical areas for each state.

to $4,700.[9] In other words, in 1965, Spanish-American families in Los Angeles had considerably higher incomes than Negro families, but the gap between the two groups had narrowed since the beginning of the decade.

The incidence of poverty among Spanish-American families rose slightly from 22 percent in 1960 to 24 percent in 1965. For Negro families, the proportion in poverty was about 28 percent in both years.

Many factors contributed to the decline in income of Spanish-American families in East Los Angeles and of Negro families in South Los Angeles. One important factor, particularly for Negro families, was the change in family composition within the area. In 1960, about 73 percent of all Negro families in South Los Angeles were married couples living in their own households. By 1965, this proportion had dropped to 68 percent. In the case of Spanish-American families in East Los Angeles the decline was from 78 percent to 75 percent. These figures, which suggest an increase in the prevalence of "broken" homes within the area, are supported by other census data which show that the proportion of children living with both parents in these areas also declined. Since the incomes of broken families are far lower, on the average, than those in which a husband and wife are both present, this change in family composition tended to reduce the average income for the area as a whole.

Selective out-migration may also have contributed to the decline in median family income in these areas. Only about one-half of the Spanish-American families in the city of Los Angeles lived in East Los Angeles in 1960. This proportion probably dropped by 1965. In the case of Negroes, the proportion of the entire city population living in South Los Angeles dropped from three-fourths in 1960 to about one-half in 1965. If we assume that the more successful families tended to move to more desirable neighborhoods and were replaced by lower income groups moving in from other parts of the state or the nation, average family income for each area would tend to be depressed.

Jew, Catholic, Protestant

About 66 percent of the population in the United States is Protestant, 26 percent is Catholic, and 3 percent is Jewish. The remaining 5 percent include people of other religions, those who profess no religious affiliation, and those who did not report their religion. In this section we shall focus on the three largest religious groups and see what differences there are in economic status as reflected in education, occupation, and income.

The Jews are one minority group in America who are not economically underprivileged. The influx of Jewish migration started toward the end of the last century. The great majority of them came with literally nothing but the shirts on their backs. Professor Will Herberg states in *Protestant-Catholic-Jew* that most of them "went into shops and factories, in light industry, or in building and allied trades; they became wage workers and built up a very considerable labor movement. But this process of proletarianization was not a lasting one; almost immediately a reverse process of deproletarianization set in. . . . Some of them very soon left the shop to go into business; others proved able to combine long hours in the sweatshop with after-work study that gained them coveted degrees and licenses in medicine, law, and accountancy."[10] The way in which these people have flourished in America is a tribute to themselves and to the United States.

Income

The average income of Jewish families is considerably higher than that of Protestants or Catholics. About one out of every four Jewish families had an income over $10,000 in 1957 as compared with less than one out of fifteen for Catholics and Protestants. Overall, Catholics have higher incomes than Protestants, largely because they are more concentrated in larger cities and work at nonfarm jobs.

TABLE VI-9

Family Income and Religion: 1957

Income level in 1956	Protestant	Catholic	Jewish
Under $2,000	17%	11%	8%
Between $2,000 and $4,000	24	19	14
Between $4,000 and $5,000	15	16	12
Between $5,000 and $7,000	22	28	21
Between $7,000 and $10,000	15	18	20
$10,000 and over	7	8	25

U.S. Bureau of the Census, *Current Population Survey*, March 1957.

The higher incomes of Jewish families are in large measure due to the fact that the working members are better educated. Most of the well-paid jobs in our society require college training or high-level managerial or technical responsibility. Since a large proportion of the Jewish family heads are college-trained and work at professional and managerial jobs, it is not surprising that many of them are in the upper income brackets.

TABLE VI-10

**Educational Status and Religion of
Persons 25 Years Old and Over: 1957**

Schooling completed	Protestant	Catholic	Jewish
Elementary school	77%	77%	82%
High school	41	40	59
College (4 years)	8	6	17

Note: In this and similar tables, figures do not add to 100% because categories overlap; e.g., a high school graduate is counted as having completed both elementary and high school.

See Table VI-9 for source.

Education

The figures on educational attainment show that the proportion of college graduates is far greater among the Jews than it is in either of the two other groups shown. One out of every six Jewish adults is a college graduate. This proportion is twice that among Protestants and nearly three times the Catholic rate. Protestants have somewhat higher college attendance rates than Catholics, but the difference in education between the two groups is not very striking.

Occupations

The figures on occupational distribution show that the Jews have not only acquired education but have also been given the opportunity to use their training. More than half of the employed Jewish men are professional or managerial workers. These are the two highest paying major occupation groups. The comparable proportion for Catholics and Protestants was less than one out of four. The second most important occupation group for Jews was clerical and sales. Over one-fifth of the men worked in these occupations. Altogether about 77 percent of the Jewish men worked in white-collar jobs as compared with only one-third for Protestants and Catholics.

The major difference in occupational distribution between the two Christian religions is the greater concentration of Protestants in agricultural jobs. About 9 percent of the Protestants were farmers as compared with only 4 percent of the Catholics. There is a correspondingly greater proportion of Catholics in blue-collar jobs, reflecting their greater concentration in urban areas.

TABLE VI-11

**Occupational Status and Religion
of Employed Males 18 Years Old and Over: 1957**

Occupational group	Protestant	Catholic	Jewish
Professional or managerial worker	23%	21%	55%
Farmer	9	4	–
Clerical or sales worker	12	13	22
Craftsman	20	23	9
Semiskilled worker	20	22	10
Service worker or laborer	16	17	3

See Table VI-9 for source.

VII

America's Fight with Poverty

AN OVERVIEW

During the past decade, America has been engaged in another round in the perennial bout with poverty. This is not a new battle. It has been going on since the founding of the Republic. By and large, it has been most successfully waged. We now find, however, as we examine ourselves closely, that despite the generally high levels of living that prevail, millions are not sharing fully in the abundance that has been created. Although incomes were at an all-time high in 1968, 25 million people were in families with incomes below the poverty line. This is a large number—many think too large—and much thought and effort have been devoted to reduce it. In 1969 about $24 billion was spent in federal aid to the poor, in contrast to $12 billion in 1964.[1]

To fully appreciate the extent to which America's bout with poverty has been a success, one need only look at the long way we have come in the short span of 180 years. Today the majority of our families are well provided with the good things in life. They have decent homes, good schools, some security in old age, and generally live in an abundance that was unheard of only a short time ago and that still seems unreal in many parts of the world. But it was not always so. Only yesterday, in the span of history, settlers came to these shores with very little. They cleared a continent, battled the hostile forces of man and nature, settled the land, and hacked a new society out of the wilderness. The fruits of their efforts are now taken for granted by Americans and by people in other parts of the world as well, but they were purchased at a price. It took courage for families to uproot themselves from the comforts of the Atlantic shores and fan out into a hostile land inhabited by Indians. It took foresight to defer the immediate gratification of wants and to plow back the surpluses that accrued from agriculture and shipping into the construction of a network of roads, canals, and railroads that facilitated the development of the country. It took faith in democratic ideals to open our shores to Europe's unwanted millions, to make good farmland available to them at a low price, and to entrust to them the creation of local schools in which to educate their children. It took a willing endurance of suffering to engage in the bloodiest war in our history to correct the evil of slavery that had been unwisely tolerated for too long. These are the secrets of America's success in its fight with poverty. They are the true and enduring sources of our economic growth, which is the foundation of any anti-poverty program. But economic growth has not been the only weapon in the arsenal used against poverty, not today and not in the past. It has been combined with various other measures to relieve the suffering of those bypassed by economic progress. We might begin this examination of America's fight with poverty with a brief review of programs that have been used in the past.

Anti-poverty programs at the turn of the century

Poverty first became recognized as a social problem in the United States about a hundred years ago. It existed before that time, to be sure, but it was regarded as an individual rather than as a social problem requiring social action. The prevalent American attitude in the pre-Civil War period was that a man's misfortunes were his own affair and that there was little that society could or should do about them. If things did not go well in the East, young men were exhorted to go West. It was a big, rich, unsettled country, and if a man could not find his niche, he had no one to blame but himself. This view could develop and be sustained only in a predominantly rural society with an abundance of unoccupied good land. With industrialization and immigration came vast urban slums.

It soon became apparent, in urban areas at least, that new forces were in operation and that the old clichés no longer fit. As one writer has put it, "poverty might be dismissed as a personal matter, but the slums could not be brushed aside so easily."[2] The slums were largely attributed to immigration. It is easy for us to wonder today, with the benefit of fifty years or more of hindsight, why it was ever doubted that the Irish, German, Italian, and Polish immigrants could be absorbed into the mainstream of American life. Their contemporaries, however, had an entirely different view of the matter. Many of the charges that are now being leveled at our new "immigrants"—Negroes, Mexicans, Puerto Ricans, and hillbillies—were leveled at the forebears of those who are now most vociferous. Pauperism, crime, intemperance, disease, and political corruption were all attributed to the millions who came to our shores after the Civil War. By the close of the century "there was suspicion at nearly all levels of society that the immigrants, if not actually bent on the destruction of American institutions, were nevertheless quite capable, either through illiteracy or political immaturity, of subverting the foundations of the republic."[3]

The early leaders in the fight for anti-poverty programs were the private charities and the settlement houses. They were soon joined by the labor unions and by religious and civic organizations. Located at the centers of our largest cities, social workers developed an intimate knowledge of the circumstances and needs of the urban poor. Those were the days before the nation had large government programs to prepare facts about the poor and design policies to help them. At that time philanthropic organizations attempted to meet this need, and although the effort seems small today, relative to the huge sums that are now being spent for this purpose, the accomplishments were great.

The targets of the poverty fighters at the turn of the century were various social evils that required change: poor housing, poor schools, bad working conditions, low wages, and unemployment. These efforts led to major social reforms: public health and housing regulations, abolition of child labor, regulation of hours of work and working conditions, and workmen's compensation. The whole tenor of the fight against poverty then called for social reform, not rehabilitation.

Anti-poverty programs of the thirties

Still fresh in many minds is the massive attack on poverty which took place under Franklin D. Roosevelt during the thirties. At that time, under the impetus of a worldwide depression, the now familiar anti-poverty tools were forged—social security, old-age assistance, aid to dependent children, unemployment compensation, and the rest. The motivation for the attack on poverty in the thirties, however, was different from what it had been in the past. The reform movement in the early part of the century had been conducted in the interest of social justice. Poverty had been considered evil because of its debilitating effects on the poor and because of the social costs associated with crime and illness. Lurking in the background had been the notion that reform was required to protect society from possible ravages by the poor. The more sophisticated concept that the poor might be converted into a vast new market through a redistribution of income had to await the depression of the thirties. During that period a mass technology brought problems of distribution to the fore. The big question then was one of distributing the vast output that was potentially possible. Getting the economy moving again was the important goal, and if that could be done by giving money to the poor, so much the better. It was in the light of these circumstances that the anti-poverty measures of the thirties were conceived. In both periods poverty was blamed on the times, on the economic system. During the earlier period, however, reforms had been made to protect the poor from the inequities caused by the system and, incidentally, to protect society from the poor. During the later period the reforms were made not only to relieve the misery of the poor but also to improve the operation of the economy by redistributing incomes.

The current attack on poverty

The major emphasis in the fight against poverty today is rehabilitation rather than reform. At the turn of the century it had been the consensus that society had to be changed. This led to the adoption of a variety of social reforms. During the depression it was the income distribution mechanism that had broken down. This led to income-maintenance programs. Today it is felt that the poor themselves must be changed if they are to be brought into the mainstream of American life. As a result, we have developed a variety of programs to cater to the diverse needs of the poor. The welfare system today consists of three major types of programs.[4]

1. Programs which provide money to persons who are not in the labor force. These programs include Old-Age, Survivors and Disability Insurance; public assistance under the Social Security Act; pensions for needy veterans; and general assistance for the needy provided by some states and localities.

2. Programs designed to help workers. Included here are manpower training programs, aid to depressed areas, unemployment insurance, minimum wage protection, the creation of jobs, and work relief.

3. Programs that provide goods and services directly to the poor. These include child care, subsidized housing, medical services and drugs, and the distribution of food.

Despite the considerable increase in expenditures for welfare in the United States in recent years, the present program is under serious attack and it has relatively few defenders. This dissatisfaction was very well summed up by Arthur Burns, chairman of the Federal Reserve Board, as follows:

> The Federal Government has tried to solve these complex problems by spending large sums of money on projects that have often been hastily devised. Hundreds of grant-in-aid programs dealing with health, education, welfare and other local needs were established in quick succession. Several regional commissions were established to seek better balance in economic development and social improvement. An Economic Development Administration was established to aid local communities, both urban and rural, that suffer from excessive unemployment or inadequate incomes. More recently, a Model Cities Program was established, aspiring to achieve what our best city planners can contrive. By proceeding in all these directions, we have created a costly governmental maze that involves much duplication and waste, that often hampers the constructive efforts of local officials and, perhaps worst of all, that practically defies full understanding or evaluation.[5]

This bleak summary fails to mention much of the good that has been accomplished. Chapter V showed that the reduction of income differentials between Blacks and whites began in 1965, about the time the big increase in poverty expenditures began. An examination of poverty statistics (see Table VII-5) shows that large and consistent annual reductions in the number of poor also began that year. These changes, no doubt, were primarily associated with the general improvement in economic conditions stemming from the stepped-up activities in Vietnam. There was less unemployment and more jobs for all—Black as well as white, poor and nonpoor. But who is to say that the anti-poverty programs and the general increase in awareness of the problems of racism and poverty in our society generated by those programs were not also major factors? Employment conditions were as favorable during the Korean war as they were in the late 1960's, but the income gap between Blacks and whites was much wider in the earlier period.

Dr. Burns's bleak summary also ignores the fact that by focusing on the problem and by providing training programs we have reduced the school dropout rate among teen-age Negro boys appreciably. Thanks to Head Start, one-fifth of the Negro 3- and 4-year-olds are now enrolled in schools where they at least stand a chance of learning useful things they would not be taught at home.

There are many other benefits of poverty expenditures that have been omitted from the very unfair and biased picture presented by Dr. Burns. But perhaps most important of all is the omission of the fact that many of the hastily devised programs were created in the heat of battle, in some cases while some of our cities were literally burning. Some action—any action at all—at such a time was better than waiting to achieve greater understanding.

But when all is said and done, there can be little doubt that Dr. Burns has expressed a sentiment which is widely held. There now seems to be general agreement that the efforts made to combat poverty in the past have not been successful and new paths are now being suggested. Some of them are examined in the next chapter.

The concept of poverty

It is trite, but true, to say that poverty is a concept that is not easily defined. Poverty will surely have a different meaning in India or China than in the United States. There is no more agreement about who is poor even at a given time and place than there is about what is beautiful or ugly. This question is often overlooked, but it is essential to an understanding of the subject and it is largely responsible for the wide range that exists in estimates of the numbers of poor in the United States. There is no objective definition of a poor man. The standards of poverty are culturally determined. They can arbitrarily be defined for a given time and place, but they vary from place to place and they differ from time to time for a given place.

The term poverty may connote hunger, but this is not what is usually meant in discussions about poverty in America. Consider, for example, the facilities available to the poor. Tunica County, Mississippi, is the poorest county in our poorest state. About eight out of every ten families in this county had incomes under $3,000 in 1960 and most of them were poor by national standards; yet 52 percent owned television sets, 46 percent owned automobiles, and 37 percent owned washing machines. These families might have been deprived of hope and poor in spirit, but their material possessions, though low by American standards, would be the envy of the majority of mankind today.

There are dangers in associating poverty with the absence of certain material possessions, such as adequate housing, a TV set, a washing machine, or even an automobile. Ignoring for the moment the very real possibility that our measuring device is much too gross, it is very likely that for some poor families material possessions may be merely relics of an earlier affluence. Others among the poor may obtain such items as hand-me-downs from more prosperous friends or relatives, as gifts, or even by the very expensive process of "paying a penny down and a penny forever." Far from being a symptom of affluence, the ownership of an automobile or a television set may be a cause of poverty, because it is purchased in lieu of a good diet, medical care, education, or other goods that would yield a much greater return in terms of increasing productivity. Television presents a very special problem for poor people in an affluent society. Any man who cannot afford to buy a television set when all of his neighbors have them is probably going to feel poor. And many of those who do have television sets are made to feel poor because they are constantly bombarded by ads for products which they cannot afford. Poverty in its truest sense is more than mere want; it is want mixed with a lack of hope. This is very difficult to measure in any quantitative sense.

The immigrants who came to this country in the early part of this century were poor; but their poverty was mixed with hope. They escaped from political oppression and religious persecution to a new world where freedom would be theirs. Even if they were too poor and uneducated to enjoy it themselves, they had the hope that their children would share in it one day. Many of the poor today have "adequate" homes, television sets, telephones, and other appurtenances of the "good life," but they have no hope for either themselves or their children. This is one of the factors that make our problem today even worse, in a certain sense, than it was in the past.

111

There is a growing body of evidence to support the view that much of our poverty is handed down from father to son, and that a large proportion of those who will be impoverished adults tomorrow are children of the poor today. For example, a study made in 1963 of families receiving Aid to Dependent Children shows that over 40 percent of the mothers or fathers of these families were raised in homes where some form of assistance had been received at some time.[6] Nearly half of these cases had received Aid to Families with Dependent Children. Here is another example: education, as we all know, is very important for any chance of a well-paying job, yet one-fourth of the young people 18 to 24 years old in families receiving Aid to Dependent Children did not go beyond the eighth grade.[7]

Still another example can be drawn from the field of education. About one-third of the youths in low-income families do not complete high school. The fathers of these school dropouts also tend to be uneducated—60 percent of the low-income families are headed by people who did not go beyond the eighth grade. The pattern is clear. Parents who are uneducated tend to have low incomes because they are not trained to do skilled work. They also have little interest in education, perhaps because they were brought up in an environment where education was not considered important. As a result, their children also lack interest in education, and they tend to become the poor of the next generation. This is part of the vicious cycle whereby poverty is handed down from one generation to the next.

Poverty and the Negro

An attempt has been made to show, in the preceding discussion, that anti-poverty programs do not develop out of thin air. They represent attempts by society to come to grips with the underlying social and economic problems at different points in time. The declaration of "war on poverty" in America in the sixties was our answer to dislocations that were caused by technological change. Just as unemployment sparked the adoption of a social security program during the thirties, the recognition that millions of families were being systematically excluded from the mainstream of economic life sparked new legislation such as the Economic Opportunity Act, the Elementary and Secondary

Education Act, and manpower training programs, designed to improve the skills of the labor force.

The Negro has played a special role in shaping the anti-poverty program of the past decade with its emphasis on education, training, and rehabilitation rather than money handouts. During the thirties, Negroes were largely tucked away in the rural South, where they worked for the most part as subsistence farmers or sharecroppers. Although their need then was as great as, and perhaps even greater than, that of other parts of the population, they operated largely as passive agents in the war on poverty waged at that time. During the depression the unions and their leaders sparked the drive against poverty. The target was income maintenance to combat the effects of unemployment. The unions organized the millions of unskilled workers who had been unorganized; they marched, sang, and struck. They were the prime movers in obtaining passage of the social security laws that characterized the anti-poverty measures of the depression.

In the sixties it was primarily the Negro leadership that focused attention on the poor. Negroes have been particularly hard hit by the rapid economic changes in recent years. There is a large dissident element among Negro youth that does not need government statistics to tell them they are being bypassed by society as were their fathers and grandfathers before them. They are aware that the economy is producing jobs that are vacant—jobs as delivery boys, busboys, handymen, and other menial tasks—but they are not inclined to flock to them. Their attitude is summarized in the statement by Bayard Rustin that "to want a Cadillac is not un-American; to push a cart in the garment center is."[8] There is one major difference between these young men and their forebears. Negro youth today will not stand idly by. In all regions of the country, a revolution is in progress—a revolution that demands rights, dignity, and jobs. This revolution is undoubtedly responsible in large measure for the attack on poverty during the sixties.

The rural poor, the aged poor, and even the poor hillbillies in Appalachia and the Ozarks could not arouse the nation to their urgent needs. They continued to suffer year after year in quiet desperation while they lived in hovels and suffered other indignities of body, mind, and spirit and their children were poorly educated. Action came only recently. It followed a prolonged period of marches, sit-ins, and other forms of protest by the Negro community.

The gradual reduction of poverty

Ample evidence exists that poverty in the United States is gradually being reduced. The official poverty statistics of the federal government show that the number of people in poverty dropped from 40 million in 1959 to 25 million in 1968. In less than a decade, the incidence of poverty dropped from 22 percent of the population to 13 percent.

The long-run change in the incidence of poverty is more difficult to measure; but the scanty evidence that is available presents a favorable picture. One way to measure this change is to examine the proportion of families with incomes insufficient to purchase a subsistence budget. In this case, subsistence must be thought of not as starvation but as a minimum adequate level of living for this society. Such a budget would provide the least amount that is compatible with the maintenance of a family's health, efficiency, and social acceptability. One example of a subsistence budget is that used by the New York City Welfare Department to determine which poor families in the city can qualify for public assistance payments.

Estimates of the change in the proportion of families with incomes below the subsistence budget for various periods are shown in Table VII-1. In 1935 the cost of a subsistence budget (measured in 1960 dollars), as subsistence was defined in that year, was $1,741, and 28 percent of the families had incomes below that amount. In 1960 the cost of a subsistence budget (also measured in 1960 dollars), as subsistence was defined in that year, had risen to $2,422, but only 10 percent of the families had incomes below that amount. On the basis of the 1960 budget, nearly half of the families would have been considered poor in 1935. These figures bring out two very important points. First, the quantity of goods and services that is considered necessary for subsistence tends to rise over time. The growth rate in the poverty line in recent years appears to be in the neighborhood of 1 percent per year. There are some who fail to understand the reason for the upward movement of the poverty line, but the answer is really quite simple, especially in a democratic society. The poor have eyes and they have a vote. They see those above them increasing their levels of living each year and it is inevitable that they will demand their share or that self-appointed or elected spokesmen will demand it for them

The second and perhaps more significant point suggested by these

TABLE VII-1

Families with Incomes Below Poverty Line*: 1935–1960

Year	Poverty line†	Percentage of families in poverty	
		Contemporary definition	1960 definition
1935	$1,741	28%	47%
1941	1,613	17	31
1950	2,213	13	26
1960	2,422	10	10

*Poverty line based on N.Y. Welfare Department Budget.
†In 1960 dollars.

Herman P. Miller, "Changes in the Number and Composition of the Poor," in Margaret S. Gordon, ed., *Poverty in America.* San Francisco, Chandler Publishing Co., 1965, p. 98.

figures is that there has been a marked reduction in the proportion of families living under distressed conditions. In 1935 over one-fourth of the families had incomes below the subsistence level as compared with only one-tenth of the families in 1960. These figures show what most Americans know to be true. More people in the United States are living better than ever before and the proportions living at the lowest levels have been reduced dramatically.

Outlook for the future

Many have dreamed about ultimate victory in the fight against poverty. Around the turn of the century, David Lloyd George requested funds from the British Parliament to wage "warfare against poverty."[9] His confidence in the outcome was reflected in his belief that within his own lifetime he would see "a great step towards that good time when poverty . . . will be as remote to the people of this country as the wolves which once infested its forests." In 1928 Herbert Hoover also saw victory in sight against this most ancient of man's enemies. He declared, in accepting the presidential nomination, "We shall soon with the help of God be in sight of the day when poverty will be banished in this nation."[10] Despite the predictions of such able and farsighted men as Lloyd George, Herbert Hoover, and many others, poverty still remains. It is a different kind of poverty from the one they had in mind; but even by the standards of 1900, poverty remains a problem in America. Now, once again, there is talk about ultimate victory. Can this be just a pipe dream after all? In what way are the present prospects for success better than those of the past? At least three major differences can be detected:

1. At the turn of the century a large proportion of the people were poor even by the low contemporary standards that were used at the time. By today's standards all but a very small part of the population would have been considered poverty-stricken. Although conditions had improved by the prosperous twenties, over half of the families had incomes below the poverty line as it is defined today. With victory so far away, it is difficult to see how anyone could have been very confident about the outcome.

2. Productivity has been growing rapidly in recent years. There is good reason to believe that this trend will continue and that it will provide us with far higher incomes than we have had in the past. Part of the increase will undoubtedly be devoted to the eradication of poverty. The prospects for growth are far, far greater than the average citizen realizes. Here is how the matter was summed up by the Council of Economic Advisers in 1965:[11]

> If average productivity gains until the year 2000 no more than match those of the last seventeen years, output per man-hour will be 3 times as great as that today. If working hours and labor force participation rates were to remain unchanged, average family income would approximate $18,000 in today's prices.

With this kind of leverage, the allocation of a small additional fraction of our income to the eradication of poverty becomes a real possibility.

3. We appear to have mastered that old bugaboo of capitalism—cataclysmic depressions. It is now over a quarter of a century since there has been a major depression in the United States, and judging from the frenzied activity displayed by the government at every minor turn in the business cycle, we have reason to hope that great depressions, like bubonic plagues, are things of the past. This freedom from

fear of want for society as a whole has permitted us to devote our creative energies to the elimination of want for the poorest segments of society.

If the above observations are correct, the great day may nearly be here when it will be possible for all Americans to have their basic physical needs met at currently acceptable standards without taking a pauper's oath and without losing dignity and self-respect. Dire poverty in the United States rests on a very weak foundation. Even if allowance is made for moderate increases in the poverty line, its ultimate defeat is only a matter of time—ten years or twenty at the most.

POVERTY DEFINED

We can talk all we want about poverty, but if there is going to be scientific understanding there must also be measurement. "In this life," thunders schoolmaster Thomas Gradgrind in Dickens' novel *Hard Times*, "we want nothing but Facts sir; nothing but Facts." Statistics are dull and often wrong, but they are necessary if we are to go beyond impressions and value judgments in thinking about poverty.

No hard and fast line separates the poor from the rest of society, just as no line separates the sick from the well, the happy from the depressed, or the sensitive from the vulgar. Poverty, like the other conditions of man, can best be described as a continuum rather than a fixed point.

An arbitrary line must be drawn if poverty is to be measured, but where and how? After several years of experimentation, the federal government has developed a poverty measure by which families are called poor if their income is below a specified level prescribed by the Social Security Administration. This level takes account of such factors as family size, number of children, and farm-nonfarm residence, as well as the amount of family income. Any family of a given type with an income below the amount shown in Table VII-2 would be classified as poor.

The poverty level is based on a minimum nutritionally sound food plan (the "economy" plan) designed by the Department of Agriculture

TABLE VII-2

Poverty Income Threshold: 1968

Size of family	Nonfarm	Farm
1	$1,748	$1,487
2	2,262	1,904
3	2,774	2,352
4	3,553	3,034
5	4,188	3,577
6	4,706	4,021
7 or more	5,789	4,916

U.S. Bureau of the Census, *Current Population Reports*, Series P-60, No. 68, p. 11.

for "emergency or temporary use when funds are low." Assuming that a poor family should spend no more than one-third of its income for food, the cost of food included in the economy plan is used to determine the minimum total income requirements for a given type of family. A household is statistically classified as poor if its total money income is less than three times the cost of the economy food plan. As applied against 1968 incomes, the poverty level of nonfarm residents ranges from $1,748 for a person living alone to $5,789 for a family of seven or more persons; it is $3,553 for a nonfarm family of four. The poverty line for farm families is set at 85 percent of the level of nonfarm families to make allowance for the fact that some of the income received by farmers is in the form of goods produced and consumed on the farm.

At the core of this definition of poverty is the food plan designed by the Department of Agriculture. In determining the proportion of total family income that should be consumed by food requirements, it was noted that the percentage of income spent for necessities, in particular food, reflects the relative well-being of both individuals and the society in which they live. In general, families that need to use about the same proportion of their income for a given level of food expenditure are considered to share the same level of living. For families of three or more persons the poverty level was set at three times the cost of the economy food plan. This was the average food-cost-to-family income relationship reported by the Department of Agriculture on the basis of a 1955 survey of food consumption.[12] For smaller families and persons residing alone, the cost of the economy food plan was multiplied by factors that were slightly larger to compensate for the relatively higher fixed expenses of these smaller households.

Table VII-3 shows the food budget on which the poverty standard shown in Table VII-2 is based. If a poor family spent its money carefully, it could provide the man of the house with the weekly quantities of food shown. Note that these are not the foods that a poor man would actually eat. They represent only what a poor man could afford to eat if he spent his money wisely. Also shown for comparison is the menu for a moderate-cost budget, which provides a much higher standard of living. The major difference between these two budgets is the amounts of meat, fruits, and vegetables that are provided. The moderate budget provides 5 pounds of meat, poultry, and fish per week as compared

TABLE VII-3

Family Food Plan for Men 20–35 Years Old: 1964

	Weekly quantity	
Food	Moderate cost	Economy*
Milk, cheese, ice cream	3 1/2 qts.	3 qts.
Meat, poultry, fish	5 lbs.	2 lbs.
Eggs	7	5
Dry beans, peas, nuts	1/4 lb.	1/2 lb.
Flour, cereal, baked goods	4 lbs.	4 1/2 lbs.
Citrus fruit, tomatoes	2 1/4 lbs.	1 1/2 lbs.
Green and yellow vegetables	3/4 lb.	3/4 lb.
Potatoes	3 lbs.	4 1/4 lbs.
Other fruits and vegetables	6 1/2 lbs.	3 1/2 lbs.
Fats, oils	1 lb.	7/8 lb.
Sugar, sweets	1 1/4 lbs.	1 1/8 lbs.

*Poverty level.

U.S. Department of Agriculture, Agricultural Research Service, *Family Food Plans, 1964*, CA 62-19, November 1964.

with only 2 pounds in the poverty budget, and 6½ pounds of certain fruits and vegetables as compared with only 3½ pounds in the poverty budget. It is assumed that poor people will eat more bread and potatoes and less meat and vegetables than those who are better off.

The current poverty index has several serious shortcomings. First, the relationship between food expenditures and the total budget is based on information obtained in 1955. A similar study conducted in 1965 showed that families, on the average, spend 28 percent of their income on food rather than 33 percent. On this basis, the cost of the food budget should be multiplied by 3½ rather than by 3, and the poverty line should be set at a considerably higher level. This change has not been made. Second, no allowance is made for regional variations in the cost of living, and the farm-nonfarm differential of 85 percent is quite arbitrary. Third, the food items on which the poverty line is based were developed for "temporary or emergency use" and are inadequate for a permanent diet. Finally, and perhaps most important of all, a fixed standard is used for measuring poverty. In the present poverty index no allowance is made for changing the content of the poverty budget. It is assumed that poor people will maintain the same level of living even though the levels of living of everyone else will be rising. A fixed standard is suitable for measuring changes in poverty over a period of several years. For the long run, however, a relative standard is preferable or periodic modifications must be made in the fixed standard. This practice is followed by the Labor Department, which periodically revises the market basket that is used as the basis for the Consumer Price Index.

The essential fallacy of a fixed poverty line is that it fails to recognize the relative nature of "needs." The poor will not be satisfied with a given level of living year after year when the levels of those around them are going up at the rate of about 3 percent per year. Old-timers may harken back to the "good old days" when people were happy without electricity, flush toilets, automobiles, and television sets; but they must also realize that once it becomes possible for all to have these "luxuries," they will be demanded and will quickly assume the status of "needs." For these reasons, it is unrealistic in an expanding economy to think in terms of a fixed poverty line.

Various proposals have been made for defining poverty on a relative rather than on an absolute basis. Victor Fuchs, for example, has suggested that we "define as poor any family with an income less than one-half that of the median family."[13] On this basis he concludes that the incidence of poverty did not change at all during the postwar period.[14]

An alternative proposal is presented in the numerical example shown in Table VII-4. This table, based on figures shown in Table VII-5, shows the change in the number of poor persons between 1959 and 1968, using the current definition of poverty, which is the fixed standard. It shows that in 1959, 39.5 million Americans were counted as poor; in 1968 the number was estimated at 25.4 million—a drop of 14 million in nine years. During this period, the incidence of poverty—that is, the proportion of persons in poor households relative to the total population—dropped by nearly half, from 22 percent to about 13 percent. Note also that in 1959 the poverty cutoff point for a four-person family ($2,943) was 54 percent of the median income for all families ($5,417) and that in 1968 the poverty cutoff point for a four-person family ($3,531) was only 41 percent of the U.S. median family income ($8,632). Now if we assume the ratio of the cutoff point for a four-person family to that for the average family in 1968 should have been the same as in 1959, then the poverty cutoff point would have been

TABLE VII-4

Incidence of Poverty Under Alternative Definitions

	Number of poor (millions)	Percentage of total population
Fixed standard (current definition)		
1959	39.5	22%
1968	25.4	13
Variable standard*		
1968	34.6	18

*Example:		
Nonfarm families	1959	1968
A. Median income, total U.S.	$5,417	$8,632
B. Poverty cutoff, 4-person family with male head	$2,943	$3,531 ($4,661)
Ratio of B to A	54%	41%

TABLE VII-5

Persons in United States Below Poverty Level, by Color: 1959–1968

Year	Number (millions)			Percentage		
	Total	White	Nonwhite	Total	White	Nonwhite
1959	39.5	28.5	11.0	22%	18%	56%
1960	39.9	28.3	11.5	22	18	56
1961	39.6	27.9	11.7	22	17	56
1962	38.6	26.7	12.0	21	16	56
1963	36.4	25.2	11.2	19	15	51
1964	36.1	25.0	11.1	19	15	50
1965	33.2	22.5	10.7	17	13	47
1966	30.4	20.8	9.7	16	12	42
1966*	28.5	19.3	9.2	15	11	40
1967	27.8	19.0	8.8	14	11	37
1968	25.4	17.4	8.0	13	10	33

Note: Sums of tabulated figures in this chapter may not equal totals because of rounding.

*Revision in series.

U.S. Bureau of the Census, *Current Population Reports*, Series P-60, No. 68, Table 1.

$4,661 in 1968 and we would have found 35 million poor people representing 18 percent of the total. In other words, if we had used a relative standard, we would have concluded that there was little change in the number of poor.

Although the fixed standard now used to measure the extent of poverty has serious limitations, there are understandable reasons for retaining it. The general public has become familiar with the present method and accepts the numbers associated with it. Any significant change would raise doubts and create some confusion. The fixed standard also provides a simple method for measuring changes over time. It identifies the number of people each year whose incomes are inadequate to purchase a fixed bundle of goods and services.

At the same time, however, we must recognize that the use of a constant standard exaggerates the improvement that is made over time. If the poor are identified by a constant market basket, no allowance is made for a rise in the standard of living among poor families. The standard of living of the average family, however, goes up each year because its income is going up. By using a constant standard many people are moved above the poverty line each year, but their position relative to others is unaltered. They continue to be unable to afford many of the goods and services that are widely enjoyed by others. Their status in the census tabulations is changed from poor to nonpoor, but their feelings of deprivation remain unchanged. If this definition remains in use long enough, poverty will in time be eliminated statistically, but few people will believe it—certainly not those who continue to have housing, education, medical care, and other goods and services that are far below standards deemed acceptable for this society.

WHO ARE THE POOR?

Although poverty remains an urgent national problem, we have been successful in whittling away at it and there is good reason to be optimistic about the prospects for future progress. From 1948 to 1968 the incidence of poverty dropped at the rate of about one percentage point per year. The rate of decrease was fairly constant throughout the period, which is no mean accomplishment in view of the many factors tending to depress that rate. It was much easier to reduce poverty by one percentage point in 1948 when about one-third of the families were below the poverty line than it was in 1968, when only one-eighth were below that level. Also, the closer we get to the very bottom of the income distribution, the more we find the hard-core poor whose incomes arise largely outside of the labor market and are not necessarily responsive to economic growth. Finally, although economic growth tends to reduce poverty by pushing families above the poverty line, it also tends to increase it in a statistical sense by making it possible for the young and the old to maintain their own residences, thereby creating low-income families that might not otherwise exist as independent units. Although the undoubling of families acts as a brake on the reduction in poverty, those families that choose to live alone on a lower income may feel "better off" than those who live with others and have a higher combined income as a result.

All groups have shared in the reduction of poverty. While the size of the U.S. population increased at the rate of about 2½ million per year during the past decade, the number of whites in poverty dropped from 29 million in 1959 to 17 million in 1968, a decline of over 1 million per year. The number of nonwhites in poverty dropped from 11 million to 8 million during the same period, representing a decline of about 350,000 per year. In 1959, 56 percent of the nonwhites were poor as compared with only 33 percent in 1968.

There are many different ways to classify the poor. One useful way is to identify four different groups of people: children in poor families, the aged, adults of working age who are employed, and adults of working age who are not employed. The causes of poverty are different for each group, and different programs are needed to improve their lot.

Poor kids

There were about 11 million poor kids in the United States in 1968. Two-fifths of them were black and many lived in large families. These children are of particular social concern because they are the most likely candidates for the next generation of poverty. Most of these children in poor families will rise above their environment. They will become educated, useful citizens, who will marry, raise a family, and lead wholesome, productive lives. The number who "make it" should be greater in the future than they have been in the recent past because we are now more aware of their problems and are trying in small ways to correct them. But far too many will fall by the wayside. Some have been scarred by physical handicaps. They have lived too long with hunger, illness, pain, and malnutrition. Their formative years were spent in substandard, overcrowded housing and they attended substandard, overcrowded schools. These are the children who will become street corner men. Others have experienced severe emotional trauma for which they and society may pay forever. They have been reared in unstable homes by unstable parents. They regularly experience anger, fear, frustration, and violence. Rape, drug addiction, and drunken brawls are as

TABLE VII-6

Persons in United States, by Poverty Status: 1968

	Total (millions)	Below poverty level	
		Number (millions)	Percentage of total
All persons	197.6	25.4	13%
In families	183.8	20.7	11
Head	50.5	5.0	10
Under 65 years	43.4	3.8	9
65 years and over	7.1	1.2	17
Family members	133.3	15.6	12
Under 18 years	70.0	10.7	15
18 to 64 years	57.1	4.1	7
65 years and over	6.2	0.8	14
Unattached individuals	13.8	4.7	34
Under 65 years	8.5	2.1	25
65 years and over	5.3	2.6	49

Derived from U.S. Bureau of the Census, *Current Population Reports*, Series P-60, No. 66 and 68; and unpublished data.

common to some poor kids in the slums as family picnics are to middle-class kids in the suburbs.

Many more statistics could be cited to show the deprivation of poor kids. But facts are no substitute for feeling. What is it like to be a poor kid or the parent of a poor kid? Here are some examples of how the poor see themselves, as reported in the Child Rearing Study of Low-Income Families.[15]

There was no food in the house and I didn't want them to have to go to school hungry and then come home hungry too. I felt that if I kept them home with me, at least when they cried and asked for a piece of bread, I would be with them and put my arms around them.

The Child Rearing Study found that the amount and regularity of family income make a significant difference in the child-rearing priorities of parents. Thus the mother who decided to keep her hungry children at home did not necessarily demonstrate unconcern about education or truancy. Her most urgent concern was how she would feed, shelter, and clothe eight children on her husband's earnings of $52 a week.

Some parents refused to send their children to school looking "raggedy," and one mother, who had been jailed for assaulting her husband, placed her priority on the shelter of her nine children, even though she later had misgivings about such a long separation:

> You know, I didn't have to stay in jail those two weeks. I could have paid $40 for bail and gotten out but I just kind of felt that maybe I'd stay there for a while. I had $73 on me because I had the rent money on me. One mind told me to pay the bail and the other mind said "no." So when they told me I could make one telephone call and asked me who I wanted to call I told them to just call the rent man and tell him to come and get the rent and I would stay in jail. . . .
>
> . . . The only thing that worried me while I was in jail was the children. I worried about them as they have never been separated from me before. When I got out of jail my husband came for me and asked me if I didn't want to come home to fix something to eat for the children first. I told him "no." I just wanted to get the children and I kept right on from jail to Junior Village to get them. They had been taken good care of there, but there won't be no more separations. The next separation will have to be a death separation. . . .

Many children seek their pleasures outside of the home, which affords few pleasures or comforts. In some low-income households, the floor space is nearly covered with beds. Even the living rooms and kitchens may double as sleeping quarters. Home often is simply a place to sleep and, hopefully, to eat. The close quarters, the drabness, the lack of something to do, drives children into the streets.

The late Roscoe E. Lewis, a Hampton Institute professor who lived in the Second Police Precinct area in Washington, D.C., while a member of the Child Rearing Study staff wrote this vignette of children on their own:

> . . . Occasionally you see a group of the younger ones playing "taxi" in a derelict car—taking turns at the steering wheel, starting the car off. "Where you want to go, lady?" But the larger kids are on the block, the only place where there are any "pickings."
>
> Picking begins about 8:00 A.M. The sidewalks and gutters of the block are carefully searched; drunks of the night before may have dropped a coin, or

even lost their pocketbooks or cigarettes. The yards of the few who are "family" people are investigated; there may be papers or bottles that others have missed. There are jukeboxes and the cigarette machines to be searched for unused coins; the floors of the restaurants and those bars that will let them in have to be looked over. For this age group, asking passersby for coins is child's play. Morning is a busy time for the 10- to 12-year-old group.

When "pickings" is finished the rest of the day is given over to methods of play that can be carried out on concrete sidewalks. The younger ones roll discarded automobile tires down the sidewalk—the smaller tires, which can accelerate fast, usually winning. There is a great variety of hop, skip, and jump games played by the girls; there are several different versions of playing ball among the boys. The dangerous games, "Beat the car across the street" and "make the car screech," are played occasionally by the older boys—those in the 10- to 12-year-old group. It is not a daylong game, for those who play it realize it is a dangerous game. It is played only when each one can show a stake—a nickel, a streetcar token, a couple of cigarettes, perhaps picked off the street.

Many of the parents were not ambitious in their hopes for their children, citing the completion of high school as a realizable educational goal. High school was seen as a passport to a "good" job—a job that is regular, contrasting with the seasonal work of so many low-income males; a job that pays enough to provide a modicum of security; a job that does not require the physical strain of common labor. Beyond these goals many low-income families dared not hope. One mother gave this assessment:

My husband didn't have no education and had to do laboring work. If my children could read, they could get a job driving a truck or working in a store. They could learn to use the cash register if they know how to add. They can be somebody. If you don't have no education, you have to take the first thing they give you. If you go to an employment agency, you'd get a job probably dishwashing since you had no education. I want them to do something better.

Another mother was more succinct and emphatic: "I'll be satisfied as long as they ain't doing no day's work in nobody's house and working in nobody's kitchen!"

127

TABLE VII-7
Poverty Status of Persons in Families: 1959 and 1968

	1959			1968		
		Below poverty level			Below poverty level	
	Total (millions)	Number (millions)	Percentage of total	Total (millions)	Number (millions)	Percentage of total
All families	45.1	8.3	18.5%	50.5	5.0	10.0%
Residence						
Farm	3.8	1.7	44.6	2.6	0.5	18.8
Nonfarm	41.3	6.6	16.1	47.9	4.6	9.5
Sex of head						
Male	40.6	6.4	15.8	45.1	3.3	7.3
Female	4.5	1.9	42.6	5.4	1.8	32.3
Race of head						
White (total)	40.8	6.2	15.2	45.4	3.6	8.0
Male	37.3	5.0	13.3	41.4	2.6	6.3
Female	3.5	1.2	34.8	4.1	1.0	25.2
Nonwhite (total)	4.2	2.1	50.4	5.1	1.4	28.2
Male	3.3	1.5	44.2	3.7	0.7	18.9
Female	0.9	0.7	72.0	1.4	0.7	52.9
Age of head						
14 to 24	2.3	0.6	26.9	3.3	0.4	13.2
25 to 64	36.5	5.8	16.0	40.1	3.4	8.5
65 and over	6.2	1.9	30.0	7.1	1.2	17.0

AMERICA'S FIGHT WITH POVERTY

Size of family						
2	14.5	2.9	19.6	17.4	1.8	10.5
3 or 4	18.9	2.4	12.8	20.2	1.4	7.1
5 or 6	8.9	1.8	20.2	9.8	1.0	10.2
7 or more	2.8	1.3	45.6	3.2	0.8	24.7
Employment status of head						
Employed	35.5	4.5	12.8	40.2	2.4	6.0
Unemployed	1.7	0.6	33.7	0.8	0.1	19.3
Not in labor force, or in armed forces	7.9	3.2	40.8	9.6	2.5	26.0
Work record of head						
Worked (total)	38.4	5.6	14.6	42.8	2.9	6.7
50 to 52 weeks	28.8	3.0	10.6	34.6	1.6	4.6
Full-time	27.7	2.6	9.4	33.5	1.4	4.0
Part-time	1.1	0.4	38.4	1.1	0.2	19.8
1 to 49 weeks	9.6	2.6	26.9	8.2	1.3	15.8
Unemployed	4.2	1.2	28.4	2.5	0.3	13.6
Other	5.4	1.4	25.7	5.7	1.0	16.9
Did not work (total)	5.6	2.5	45.2	6.8	2.1	30.9
Ill or disabled	1.5	0.8	52.8	1.7	0.6	37.7
Keeping house	1.7	0.9	53.3	1.6	0.8	47.2
Going to school	–	–	*	0.1	–	43.2
Unable to find work	0.2	0.1	*	0.1	–	†
Other	2.2	0.7	32.7	3.3	0.6	18.7
In armed forces	1.0	0.2	15.5	0.9	0.1	6.6

Note: Dash = less than 100,000.
*Base less than 200,000.
†Base less than 75,000.

U.S. Bureau of the Census, *Current Population Reports*, Series P-60, No. 68.

The aged poor

There were 4.6 million aged persons living in poverty in the United States in 1968. This figure excludes an additional 700,000 who lived in old-age homes or hospitals and an additional 1.7 million whose own income would have classified them as poor, but who were living with children or other relatives who were not poor.[16] The major cause of poverty among the aged is that few of them are able to work and their pensions are too small to provide an adequate level of living. Only about one-fifth of the aged poor were employed; the majority of the other four-fifths feel too old or too sick to work.

More than half of the aged poor live by themselves. The majority are women. Not too long ago many of these widows and widowers would have lived out their final years with their children. Neither they nor their children might have been happy with the arrangement, but there were no alternatives. Thanks to social security, many now have the resources to maintain their own homes or apartments. According to current standards they live in poverty; but they do have their independence and that counts for something. Increases in the coverage and amount of payments under the Social Security Law have gradually improved the economic circumstances of the 2½ million elderly poor people who live alone as well as the million or so elderly couples who are in poverty.

The working poor

About 1½ million family heads who worked full-time throughout 1968, trying to eke out a living, never made it above the poverty line. These are the farmhands, porters, janitors, waitresses, busboys, and other low-paid workers who make up over one-quarter of the poor. The reason for their poverty is quite simple: they have inadequate skills and receive low wages. A rise in the minimum wage laws would help many of them rise above the poverty line; but it would also put many others out of work entirely because they are often marginal workers who can be replaced by machines. The younger workers in this group might be amenable to training. For many of the older workers, however, some form of subsidy is essential if they are to rise above the poverty line.

A nearly equal number of family heads also did some work in 1968, but they had less than full-year employment. Many of these part-year workers are people who had one or more stretches of unemployment during the year; some were too sick to work at full-time jobs and some were women with small children to care for. Altogether, therefore, nearly half of the poor families were headed by workers who did not earn enough to raise their families above the poverty line.

The nonworking poor

In 1968, about 2 million families (40 percent of the total) were headed by a person who did not work at all. About one-third were ill or disabled, one-third were mothers with small children, and the rest were retired or were not working for other reasons. Welfare mothers constitute a significant proportion of the total in this group. Although some of these families could be moved out of poverty by providing suitable jobs or training for the family heads, the majority will probably have to depend on income-maintenance programs of one form or another.

VIII

Help for the Poor

As a society we are doing more than ever before to help the poor, but the efforts are not widely appreciated. Many people feel that we are still not doing enough and nearly everyone agrees that much of what we are doing is wrong. American programs to help the poor have been described as "welfare colonialism" and as an "ugly, diseased social growth [that] must be removed from American life."[1] Some would replace the present programs entirely with a cash subsidy in the form of a negative income tax. Others advocate family allowances, and still others argue for large cash subsidies and improved services. Nearly all of these programs would be more expensive than those we now have. They might enable the poor to live more comfortably, but none can guarantee that they would feel more comfortable or satisfied. Shakespeare might well have been thinking about this kind of a problem when he wrote, "If to do were as easy as to know what were good to do, chapels had been churches, and poor men's cottages princes' palaces."

A broad outline of the scope and magnitude of the federally funded anti-poverty program in the United States is shown in Table VIII-1. In 1969 expenditures of the federal government to help the poor amounted to $24.4 billion. This total would be increased by about 50 percent if allowance were made for state and local efforts to combat poverty, and by an additional $1 billion if the work of private charities were taken into account. Thus, according to the best estimates available, a total of nearly $40 billion was spent to combat poverty in 1969.[2]

The growing awareness of the problem of poverty in the United

TABLE VIII-1

Federal Aid to the Poor: 1961, 1964, 1969

Program	1961	1964	1969
Total	$9.7 billion	$11.9 billion	$24.4 billion
Cash assistance	8.3	9.8	13.0
OASDI	3.5	4.7	6.0
Public assistance	1.9	2.4	4.0
Veterans' payments	1.5	1.7	2.1
Unemployment insurance	1.0	0.7	0.5
Railroad retirement	0.3	0.3	0.4
Employment and training	0.1	0.2	2.0
Economic development	*	*	0.2
Education	*	*	2.1
Health	0.7	0.9	4.9
Housing	0.1	0.1	0.2
Food	0.2	0.3	0.7
Indians and trust territories	0.3	0.4	0.5
Other	0.1	0.1	0.8

Note: Sums of tabulated figures in this chapter may not equal totals because of rounding.

*Less than $50 million.

Sar A. Levitan, *Programs in Aid of the Poor for the 1970's.* Baltimore: Johns Hopkins Press, 1970.

States and the desire to alleviate it are reflected in the figures in Table VIII-1. At the beginning of the decade of the sixties, less than $10 billion was spent by the federal government on programs in aid of the poor. The lion's share of the total was given in the form of cash help. By 1964 federal expenditures increased modestly and reached a new total of nearly $12 billion. Expenditures for health, training, and other services increased at a somewhat more rapid rate than cash assistance, but even by the middle of the decade more than 80 percent of federal help was in the form of cash payments. The next five years witnessed a dramatic change in both the scope and nature of the federal government's fight against poverty. Between 1964 and 1969 federal aid to the poor more than doubled, rising from $11.9 billion to $24.4 billion. The increase in

133

federal anti-poverty expenditures during these five years alone represented more than the total amount spent for this purpose in 1964. It is significant that only a little over half of the expenditures in 1969 were in the form of cash help. The balance was in the form of expanded employment and training programs, education, health care, and other goods and services.

Cash help

Old Age, Survivors and Disability Insurance (popularly known as social security) is the single most important government program providing help to the poor. Payments to the poor under this program amounted to $6 billion in 1969, or about one-fourth of total government payments to the poor. Table VIII-2 shows that about 34 percent of all poor households received some OASDI payments in 1965 and that 22 percent of all the income received by poor families came from this source. There is no reason to believe that these numbers have changed much since 1965. This program was the major source of livelihood for that one-third of the poor households which received payments under it. These families averaged $916 from the program in 1965 and these payments accounted for 64 percent of their income.

Table VIII-2 also shows how much more important this program is to poor families than to those which are not poor. Since the aged constitute a much larger proportion of the poor population than of the total population, only 19 percent of the nonpoor households received income from this source as compared with 34 percent of the poor. Even more significant is the fact that these payments constituted only 3 percent of the total income received by the nonpoor, as compared with 22 percent for the poor. Since payments under this program are tied to previous earnings, the incomes received from OASDI by the nonpoor are considerably greater than those received by the poor.

In addition to making income payments for retired workers who earned credits under OASDI, the Social Security Act provides for payment on the basis of need alone to four groups of needy people: Old Age Assistance, Aid to the Blind, Aid to the Permanently and Totally Disabled, and Aid to Families with Dependent Children. Although AFDC is the largest and most controversial of these four programs, it accounts

TABLE VIII-2

OASDI and Public Assistance Payments to Poor and Nonpoor: 1965*

	OASDI	Public assistance
Poor		
Percentage of households receiving aid	34%	19%
Mean income from source for all poor	$312	$192
Mean income from source for recipient	$916	$994
Percentage of income of all poor from source	22%	13%
Percentage of income of recipient from source	64%	69%
Nonpoor		
Percentage of households receiving aid	19%	2%
Mean income from source for all nonpoor	$253	$22
Mean income from source for recipient	$1,335	$1,107
Percentage of income of all nonpoor from source	3%	†
Percentage of income of recipient from source	16%	14%

*This table is intended to show general magnitudes rather than precise numbers.

†Less than ½ of 1 percent.

See Table VIII-1 for source.

for less than half of the funds paid out as public assistance. In 1968, for example, a total of $6.3 billion was paid out to the total population under these four programs, plus general assistance which is paid by states and localities to people who do not qualify under one of the four programs. Only $2.8 billion or about 45 percent of the total was paid to AFDC recipients.

About one-fifth of the poor households in the United States received some payments under one of the public assistance programs in 1965. These payments accounted for 13 percent of all the income received by the poor. As in the case of OASDI payments, those families which received public assistance payments were largely dependent upon this income. They received an average of about $994 per household and this income accounted for 69 percent of their total receipts from all sources.

Help for the employable poor

The chief way in which the government helps the employable poor is through training programs which improve their skills, thus making possible gainful employment. In addition, there are some programs which create jobs directly for the poor; and finally there are programs which improve the operation of the labor market by attempting to match up people and jobs. Table VIII-3 presents a listing of the various manpower programs in operation in 1969 and the amount spent for each. The total for training, job creation, and employment market services was $2.4 billion.

These programs try to cater to the very diverse needs of the labor force for training and guidance. They include efforts directed to specific kinds of workers as well as broad comprehensive programs which attempt to change patterns of behavior. The help offered to the poor by these programs has been summarized in the following way:[3]

1. Outreach to find the discouraged and undermotivated and encourage them to partake of available services;
2. Adult basic education to remedy the absence or obsolescence of earlier schooling;
3. Prevocational orientation to expose those of limited experience to alternative occupational choices;
4. Training for entry-level skills for persons lacking a rudimentary education;
5. Training allowances to provide support and incentives for those undergoing training;
6. Residential facilities for those who live in sparsely populated areas or who have a home environment that precludes successful rehabilitation;
7. Work experience for those unaccustomed to the discipline of the work place;
8. Job development efforts to solicit job opportunities suited to the abilities of the disadvantaged job seeker;
9. Subsidized private employment for the disadvantaged;
10. Job coaching to work out supervisor-worker relationships once a job is found;

11. Creation of public-service jobs tailored to the needs of job seekers who are not absorbed in the competitive market;

12. Supportive services—such as medical aid and day care centers for mothers with small children—for those who need corrective measures to enter or resume positions in the world of work; and

13. Relocation allowances for residents in labor-surplus areas coupled with special inducements to employers to bring jobs to those stranded in depressed areas.

Provision of goods and services

Education and health are the two major forms of goods and services provided to the poor by the federal government. In 1969 expenditures

TABLE VIII-3

Manpower Programs and Costs: 1969

Program	Outlay (millions)
Total	$2,442
Training and remedial	1,437
Vocational education	242
Adult basic	45
Vocational rehabilitation	369
MDTA	374
Job Corps	278
Projects 100,000 and Transition	39
WIN	90
Job creation	501
NYC	321
Mainstream	38
New Careers	22
JOBS	120
Delivery agencies	504
Employment Service	341
Concentrated Employment Program	163

See Table VIII-1 for source.

for these activities amounted to $2.3 billion for education and $4.9 billion for health.

Table VIII-4 focuses on the federally supported programs which minister to the educational needs of the poor. These programs totaled $2.3 billion. About one-half of this amount was spent under the Elementary and Secondary Education Act of 1965, which provided $1.1 billion in 1969 to school districts in which large numbers of poor children were enrolled. These funds are given to the state school boards, which in turn distribute them to local school boards. The funds have largely been used for traditional educational activities. The remaining $1.2 billion spent on education for the poor went to several different programs. About $330 million was spent on Head Start programs and about $500 million was spent on higher education programs.

A classification of federal health expenditures for the poor alone, by program, is not available. Table VIII-5, however, does present this infor-

TABLE VIII-4

Federally Supported Educational Programs Focusing on Needs of Poor: 1969

Program	Outlay (millions)	Number of disadvantaged students served (thousands)
Total	$2,338	–
Head Start	330	–
Full year	–	218
Summer	–	417
Follow-Through	30	23
Elementary and Secondary Education Act	1,123	9,200
Upward Bound	30	25
College Work Study	134	89
Education Opportunity grants	125	120
Student loans	194	110

See Table VIII-1 for source.

mation for the poor and near-poor. Since total health expenditures for the poor amounted to $4.9 billion in 1969 (see Table VIII-1), one can surmise from this table that about equal amounts were spent for the poor and the near-poor. The great bulk of the federal health expenditures for the poor are under the Medicare and Medicaid programs, which were added to the Social Security Act in 1965. Medicare covers the bulk of the hospital and medical costs of the aged who are covered by social security, railroad retirement pensions, or who meet certain special qualifications. More important for the poor is Medicaid, which extends hospital and medical care services for indigent people who are covered by one of the four public assistance programs.

TABLE VIII-5

**Estimated Federal Appropriations
for Medical Aid to Poor and Near-Poor: 1970**

Program	Outlay (billions)	Eligible population (millions)
Total	$9.6	—
Medicare	2.3	7.0
Medicaid	5.8	10.0
Veterans	0.9	0.8
Children	0.2	—
Indians	0.1	0.4
Neighborhood health centers	0.1	0.8
Other	0.1	—

See Table VIII-1 for source.

New income-maintenance proposals

The continued existence of a large number of poor people and general dissatisfaction with the present American welfare system has led to the search for new ways to raise the incomes of poor families. Two general approaches have received widespread attention in recent years: family allowances and the negative income tax.

A family allowance program would provide for the payment of a monthly check to each family with children. Benefits would be paid to the family for each child under 18. All children would be eligible for such payments regardless of the family income or the employment status of their parents. This is considered to be one of the great advantages of family allowances over other forms of income maintenance. It eliminates the means test by making all children eligible. This plan also eliminates the need for a large bureaucracy with complicated regulations and investigative powers to determine eligibility. Once the existence of a child was established under the plan, the family would automatically receive a benefit. A third advantage claimed for this proposal is that it would not reduce the work incentives of the parents, since the amount received for each child would be fixed, regardless of the amount earned. Of course, above a certain income level families would have to pay taxes on the benefits received; but most poor families would not be affected by this fact. There are some major objections to this plan. One important objection is that it would distribute large amounts of money to affluent families and then attempt to recoup those funds through taxation. It seems very inefficient for the government to hand out many billions of dollars each year to families that do not need the money and then to try to recoup those funds by taxation. A second objection to the plan is that it may tend to increase the birthrate, particularly among poor families. If the payment for each child were large enough, some women might be inclined to have more children for that reason. There is no solid evidence, however, that the family allowance program has had any major impact on birthrates in those countries where it has been used.

Most industrial countries now use some variant of the family allowance principle. In some nations a fixed amount is paid for each child regardless of age, and in other nations the amount paid varies with the age of the child. In France, payments are financed by employers and amount to as much as 5 percent of the national income. In Canada, the government makes the payments, which are relatively small, amounting to $6 per month for each child under 10 years old, $8 for each child between the ages of 10 and 16 years, and $10 for 16- and 17-year-olds.

Since family allowance programs provide only for families with children, they must be regarded as a supplement to other forms of income maintenance for the aged, handicapped, disabled, and other needy groups. However, this program, if adopted, could reduce the incidence of poverty appreciably. According to estimates prepared by the Department of Health, Education and Welfare, a family allowance program paying $25 a month for each child would have removed 36 percent of all families and 45 percent of all children from poverty in 1965 at a cost of about $11 billion. A $50-a-month allowance would have cost $29 billion and would have removed two-thirds of all families and three-fourths of all children from poverty.

TABLE VIII-6

Effects of Monthly Child Allowance Program: 1965

	$25 for each child	$25 for third and subsequent children	$50 for each child	$50 for third and subsequent children
Program cost (billions)				
Payment	$20.9	$6.7	$41.2	$13.3
Tax recovery potential	9.6	2.6	12.7	3.5
Eliminating exemption*	6.5	1.8	6.5	1.8
Tax on allowance	3.1	0.8	6.2	1.7
Program results				
Reduction in welfare payments to poor (billions)	$4.2	$1.9	$8.4	$3.9
Percentage of families removed from poverty	36%	15%	64%	29%
Percentage of children in families removed from poverty	45%	25%	77%	46%

*$600 exemption and minimum standard deduction for children receiving allowance.

See Table VIII-1 for source.

The negative income tax is a new kind of income-maintenance plan which has received serious consideration and widespread support in recent years. Legislation for such a plan has been introduced by members of both political parties and President Nixon has submitted a detailed proposal for consideration by the Congress.

The negative income tax is a direct analog to the positive income tax. At present, every family that receives an income above a certain amount must pay a tax on that income. Families with incomes below the specified amount do not file a tax return and they do not pay a tax. If a negative income tax plan were adopted each family would be required to file a tax return. Those families with incomes below a certain amount would receive a payment from the government (negative tax) and those with incomes above that amount would pay a tax as they do at present.

Several different negative income tax proposals have received serious consideration. All have three things in common: a guaranteed minimum level of income which would vary with size and type of family, a specific tax rate or rates which apply to earned income up to a certain level, and a break-even point where the negative tax ends and the normal tax rate begins. The fundamental principles of the negative income tax can perhaps best be demonstrated by an example (Table VIII-7). Let us assume such a program with provisions for a minimum income of $2,600, a tax rate of 50 percent on earnings, and a break-even point of $5,200. Let us assume, further, that a family of four is headed by a totally disabled man whose wife is also unable to work because she has small children.

TABLE VIII-7

Essential Features of Negative Income Tax Plan

Earnings (A)	Deductions from government contribution* (B)	Net government contribution† (C)	Net income (A+C)
$0	$0	$2,600	$2,600
1,000	500	2,100	3,100
2,000	1,000	1,600	3,600
3,000	1,500	1,100	4,100
5,200	2,600	0	5,200

*50 percent tax.
†$2,600 minimum income.

Since this family would have no earnings, it would receive $2,600 from the government in the form of a negative income tax. This amount would represent the maximum payment by the government. Since the family has no earnings, nothing would be deducted from the government payment. Therefore, the net income of this family would be $2,600. Let us assume another family with earnings of $1,000. This family would receive a payment of $2,100 from the government, representing the basic allowance of $2,600 less one-half of the earnings. The total amount received would therefore be $3,100, or the $1,000 of earned income plus $2,100 of negative income tax payment from the government.

A family with $5,200 of earnings would receive no negative income tax payment because the one-half of its earnings which must be deducted from the government contribution of $2,600 would be exactly equal to that contribution, and would result in a net government contribution of zero. Such a family would have a net income of $5,200.

President Nixon submitted a variant of the negative income tax plan in a message to Congress in August 1969.[4] The Nixon plan would be restricted to families with children and it would be a supplement to other income-maintenance plans now in existence rather than a substitute for these plans. All families with children would be guaranteed $500 per person for the first two members and $300 for each additional family member. For a family of four, this would amount to $1,600. In addition, the first $720 of family income would not be counted and a deduction of 50 cents for each dollar would be made for earnings above this amount. In thirty states, the proposed payment would be less than the amount currently paid to welfare recipients. These states would be required to maintain the current level of benefits, but in no case would they be required to pay more than 90 percent of their current welfare cost. The federal government would make up the difference between what the states paid (i.e., up to 90 percent) and what it took to maintain the current level of benefits.

The plan has several other important features, one of the most controversial being the requirement that employable persons who accepted payments be required to register for work or job training and that they be required to accept jobs or training that was available locally. The only exception to this work requirement would be mothers of preschool children. The plan also calls for a major expansion of job-training and day-care facilities and the uniform federal payment of minimum amounts of $65 per month for the aged, the blind, and the disabled. The administration has estimated that the total costs of the plan would be about $4 billion more than was paid in public assistance in 1969.

A graphic description of how the Nixon plan would work for a family of four is shown in Table VIII-8. The key features of the plan are a minimum income of $1,600 for a family of four, a tax rate of 50 percent on earnings above $720, and a break-even point of $3,920 per year. Assume that a family of four earned $720 during the year and had no other earnings. Such a family would receive the basic government payment of $1,600, in addition to the $720 of earnings, for a total of $2,320. If a family earned $1,000, it would have 50 percent of the earnings above $720 (or one-half of $280) deducted from the basic contribution of $1,600 and would therefore receive a total of $2,460.

The main advantage of the negative income tax plan is that it eliminates the means test and provides income maintenance in a single, comprehensive plan that does not depend on state and local administration. It gives money only to the poor, in contrast to the family allowance plan, which also gives money to the affluent and then has to tax it back from them. By having a variable tax rate it is possible to minimize the incentive to stop working. Finally, this plan can also be used either as a substitute for other existing income-maintenance programs or as a supplement to them. Although advocates of the plan regard it as simple to administer through the Internal Revenue Service, critics see many administrative complexities, particularly if monthly payments are contem-

TABLE VIII-8

Nixon Negative Income Tax Proposal*

Earnings (A)	Deductions from government contribution (B)	Net government contribution (C)	Net income (A+C)
$0	$0	$1,600	$1,600
720	0	1,600	2,320
1,000	140	1,460	2,460
2,000	640	960	2,960
3,000	1,140	460	3,460
3,920	1,600	0	3,920

*Figures shown are for a family of four.

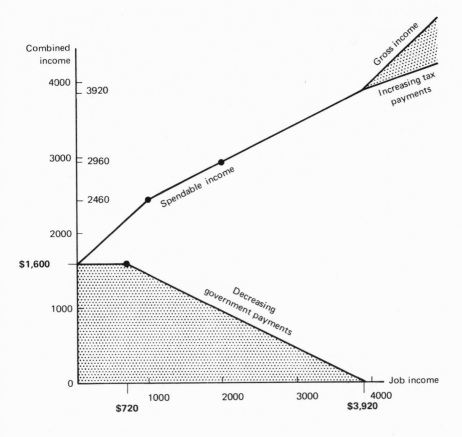

plated and if some attempt is made to take regional variations in the cost of living into account.

Perhaps the greatest uncertainty about the negative income tax concerns the impact it will have on incentives to work and to learn new skills. Little is known at present about the extent to which the heads of poor families would continue to work if they knew that their income would be guaranteed at a certain minimum level. The American public seems quite apprehensive on this point. A Gallup Poll survey conducted early in 1969 asked a sample of people if they would favor guaranteeing a family of four an income of at least $3,200 a year.[5] Two-thirds of the respondents were opposed to such a plan. In contrast, four-fifths of the people were in favor of guaranteeing to each family of four a job which would pay a minimum of $3,200 a year. Evidently most Americans are still opposed to the idea of giving people something for nothing.

Some spokesmen for the poor also have misgivings about the negative income tax. As one columnist put it recently, "In the short run, some form of income maintenance may be the only way out [but] income guarantees can be treacherous as a long-range solution."[6] The reason it is regarded as treacherous is the fear that it may induce some people to depend on subsidies rather than to develop their skills and attempt to achieve economic independence. Sar Levitan has pointed out that under the Nixon plan, "two family heads, each with three dependents, could both receive an annual income of $4,000—although one works full time at an hourly rate of $2, while the other works only half time at the same $2 per hour and makes up the difference with cash supplements, food stamps and other income in kind available under welfare programs."[7]

Based on preliminary evidence from an experimental survey being funded by the Office of Economic Opportunity, there is reason to believe that a negative income tax would not reduce the incentives of poor families to work. In mid-1968, a representative sample of 509 poor families in New Jersey was selected to participate in a program which would provide federal payments on a sliding scale similar to that described above under President Nixon's proposed welfare plan. These families were divided into two groups, one of 364 families that received benefits and a control group of 145 that did not. The families were similar in all other respects—income, education, employment, and other characteristics. The families in the subsidized group had an average size of 5.8 persons, their average income was $4,248 a year, and they received additional government payments of $1,100 a year. After ten months of operation, it was found that 53 percent of the families receiving federal subsidies had increased their outside earnings; for 18 percent, earnings had not changed; and for 29 percent, earnings had declined. In the control group, 43 percent of the families showed increases, 26 percent remained the same, and 31 percent declined.[8] The preliminary data also showed that families receiving supplementary benefits tended to reduce borrowing, buying fewer items on credit and purchasing more consumer goods such as furniture and appliances.[9] On the basis of this evidence, the report issued by the Office of Economic Opportunity concluded that a family assistance plan such as that proposed by President Nixon "is practical."[10]

IX

The Rich and the Very-Rich

We hear a lot about the poor. Congressional committees study their characteristics and devise programs for their help. They are the focal point of discussions about crime, juvenile delinquency, slums, school dropouts, and many other social problems. This is as it should be. We are a people with a conscience and we deplore the existence of poverty. President Kennedy stated the issue squarely when he told Congress: "There is a claim on our conscience from . . . the elderly, nonwhites, migratory workers, and the physically or mentally handicapped—people who are shortchanged even in time of prosperity." [1]

But how about the rich? What are they like? Their characteristics and behavior are in many ways just as important to society as are those of the poor—not because of what we can do for them but because of what they can do for us. They own most of the wealth, do most of the saving, and are primarily responsible for investments, which are the key to prosperity and full employment. There are, to be sure, some wealthy people that society could get along very well without, but, by and large, the wealthy in the United States contain some of the best and most essential talents—doctors, lawyers, engineers, entertainers, artists, plant managers, etc. While the association between ability and income is far from perfect, ordinary observation shows that many of the most talented are included among the highest paid.

The aim here is to present a statistical portrait of the rich, not to attack or defend them as an economic or a social class. Who is rich; how rich are they; and how do they get their money? What share of all the income or wealth of the country do the rich control, and how has this share changed over time? These are the kinds of questions with which we shall be primarily concerned.

Not everyone takes this dispassionate a view of the subject. In fact, some people cannot tolerate the rich at all and are quite convinced that we would be much better off without them. Ferdinand Lundberg is one such critic. In his best seller *The Rich and the Super-Rich,* he describes the wealthy as "a small and not especially qualified, mainly hereditary group [which] allocates vast economic resources in narrow, self-serving directions." He also accuses the wealthy of involving "the nation in cycles of ferocious wars that are to the interest of asset preservation and asset expansion but are contrary to the interest of the nation and the world."[2] Mr. Lundberg has many other harsh things to say about the rich. Some of them will come up later in this chapter. His views are mentioned at the outset to set the stage and to caution the reader that statistics on wealth are not just numbers. They are ideas that touch some of our deepest emotions—envy, fear, anger, and hate—and also stir the passions of those who care about social justice.

Who is rich?

When the writer, Harry, is dying in Ernest Hemingway's *The Snows of Kilimanjaro,* he thinks of the past. He remembers: "Poor Julian and his romantic awe of [the rich] and how he had started a story once that began, 'The very rich are different from you and me.' And how someone had said to Julian, 'Yes, they have more money.'"

Are the rich really so much like other people that the only difference is their money? It is hard to say without a more precise definition of terms. Who is rich? Men who earn as much as $30,000 or $40,000 a year often do not regard themselves as rich because their friends and neighbors earn so much more. Many people with incomes this high complain that after taxes and "necessary" expenses, they have very little left over. Very often writers, salaried professional men, small-business men, and even government workers, who regard themselves as comfortable but not well-to-do, are simply amazed when they look at an income distribution chart and find that they are in the top 1 or 2 percent income bracket. They just don't feel that well off and would strongly deny that they are at the top of the heap.

The writer Isaac Bashevis Singer is a good example of a man who statistically qualifies as a member of the rich but who acts and feels otherwise.[3] Since the Book-of-the-Month Club purchased two of his novels and he has three film contracts, his income "comfortably exceeds $100,000 a year." This figure is four or five times what he earned a decade ago, yet he says, "the only differences that success has made for me is that I work more and I don't have this fear, which I had for many years, that I will starve." Despite his six-figure income, Mr. Singer's life-style has scarcely changed since he came to this country thirty-five years ago. He still lives in a modest apartment on the upper west side of Manhattan and he eats his vegetarian lunch in neighborhood cafeterias. His wife works as a saleslady in Lord and Taylor. He thinks she works for the love of it; but "if you ask her," claims Mr. Singer, "she says she has to work because she needs the money to buy all kinds of gadgets." Is Isaac Bashevis Singer a rich man? Statistically, yes; by his own account, hardly.

The rich cannot be objectively defined. Any definition will be faulty in some respects. If the standard is set too low, it will include too many people with "working class" characteristics; if it is set too high, it will understate the importance of this group in the economy. Three different sets of statistics will be used to describe the rich.

The first set is based on the Census Bureau's annual survey showing the number of families with incomes over $50,000. In 1968 about 150,000 families had incomes this high. Although these figures include the not-so-rich as well as the very-rich, they do reach up to the very top 3/10 of 1 percent of the income pyramid and they present more characteristics about these families than are available from any other source.

The second set of statistics is based on a study of the distribution of wealth in the United States conducted by the Bureau of the Census for the Federal Reserve Board in 1963.[4] In this study a representative national sample of 3,600 households was asked detailed questions about various aspects of wealth—the amount of their equity in a home or business; checking and savings accounts, U.S. Savings Bonds and other liquid assets; publicly traded stocks and bonds and other assets. They were also asked detailed questions about debt, income, employment, and other subjects. Responses were obtained from 2,600 families or about 86 percent of those interviewed. The sample was designed in such a way that families which were expected to have sizable wealth were sampled at much higher rates than the rest of the population. Interviews were completed with about 532 families with wealth of $100,000 or more. A total of 245 of these families had $500,000 or more.

The third set of statistics is based on Internal Revenue Service reports on estate tax returns. Since 1942, estate tax returns are required to be filed by the survivors of each person who dies and leaves an estate of $60,000 or more. A statistical method has been devised for converting these estate tax returns into estimates of the living population classified by wealth. The IRS reports for recent years and private studies for earlier years show the number and characteristics of the top wealthholders—those with gross estates of $60,000 or more. Selected out of this group for special analysis will be millionaires—those with estates of $1 million or more.

On the basis of these three sources of data, and information from other studies that have been conducted, we should be able to paint a fairly accurate statistical portrait of the rich and the very-rich in America.

The $50,000-and-over income class

If you believe that there are large numbers in this top group who make their living by clipping coupons, you couldn't be further from the truth. In 1968 fewer than one family out of a hundred in the top income group lived entirely on unearned income—interest, dividends, rents, royalties, and the like. The other ninety-nine did paid work or were self-employed in a business or a profession.

Nearly all of these families were headed by a man who worked at a full-time job. In 1968 over four-fifths of these men worked full time throughout the year. They put in long hours and take relatively few vacations. According to a study of the economic behavior of the affluent conducted by the Survey Research Center of the University of Michigan in 1964, high-income workers are on the job, on the average, about forty-eight hours per week. One-fourth of them work sixty hours a week or more. At the $12,000 income level only one-sixth work sixty hours or more, whereas at the $200,000 income level over one-third work this much.[5]

This same study goes on to report that as for vacations, "high-income respondents were far from being self-indulgent." The report notes that "of every twelve workers, seven took vacations of no more than two weeks during the year, another three took between two and four weeks, and only two vacationed for a total of more than four weeks."[6]

Corporation executives and other salaried managers formed the biggest single occupation group among these top-income families, accounting for about four-tenths of the total. An additional two-tenths worked as doctors, dentists, lawyers, and other self-employed professionals. The remaining four-tenths were more or less equally divided among the owners of small businesses; scientists, engineers, and other salaried professional workers; and salesmen and independent craftsmen.

TABLE IX-1

Characteristics of Families with Incomes of $50,000 or More: 1968

Number of families	150,000
Wife in labor force	24%
College training:	
4 years	29%
5 years or more	36%
Head working full time 50-52 weeks	83%
Income from:	
Earnings only	12%
Earnings and other income	88%
Unearned income only	*
Head employed as:	
Salaried manager	41%
Self-employed professional	22%
Salaried professional	13%
Owner of unincorporated business	11%
Salesman	5%
Craftsman	4%
Other	4%

*Less than ½ of 1 percent.

U.S. Bureau of the Census.

Contrary to popular belief, there were only a handful of uneducated men in the top income group. About 30 percent had four years of college and an additional 36 percent had five years or more.

The majority of families in the top income groups are there because they are headed by a man whose skills are much in demand and who therefore has high earnings. It would be a mistake, however, to assume that only the husbands work in these families and that the wives and children enjoy a life of luxurious ease. On the contrary, one out of every four families in this group has a working wife.

Why do these women work? The reason varies. If you ask them, many will say, "For the money." But that is only part of the answer, and a small part. Many women who are married to successful men are well trained themselves and are not satisfied to do menial jobs around the house or to bask in the glory of their husbands' accomplishments. They seek personal and intellectual independence and often find it in a job.

In his book *The Rich and the Super-Rich*, Ferdinand Lundberg states, "Nearly all the current large incomes, those exceeding $1 million, $500,000 or even $100,000 or $50,000 a year, are derived in fact from old property accumulations, by inheritors—that is, by people who never did whatever one is required to do, approved or disapproved, creative or uncreative, in order to assemble a fortune."[7] Like many other of Mr. Lundberg's judgments, no evidence is given. It is difficult to square the very lopsided picture he paints with the detailed statistical portrait provided by the facts from the Census Bureau.

Changes in the kind of work they do

Statistics on the employment characteristics of families with incomes of $50,000 or more are not available for earlier years. In order to measure changes in employment, we shall have to use a somewhat different measure of affluence—the top 5 percent of the families. This includes families with incomes over $10,000 in 1950, over $15,000 in 1960, and over $24,000 in 1968.

Table IX-2 shows that in 1950 the dominant group within the top 5 percent were the self-employed. They accounted for over two-fifths of the total. By 1960 the importance of this group was greatly reduced, to only one-fourth; and by 1968 it was reduced still further, to only one-fifth.

TABLE IX-2

Occupations of Top 5 Percent Income Group:
1950, 1960, and 1968

	1950	1960	1968
Self-employed	42%	26%	21%
Professionals	11	11	12
Owners of unincorporated businesses	23	13	7
Farmers	8	2	2
Salaried	28	48	51
Professionals	10	18	22
Managers	18	30	29
White collar and other	30	26	28

U.S. Bureau of the Census, *Trends in the Income of Families and Persons in the United States: 1947 to 1960*, Technical Paper No. 8, 1963; and unpublished data for 1968.

In contrast, salaried managerial and professional workers, who essentially represent "brainpower," rose considerably in importance between 1950 and 1968. In the earlier period they represented only 28 percent of the total. By 1960 this proportion rose to 48 percent and by 1968 they constituted 51 percent of the total.

A closer look at the changes for specific groups shows that, within the self-employed category, doctors, dentists, lawyers, and other independent professionals held their own. Farmers dropped sharply, as might be expected in this declining occupation, and owners of small businesses also dropped sharply.

Some will argue that the distinction between the owner of an unincorporated business and the salaried corporation official is nebulous. Technically, the corner groceryman will appear in the figures as the owner of a business if he is unincorporated. Should he incorporate (upon the advice of his son-in-law, the accountant), he immediately becomes a salaried corporation official. It is generally believed that there is a tendency for small firms to become incorporated in order to take advantage of the tax laws or the limited liability provided by the corporate form of organization. According to the census figures, however, there was no great general movement from proprietorship toward incorporation during the fifties. In 1950 about 8 percent of all family heads were classified as owners of unincorporated businesses. In 1968 the comparable figure was 6 percent—a drop of two percentage points. But within the top income group, owners of unincorporated businesses dropped from 23 percent of the total to only 7 percent.

The same picture appears when the figures for salaried managers and officials are examined. In 1950 about 6 percent of all family heads were in this occupation, as compared with about 9 percent in 1968. However, their representation in the top income group increased from 18 percent to 29 percent.

The other striking and significant fact shown in Table IX-2 is the increase in the relative importance of salaried professional workers in the top income group. In 1968 there were more salaried professionals at all income levels than there were in 1950, but the increase was greatest at the top.

Significance of the big change

The big change is the persistent intrusion of brainpower into the top 5 percent. The small-business man and the farmer have given way to the engineer, scientist, college professor, plant manager, and others who deal primarily with ideas, not things. It was not too many years ago that Professor Morris R. Cohen, the eminent American philosopher, proclaimed: "Mankind has been ruled by soldiers, clergy, and lawyers, and now the businessmen control."[8] Babbitt has not yet been dethroned, but he sits uneasily on his regal couch.

There was a time when all you needed to operate a small business was a little money, a little experience, and lots of luck. Many failed, but the successful gained entry into the top income group. Some people still get to the top that way, but their number is dwindling. Small business has been taken over by the big corporation; but the change does not end there. The corporation executive today is often more than just an administrator. He must also be qualified to handle complex technical problems. Many of the people who are now called managers or officials are in reality scientists or engineers. Indeed, it is not at all unusual to find engineers and scientists directing the activities of huge corporations; and what is more important, many who have purely technical responsibilities earn as much as or more than their bosses.

Some years ago the editors of *Fortune* magazine wrote: "The tycoon is dead. . . . The mid-century businessman has had to go to school—in labor, in politics, in social welfare. The engineer's a businessman, the salesman's an economist, the research man knows advertising, the finance man knows law."[9] In much the same vein, historian Frederick Lewis Allen in *The Big Change* stated: "There is a striking difference between the type of men now rising to the top in big business and those of an earlier day. . . . Nowadays it seems quite natural to us that the great majority of big business executives should be college graduates and that many should have been trained in engineering or law."[10]

What is true for big business is equally true for big government. Thirty years ago Washington, D.C., was almost a sleepy southern town. There were some mathematicians, physicists, and statisticians, but they were few in number and hard to find. The typical government executive was a political appointee or a clerk who had worked his way up through the ranks. My, how things have changed! The government executive today is invariably college-trained and very often an acknowledged expert in his field. He is almost always supported by a team of other experts, who earn nearly as much as he does.

When the Census Bureau purchased its first electronic computer around 1950, it found that it also had to hire a young engineer to keep the blasted thing going. He was paid a base salary that nearly equaled that of the Director of the Census. With overtime payments, he earned more than the Secretary of Commerce. And so it goes in many organizations.

Automation, computers, research—these all require skill and brains, which are great in demand and short in supply. That is the simple explanation behind the rapid growth in brainpower within the top income group.

THE DISTRIBUTION OF WEALTH

In the preceding section the rich were identified in terms of their annual income. Families with incomes over $50,000 were called rich. A higher income floor would be desirable in order to learn something about the very-well-to-do. The figures, however, are just not available. Although the measure used did not get us to the very pinnacle of the income pyramid, it did get to within 3/10 of 1 percent of the top, which is not too bad.

The amount of wealth owned by families provides an alternative basis for identifying the rich. Since incomes fluctuate from year to year, the amount received during any particular twelve-month period provides an uncertain basis for identifying the rich. No doubt there are many businessmen who earn $100,000 one year and end up with a net loss the following year. Wealth provides a much more stable measure because it represents an accumulation over many years and is less likely to fluctuate than income.

The distribution shown in Table IX-3 of consumer units (families of two or more persons and independent individuals) classified by the amount of wealth they owned in 1962 is based on a sample survey conducted by the Bureau of the Census for the Board of Governors of the Federal Reserve System. Wealth is defined as the sum total of equity in a home or business, liquid assets, investment assets, the value of automobiles owned, and miscellaneous assets, such as assets held in trust, loans to individuals, oil royalties, etc. In this tabulation the wealthy are defined as those with a net worth of $100,000 or more, and the very wealthy as those with holdings over $500,000. On this basis, there were about 1½ million wealthy consumer units in the United States in 1962. They constituted only 2 percent of all consumer units, but they owned 43 percent of all the wealth. Moving closer to the very peak of the wealth pyramid, we find that there were about 200,000 very wealthy consumer units. They constituted ½ of 1 percent of all units, but they owned 22 percent of the wealth.

The portrait of the rich based on wealth-holding is essentially the same as that based on income. Some of the key facts are shown below. The majority are employed either in their own businesses or as salaried

TABLE IX-3

Distribution of Wealth: December 31, 1962

Wealth	Consumer units (millions)	Percentage distribution	
		Consumer units	Wealth
Total	57.9	100%	100%
Negative	1.0	2	*
Zero	4.7	8	*
$1 to $999	9.0	16	*
$1,000 to $4,999	10.8	19	2
$5,000 to $9,999	9.1	16	5
$10,000 to $24,999	13.3	23	18
$25,000 to $49,999	6.2	11	18
$50,000 to $99,999	2.5	4	14
$100,000 to $199,999	0.7	1	8
$200,000 to $499,999	0.5	1	13
$500,000 and over	0.2	*	22

Note: Sums of tabulated figures in this chapter may not equal totals because of rounding.

*Less than ½ of 1 percent.

Dorothy S. Projector and Gertrude S. Weiss, *Survey of Financial Characteristics of Consumers,* Board of Governors of the Federal Reserve System, August 1966, Tables A2, A16, A36.

executives; only 17 percent are retired. About one-sixth have wives who also work and a very large proportion are college-trained. Most significant of all is the fact that relatively few admit to having inherited a substantial proportion of their assets. Even among the very-rich—those with assets of $500,000 or more—only one-third reported that they had inherited a substantial proportion of their assets; 39 percent claimed to have made it entirely on their own, and an additional 24 percent admitted to having inherited a small proportion of their assets. [11] After examining this same evidence, Mr. Lundberg reached the following conclusion: "It should be evident in studying the . . . Federal Reserve figures on estates that the United States now has a well-established hereditary propertied class such as exists in Europe, which Americans have long looked upon disdainfully as the stronghold of class privilege. Great wealth in the United States, in other words, is no longer ordinarily gained by the input of some effort, legal or illegal, useful or mischievous, but comes from being named an heir. Almost every single wealth-holder in the upper half of 1 percent arrived by this route."[12] Little wonder that so many people distrust statistics and statisticians. Too many writers like Mr. Lundberg tend to see what they want to see in numbers, not what is actually there.

TABLE IX-4

Characteristics of Consumer Units
with Substantial Assets: December 1962

	Wealth	
	$100,000 or more	$500,000 or more
Number of consumer units	1,200,000	200,000
Headed by:		
Owner of unincorporated business	50%	50%
Salaried executive	33%	50%
Retired person	17%	*
With working wife	13%	17%
Average number of school years	13	15
Inherited assets:		
None	50%	39%
Small proportion	29%	24%
Large proportion	20%	34%
Not reported	1%	2%

*Less than ½ of 1 percent.

Dorothy S. Projector and Gertrude S. Weiss, *Survey of Financial Characteristics of Consumers,* Board of Governors of the Federal Reserve System, August 1966, Tables A32-A36.

THE MILLIONAIRES AMONG US

If you have given up hope of ever becoming a millionaire and you blame it on the system, you may just be looking for an alibi. Millionaires are being made every day, now more than ever before. They come from all walks of life and all ethnic and religious backgrounds. Most of them do it on their own, without inherited wealth. The key to their success according to the managing editor of the *Wall Street Journal,* who should know, is hard work, courage, and individuality. A little luck helps too, but most experts don't seem to attach much importance to it.

Wallace Johnson is an excellent example of the new breed of millionaires. In 1940 he borrowed a small sum from a finance company to build homes in Memphis, Tennessee. By 1964, at the age of 63, he presided over sixty-eight companies. He is one of the nation's leading home builders and is a co-founder of the Holiday Inn motels.

John Ballard is another classic case of the rise from rags to riches. In 1909 he came to work for Bulova as an office boy for $4 a week. By 1935, at the age of 42, he was president of the company; and by 1959 he was forced into compulsory retirement at the age of 65. Despite his handsome pension and accumulated wealth, he went to work as president of Bulova's competitor, the Gruen Watch Company.

Most of us believe that great fortunes are a thing of the past. It is widely held that during the roaring twenties and earlier—before the tax collector came in for a heavy take—a man could keep what he made and thereby amass a fortune, which he could squander, save, or pass on to his heirs. Since the depression, however, big government spending programs have required that income taxes (in theory) take as much as 91 cents of every dollar received by the living rich, and estate taxes (in theory) take much of what remains. Despite the recent reduction in tax rates, the feeling persists that a mortal blow has been dealt to the millionaire class.

Nothing could be further from the truth. The rich among us are flourishing like never before. And this includes not only mere millionaires, but multimillionaires as well. The number of people whose net worth is over a million dollars is growing by leaps and bounds. According to estimates published by the National Bureau of Economic Research

159

there were only 27,000 millionaires in 1953, when a very comprehensive study was made by Professor Robert Lampman, of the University of Wisconsin and formerly on the staff of the President's Council of Economic Advisers.[13] More recent figures published by the Internal Revenue Service show that by 1962 the number of millionaires had risen to 67,000;[14] and, according to *U.S. News and World Report*, the number in 1969 was 200,000.[15] These figures suggest that during the years 1962-1969 the number of millionaires increased by 200 percent whereas the general population increased by a mere 8 percent and the value of common stocks rose by 54 percent.

Statistical profiles of millionaires

The most recent figures on the characteristics of millionaires are those for 1962. A federal tax return must be filed for each estate valued at $60,000 or more. Each return contains the age and sex of the deceased as well as the type and value of the property left. This information about the dead is converted to statistics for the living by the use of a procedure which assumes that death draws a random sample of the population within each age and sex group. By multiplying the deaths in each age and sex group by the inverse of the death rate for that group, and summing the results for all ages, we obtain estimates of the living population by size of estate. This procedure, which was used by Professor Lampman to provide national statistics for 1953, has been extended to 1958 and more recently to 1962 by the Internal Revenue Service.

Sex

Each of us has his own mental image of a millionaire. Popular books on the subject portray the typical millionaire as a self-made man, who is a very hard worker, highly imaginative, and willing to take risks after thoughtful study. The pattern varies from case to case but nearly all agree that the millionaire is typically a man.

The facts do not support this picture. The men may make the money in the first place, but somehow or other the women manage to get their hands on it. The holders of big wealth are as likely to be women as men. In 1962 nearly half of all millionaires were women.

Why are so many millionaires women? The answer is at best speculative. Part of the answer may be in the greater durability of women. Men who work hard for a lifetime may barely squeak out an estate of $1 million before they die. The women who inherit these fortunes live on to reap the harvest.

Another possibility suggested by the age data below is that very rich old men marry young women who outlive them and inherit their wealth.

Or can it be that women are just smarter than men and invest more wisely?

TABLE IX-5

Number of Millionaires, by Sex: 1962

Wealth (millions)	Both sexes	Men	Women
Total number	67,442	36,756	30,687
$1 to $2	43,690	23,406	20,284
$2 to $3	10,417	6,139	4,278
$3 to $5	7,211	3,894	3,316
$5 to $10	4,277	2,079	2,198
$10 and over	1,847	1,237	611

Internal Revenue Service, *Personal Wealth: Supplemental Report to Statistics of Income, 1962*, Tables 16-18.

Age

Although there are some who get rich quick, the available evidence suggests that most of those who make it travel a long, hard road that takes a lifetime. The average age of millionaires is about 60, with the women just slightly younger than the men. There is not too much difference in the age of male and female millionaires until we get to the top class, those with $10 million dollars or more. Here we find the men average about 58 years as compared with a mere 40 years for the women. As always, the statistics end just where they become most interesting. Who are these very rich young millionairesses? How do they get their money? We can only speculate. Some are undoubtedly the younger daughters of rich men who have inherited their father's wealth. Others are younger daughters of poor men who married well and inherited fortunes.

TABLE IX-6

Average Age of Millionaires, by Sex: 1958

Wealth (millions)	Men	Women
Total	61	58
$1 to $2	59	60
$2 to $3	62	56
$3 to $5	68	63
$5 to $10	63	67
$10 and over	58	40

Herman P. Miller, "Millionaires Are a Dime a Dozen," *The New York Times Magazine,* November 28, 1965.

Sources of wealth

Stocks are without a doubt the favorite investment of the rich. Exactly one-half of the assets of millionaires are tied up in corporate stocks, often stocks of businesses they directly control and operate. It is significant that this small group, which constitutes far less than 1 percent of the population (2/10 of 1 percent to be exact), own 7 percent of all the privately held wealth and 21 percent of all the stock in corporations.

Real estate and tax-free state and local bonds are two other favorites in the investment portfolios of the wealthy. Together these two types of assets account for about one-sixth of all assets owned by millionaires. As might be expected, government bonds, corporate bonds, and life insurance rank very low as investment preferences among the rich. Although real estate is holding its own in the investment portfolios of the wealthy, tax-free bonds are declining in popularity. Between 1953 and

1958 the proportion of total assets among millionaires invested in state and local bonds declined from 13 percent to 6 percent. Although this decline has been attributed to reductions in income tax rates, there is some evidence that the disenchantment with state and local bonds had set in before tax rates were reduced.

The importance of corporate stocks in the portfolios of the very-rich can hardly come as a surprise. What better way is there to make money in a capitalistic society than by owning capital? Stewart Alsop tells the story of a Communist leader who escaped from the Soviet Union to New York City without a penny to his name. Within a few years he was living in the height of luxury on Park Avenue. When asked how he did it he replied, "Very simple. In Communist Russia, way to get ahead is to be a Communist, so naturally I am a Communist. In capitalist America, way to get ahead is to be a capitalist, so naturally I am a capitalist." [16]

The new millionaires

Although statistics on the subject are lacking, there is general agreement that most of the new fortunes have come from self-employment in a business. The reason is not hard to find. The salaried man, no matter how highly paid, cannot accumulate a fortune. During most of the postwar period, top executives who earned as much as $200,000 a year might have paid as much as $150,000 in taxes; and they could keep only $1 out of every $10 they made above that amount. The situation for rich men has improved somewhat lately, but it would still be extremely difficult—virtually impossible—to accumulate a million dollars out of wages and salaries.

The obvious path to riches is to build up equity in a business. It's a thorny path and millions of those who try fail; but the returns are great for the few who succeed. As an encouragement to investment and economic growth, the government permits the owners of capital assets (like stock in a business) to retain three-fourths of the profits they make from the sale of these assets. Unlike the successful salaried man who pays most of what he makes each year in taxes, the successful entrepreneur who has built up equity over a period of years can keep most of what he has made when he gets ready to sell. Similar tax advantages in real estate and securities and generous depletion allowances in oil, mining, and tim-

TABLE IX-7

Sources of Wealth of Millionaires: 1958

Source	Amount (billions)	Percentage distribution	Share of total United States wealth
Total	$108.2	100%	7%
Real estate	9.2	9	2
Federal bonds	2.1	2	3
State and local bonds	6.6	6	42
Other bonds	0.7	1	14
Corporate stock	54.5	50	21
Cash	3.8	3	18
Notes and mortgages	2.7	2	6
Life insurance equity	0.6	1	6
Miscellaneous	28.0	26	10

James D. Smith and Staunton K. Calvert, "Estimating the Wealth of Top Wealth-Holders from Estate Tax Returns," *Proceedings of the American Statistical Association,* September 1965, Tables 1 and 2.

ber have also made these lucrative fields for the creation of new millionaires. According to the impressionistic judgment of several noted authorities, the new millionaires are concentrated in certain tax-sheltered businesses like oil, insurance, savings-and-loan institutions, and real estate.

There are only minor variations in the accepted formulas for success. Nearly all accounts stress hard work, imagination, courage, and frugality. But the formula is undoubtedly different for women than for men, and as we have seen, the fair sex cannot be ignored in discussions of millionaires. In his book on the background of eleven millionaires, Charles Sopkin writes, "All of my millionaires own a first-rate tax man . . . ; all . . . were touched in one way or another by the depression of the thirties— and the fear of another depression seems to be the driving force in their lives. All . . . work seven days a week and put in eighteen-hour days." [17] My father remembers the depression very well and he worked around the clock most of his life, but he never owned more than a little candy store. True, he never had a first-rate tax man, but he never needed one.

The word "luck" is hardly ever mentioned by millionaires or the men who write about them. This no doubt reflects a bias on their part. Luck may not be as important in acquiring a million as many poor people like to think, but it is probably more important than many of the rich would have us believe.

There's still life in the old system

These findings do much more than satisfy the idle curiosity that most of us have about the very-rich. They provide important insights into a major aspect of American life. They can excite the imaginations of the staunchest defenders and the severest critics of our society. The editors of *Time* magazine were quick to interpret the results as living proof of the vitality of the capitalist system. "Becoming a millionaire," says *Time,* "is still an eminently realizable goal for many Americans." And so it is; but the figures also shatter the propaganda that right-wing conservatives have been spreading about the socialization and communization of America as a result of big spending programs. The steady and perhaps even accelerating growth in the number of millionaires plays havoc with the idea that high taxes are ruining the rich and destroying one of the major dreams of American youth.

The rapid rise in the number of millionaires in so brief a period suggests that large numbers of Americans are still finding it possible to work their way to the top without the help of inherited wealth. Wallace Johnson and John Ballard are only two of the many cases that could have been cited to show that the rags-to-riches legend may still be a living reality and not just a relic of our youthful, romantic past. Perhaps even more significant in these figures is the suggestion that the very-rich are not hurt so much as they think or pretend by the steep tax rates of recent years. Much of the rapid rise in the number of millionaires reflects the ability of the rich to use loopholes in the law to good advantage, but clearly more than that is involved. One analysis attributes the rise to "a rapidly changing American technology, the shift to a service economy, and the insatiable appetite for new and better ways of doing things." In other words, the way to get ahead may still be to build a better mousetrap.

X

The Cash Value of Education

"Let ignorance talk as it will, learning has its value." Thus wrote the French essayist La Fontaine three hundred years ago. He was so right. Every study of the relation between earnings and education shows that the more highly educated the man, the greater his earnings. There are many exceptions to be sure. Differences in talent, home environment, family connections, drive, imagination, and just plain old luck cause some people to do well and others poorly. And immaterial factors—the color of a man's skin, for example—make education more worthwhile to some than to others.

Perhaps it is regrettable to stress the value of education in such crass terms. Education tends to produce a richer and more varied life and it is fundamental to the operation of a democratic society. For these reasons alone, it is worth its cost in time, money, and effort even if the economic advantages should cease to exist. The main reason for focusing on the economic advantages is a simple one. At present, they are the only ones that can be measured even approximately.

But there is at least one more reason for stressing the payoff from education—to convince our poor, whose children are badly in need of schooling, that it may help them out of their present dilemma. There are still many in our society who have had little experience with education, and they do not see its value. It is a simple point, but a fundamental one that is often overlooked. Many social workers have observed that the poor today lack the interest in education that characterized the immigrant poor who lived in the same slums twenty or thirty years ago.

If this is the case, it could perpetuate the vicious circle which transmits poverty from one generation to the next. This point is well made in Christopher Rand's study *The Puerto Ricans*: "The Jewish immigrants felt that success would come through education . . . and the Italians were somewhat the same. In the garment trade twenty years ago a high percentage of the workers had kids going through college, but this is no longer the case. . . . You don't have a ferment these days to get out of the slums by educational achievement, but by financial achievement, and the Puerto Ricans reflect this. The Puerto Rican kids here dream of quick money, not of intellectual attainments."[1] Rand's observation undoubtedly applies to Negroes as well.

There is some justification for the feeling by Puerto Ricans, Negroes, and other minority groups that education does not do as much for them, financially, as it does for others. James Baldwin writes in *Nobody Knows My Name*: "It is not to be wondered at that a boy, one day, decides that if . . . studying is going to prepare him only to be a porter or an elevator boy—or his teacher—well, then, the hell with it."[2]

Emphasis on the negative aspects of the situation, important though it may be as a stimulus to improvement, should not obscure an equally important fact—that schooling does pay off for nonwhites, even though to a far lesser degree than for whites. And even if the payoff from an education is not immediate, it is still important if nonwhites are ever to advance out of their low economic status.

An investment in education is much like buying insurance. No insurance company can tell you how long you are going to live; but they do know your chances of living a given number of years if they know your age, sex, and several other things about you. The same thing holds for education. No one can tell you how much you will earn in a lifetime on the basis of your education. We can estimate your chances.

The figures in Table X-1 show the average amount of money earned per year by men with different amounts of schooling. Several different periods during the past thirty years are listed to show how the relationship has changed.

In every year for which data are shown, the completion of an additional level of schooling was associated with higher average incomes. In 1968, elementary school graduates made $5,096, high school graduates made $7,731, and college graduates made $11,257. In that one year the difference between the incomes of the average high school and the average college graduate was considerably greater than the cost of a year of college. This finding parallels that obtained in numerous other studies dating back to the early part of this century.

Although the income levels have changed considerably during the past thirty years, the basic relationship between the extent of schooling and income appears to have remained much the same. These facts belie the dire expectations of some analysts—"a college degree isn't worth anything any more." They also show how wrong were those men who opposed the vast expansion of college training programs after World War II. Professor Seymour Harris of Harvard wrote in 1949 that the persistent increase in the supply of college-trained workers would so flood the market that "college students within the next twenty years are doomed to disappointment after graduation, as the number of coveted openings will be substantially less than the numbers seeking them."[3] The same concern was expressed by James B. Conant, then president of Harvard, and Chancellor William J. Wallin of the New York State Board of Regents.[4]

These gloomy warnings were fortunately ignored. At some risk and considerable expense, the schooling of the American population increased tremendously during the postwar years. The demand for these more highly trained workers has kept pace with the supply so that they are, by and large, fully employed.

In the light of history, the fears that we might have been creating a surplus of college graduates have proved unwarranted. But today there is a similar concern in some quarters about the relationship between income and education. Now the concern is that the gap between the educated and the uneducated may be widening, thereby creating a "permanent under-class" in our society. Although it is possible that such a class already exists or that it is in the process of being formed, the figures on education do not support this thesis.

In a speech made in June 1969, Governor Andrew F. Brimmer of the Federal Reserve Board pointed out that the earnings gap between Black college men and Black high school graduates is widening and that the same is true for Black high school and elementary school graduates. The result, according to Brimmer, is that there is "a general tendency for income differentials within the Negro community to widen in recent years. . . . These figures seem to underline the conviction held by an increasing number of observers: a basic schism has developed in the black community, and it may be widening year by year."[5]

These are frightening words coming from a respected Negro econo-

TABLE X-1

Relationship of Education to Income, for Men Aged 25 and Over

Schooling completed	Mean annual income			
	1939	1949	1959	1968
Elementary school				
Less than 8 years	NA	$2,062	$2,551	$3,333
8 years	NA	2,829	3,769	5,096
High school				
1 to 3 years	$1,379	$3,226	$4,618	$6,569
4 years	1,661	3,784	5,567	7,731
College				
1 to 3 years	$1,931	$4,423	$6,966	$8,618
4 years or more	2,607	6,179	9,206	11,257

NA = not available

Herman P. Miller, "Annual and Lifetime Income in Relation to Education: 1939-1959," *American Economic Review*, December 1960, Table I; and U.S. Bureau of the Census, *Current Population Reports*, Series P-60, No. 63, Table 4.

mist, who holds one of the top government jobs. They are not supported by the facts,[6] but with a little journalistic fuel, they make a great fire. Thus, for example, one columnist cites Dr. Brimmer's conclusion as evidence that "the threat in the 1970's may be less one of two nations— one black and one white—growing apart from each other than of a permanent under-class emerging, which is increasingly alienated from a middle class that includes blacks as well as whites."[7] This theory is not supported by changes in the relationship between income and education. Table X-1 shows that in 1949 and 1959 the incomes of college graduates were two-thirds greater than those of high school graduates; by 1968 the differential was less than 50 percent. In 1949 high school graduates made one-third more than elementary school graduates; this differential rose to nearly 50 percent in 1959 and it remained at that level in 1968. Thus, the evidence shows that during the sixties there was no change in the income differentials of elementary and high school graduates, and a narrowing of differentials between high school and college graduates.

Table X-2, which shows data on changes in income differentials, by education, for Blacks and whites during the 1960's, does not support Governor Brimmer's allegation that the differentials are widening.

TABLE X-2

Median Income by Schooling Completed, for White and Nonwhite Men Aged 25 and Over: 1958–1968

| Year | Elementary school graduate | High school graduate | 1 or more years of college | Percentage difference between high school and | |
				Elementary school	College
White					
1958*	$3,276	$4,654	$5,810	42%	25%
1961*	3,617	5,155	6,379	43	24
1963*	3,749	5,600	6,829	49	22
1964	4,043	6,389	8,204	58	28
1966	4,611	7,068	9,023	53	28
1967	4,881	7,378	9,463	51	28
1968	5,184	7,875	9,980	52	27
Nonwhite					
1958*	$2,328	$2,994	$3,679	29%	23%
1961*	2,505	3,381	4,246	35	26
1963*	2,740	3,821	4,070	40	7
1964	3,455	4,237	5,429	23	28
1966	3,681	5,188	5,928	41	14
1967	3,711	5,427	7,110	46	31
1968	4,304	5,810	7,511	35	29

*Data for these years are for men 14 years old and over.

♦U.S. Bureau of the Census, *Current Population Reports*, Series P-60, annual issues.

Among white men, the income differential between elementary and high school graduates was about 50 percent in each of the years for which figures are available during the decade 1958–1968. In some years the differential was a little greater and in some years it was a little less, but there is no discernible trend. The same is true for the differential between high school graduates and men with one or more years of college.

In the case of nonwhites the ratios fluctuate somewhat erratically, reflecting perhaps the relatively small size of the sample on which they are based. But even here there is no trend. In 1968 nonwhite high school graduates made 35 percent more than elementary school graduates. The same differential existed in 1961. Nonwhite college men made 29 percent more than high school graduates in 1968. In 1964 the differential was 28 percent and in 1961 it was 26 percent. This change can hardly be called a trend.

Not only does completing college increase income, but each higher degree also increases income. The figures in Table X-3 show that in 1966 men who held a bachelor's degree as their highest degree had median earnings of $9,100; the median of those who held a master's degree was $9,300; and for those who held a doctorate or professional degree the median was $12,900. The men who held the doctorate or professional degree had median annual earnings that were $3,800 higher than for the men who held only a bachelor's degree.

The quality of the college that a man selects to attend also affects his future income. The better the college, the higher the income. The figures in Table X-3 show that men who were graduated from a low-ranking college had median earnings in 1966 of $7,900; those who were graduated from medium-ranking colleges had median earnings of $9,800; and those who were graduated from a high-ranking college had median earnings of $11,700—about $3,800 higher than the earnings of men who were graduated from a low-ranking college.

Although income generally tends to increase with education, the completion of a given level of schooling (e.g., the fourth year in high school) yields a greater return than any of the years leading up to graduation. The difference may reflect a selection in terms of ability between those who do and those who do not complete their schooling. Or it may represent the commercial value of a certificate or title. Thus in 1967, men who finished high school received on the average an annual income of about $1,500 more per year than men who left school before graduation.

171

TABLE X-3

Earnings of Male College Graduates
by Highest Degree Taken
and by Rank of College: 1966

Highest degree and rank of college	Median earnings
All degrees	
All ranks	$9,489
Low rank	7,881
Medium rank	9,752
High rank	11,678
Bachelor's	
All ranks	$9,096
Low rank	7,641
Medium rank	9,324
High rank	11,305
Master's	
All ranks	$9,339
Low rank	8,327
Medium rank	9,407
High rank	10,555
Doctorate or professional	
All ranks	$12,900
Low rank	11,842
Medium rank	13,785
High rank	16,087

U.S. Bureau of the Census, "Men with College Degrees: March 1967," *Current Population Reports*, Series P-20, No. 180.

Although education has a direct impact on the income of those women who work, its value is much more indirect for the large proportion who do not work. To most girls, education provides a greater opportunity to marry a man who will be financially successful; it also provides more in the way of intangibles that may be more important than money—the kind of man she may marry, her influence on his life, and the environment for her children.

Women earn less than men. This is partly due to the fact that many women work only part of the time. It is also true that many women are paid less than men for the same kind of work; but this difference can be exaggerated. University of Michigan Professor James Morgan and his associates report that "one economist who made crude adjustments for differences in hours worked, education, and age differences within occupations, concluded that market discrimination accounts for less than 10 percent of the difference in annual earnings of men and women."[8] But for women, just as for men, there is a direct relationship between education and income. A comparison of the income of women in 1968 who were year-round, full-time workers (Table X-4) shows that women who were high school graduates had an annual income which was $1,700 higher than that of the women who had not completed elementary school; and the women who had completed four or more years of college had an annual income which was $2,500 higher than that of high school graduates.

Schooling pays—even for a bricklayer

Everyone knows that it pays to go to college. But does schooling pay off if you are only going to be a carpenter, a plumber, or a bus driver? Definitely. The figures in Table X-5 show the earnings of two groups of white males in their prime years. Nonwhites and men in other age groups are omitted in order to focus on one thing only—the effect of education on earnings. One group never went beyond the eighth grade and the other group finished high school. The figures show that in many occupations the high school diploma is worth about $1,000 a year—roughly $40,000 over a working lifetime.

Why the difference? There are many reasons. High school graduates have higher IQ's. This is partly due to their greater education. It may also reflect greater native intelligence and aptitude to learn. But there are other reasons.

Employers give preference to high school graduates. With a diploma you can drive a bus for a transcontinental bus company; without it, you're lucky to get a job with the Podunk Transit Company. The car-

THE CASH VALUE OF EDUCATION

TABLE X-4

**Mean Income and Education of Women
Aged 25 and Over: 1968**

Schooling completed	Income	
	All women	Year-round full-time workers
Total	$3,023	$4,930
Elementary school		
Less than 8 years	$1,664	$3,222
8 years	2,153	3,744
High school		
1 to 3 years	$2,616	$4,067
4 years	3,321	4,904
College		
1 to 3 years	$3,717	$5,699
4 years or more	5,349	7,416
4 years	4,639	6,680
5 years or more	6,720	8,489

U.S. Bureau of the Census, *Current Population Reports*, Series P-60, No. 66, Table 41.

penter who is a high school graduate has a regular job with a big construction firm. He works regularly, good weather and bad. The uneducated carpenter works by the day. He gets a job, finishes it, and goes down to the union hall to get another. Whenever work is slack, he is the first to be laid off.

Unions also prefer high school graduates. Increasingly, the diploma is becoming a prerequisite to qualify for apprentice training. According to one study "virtually all registered apprenticeship programs require a minimum of two years of high school education or its equivalent. Skills are becoming more complex, and so is related classroom training, an essential ingredient in all registered apprenticeship programs. Many apprenticeship programs, therefore, are raising their educational standards and accepting nothing less than a high school diploma or its equivalent."

TABLE X-5

Relationship of Education to Income,
by Occupation, for White Men
Aged 35 to 44: 1959

Occupation	Average earnings		Income differential
	Elementary school graduates	High school graduates	
Toolmakers	$6,700	$7,300	$600
Electricians	6,100	6,600	500
Plumbers	5,700	6,700	1,000
Firemen	5,300	6,100	800
Truck drivers	5,200	5,700	500
Bricklayers	5,100	6,300	1,200
Mechanics	5,000	5,900	900
Carpenters	4,800	5,700	900
Bus drivers	4,400	5,400	1,000

U.S. Census of Population: 1960, Vol. II, Part 7B, *Occupation by Earnings and Education.*

An official of the General Electric Company reports that at one time the Schenectady plant "used to screen applicants by means of a simple test based on the three R's. Now the company accepts only apprentices who have high school diplomas and who have earned superior grades in mathematics and science."[9]

The reasons are varied, but the facts are clear. Education pays off.

Lifetime earnings

Estimates of lifetime earnings provide better measures of financial returns associated with education than the annual earnings shown above. Table X-1 shows that the difference in average income between high school and college graduates in one year was more than enough to pay for the cost of a year in college. So you can well imagine that the difference in income over a lifetime will be enormous.

THE CASH VALUE OF EDUCATION

Figures on lifetime earnings for men with less than eight years of elementary school (see Table X-6) were prepared according to standard techniques of life insurance practice. The procedure can best be explained by the following example, for men with less than eight years of elementary school:

Step 1. Out of every 100,000 male children born in 1966, 96,019 could expect to survive to age 18.

Step 2. Out of the 96,019 who survive to age 18, 94,830 will survive to age 24. Between the ages of 18 and 24 they will have lived 668,120 man-years. Assume that each year they receive a mean income of $2,460 (this was the mean income in 1966 of men 18 to 24 years old). The total expected income from age 18 to 24 is $1,644,000,000

Step 3. Out of the 94,830 who survive to age 24, 92,964 can be expected to survive to age 34. Between the ages of 25 and 34 they will have lived 939,387 man-years. Assuming a mean income of $4,099 per year gives them a total expected income of $3,851,000,000

Step 4. Out of the 92,964 who survive to age 34, 89,461 can be expected to survive to age 44. Their total man-years of life for that period will be 914,522. Assuming a mean income of $4,483 per year gives them a total expected income of $4,100,000,000

Step 5. Out of the 89,461 who survive to age 44, 81,096 can be expected to survive to age 54. Their total man-years of life during that time will be 858,737. Assuming a mean income of $4,414 per year gives them a total expected income of $3,790,000,000

Step 6. Out of the 81,096 who survive to age 54, 64,073 can be expected to survive to age 64. Their total man-years of life then will be 733,714. Assuming a mean income of $3,945 per year gives them a total expected income of $2,895,000,000

Step 7. Out of the 64,073 who survive to age 64, the total man-years of life for those 65 years old and over will be 825,139. Assuming a mean income of $2,225 per year gives them a total expected income of $1,836,000,000

Step 8. Adding up all of the amounts listed above leads to the conclusion that the 96,019 men who reach age 18 will receive about $18.1 billion during their lifetime. The average for each one is therefore $189,000

On the basis of conditions in 1966, a male elementary school graduate could expect to earn during his lifetime about $58,000 more, on the average, than the one who quit before completing the eighth grade. This large difference cannot be entirely due to the completion of several additional years of elementary school. You just don't learn that much in

176

TABLE X-6

Education and Lifetime Earnings for Men*

Schooling completed	Earnings† (thousands)
Total	$321
Elementary school	
Less than 8 years	$189
8 years	247
High school	
1 to 3 years	$284
4 years	341
College	
1 to 3 years	$394
4 years or more	542
4 years	508
5 years or more	587

*Based on 1966 dollars.
†From age 18 to death.

U.S. Bureau of the Census, "Annual Mean Income, Lifetime Income, and Educational Attainment of Men in the United States, for Selected Years, 1956 to 1966," *Current Population Reports*, Series P-60, No. 56, p. 9.

grade school. The chances are that failure to complete elementary school is, by and large, symptomatic of other traits that lead to low productivity and low income. Here again caution must be exercised lest the figures be misunderstood, for there are exceptions.

The difference between the expected lifetime earnings of the average male elementary school and high school graduates is equally striking. In 1966, the average elementary school graduate could expect lifetime earnings of about $247,000 as compared with about $341,000 for the average high school graduate—a difference of $94,000.

A college degree is required for many, if not most, high paying jobs. And the greatest gains associated with additional schooling appear at

THE CASH VALUE OF EDUCATION

the college level. In 1966, a man with four years of college could expect to earn about $508,000 during his lifetime as compared with $341,000 for the average high school graduate. During his lifetime, the average college graduate earns about $40,000 *extra* for each year of college. Even if these earnings are matched against the high cost of college training—a cost generally borne by the parents rather than the children—the rate of return is substantial.

The lifetime earnings of women also increase with each year of educational attainment. The figures in Table X-7 show that the lifetime income of women who are high school graduates is $50,000, or 44 percent, higher than that of women who only finish elementary school.

TABLE X-7

Education and Lifetime Income for Women*

Schooling completed	Income† (thousands)	
	All women	Year-round, full-time workers
Total	$154	$250
Elementary school		
Less than 8 years	$95	$167
8 years	115	184
High school		
1 to 3 years	$132	$213
4 years	165	249
College		
1 to 3 years	$188	$312
4 years or more	270	375
4 years	232	326
5 years or more	342	436

*Based on 1966 dollars.
†From age 25 to death.

U.S. Bureau of the Census.

The lifetime income of women with four years of college is $67,000, or 25 percent, higher than that of women who are high school graduates.

For both men and women a substantial cash value is associated with increased education.

Gains are much less for nonwhites

The association between earnings and education is not the same for all groups. It would be most surprising if it were, in view of the obstacles that restrict entry of Negroes and other minorities into many of the better paying jobs.

An examination of the figures separately for the two racial groups shows that education pays off for each, but the returns are far greater for whites. In Table X-8 occupations have been selected for which annual earnings estimates are available for whites and nonwhites. The figures shown in this table are from the 1960 census. The level of earnings of nonwhites and whites in each of the occupations shown has undoubtedly increased since that time and the ratio of the earnings of nonwhites relative to whites has probably also increased. The figures shown, however, are the only ones available at this writing and they undoubtedly still have much relevance.

In most occupations, nonwhite men earned about three-fourths as much as whites with the same amount of schooling. In nearly every occupation nonwhite high school graduates earned less than whites who never went beyond the eighth grade. The reasons for these differences undoubtedly vary according to the occupation. In the highly unionized crafts, many nonwhites may have to work for lower pay on nonunion jobs because they are not permitted to join the unions. Even when they are union members, they may not be able to get the better jobs with large companies, where they are assured of regular employment. In those occupations that are not highly unionized, nonwhite workers, regardless of education, may be the first dismissed during slack periods. As a result, their annual earnings are lower than those of whites even though they are paid at the same hourly rate.

Even when nonwhite men are educated and are employed in a trade or profession, their earnings are far below those of whites with the same number of years of schooling and doing the same kinds of work. This is one cause of the low economic status of nonwhites. A more important cause is their concentration in low-paid occupations such as

TABLE X-8

Education and Earnings, by Occupation, for White and Nonwhite Men Aged 25 to 64: 1959

Occupation	Elementary school graduates			High school graduates		
	White	Nonwhite	Ratio of non-white to white	White	Nonwhite	Ratio of non-white to white
Craftsmen, foremen, etc.						
Overall	$5,300	$3,800	72%	$6,100	$4,500	73%
Brickmasons, stonemasons, tile setters	5,100	4,000	78	6,100	3,900	63
Carpenters	4,400	3,200	72	5,400	4,100	76
Compositors, typesetters	6,000	*	*	6,400	4,600	72
Electricians	6,100	*	*	6,400	5,600	87
Linemen, servicemen (telegraph, telephone, power)	5,800	*	*	6,300	5,200	82
Machinists	5,500	4,300	79	6,000	5,100	85
Mechanics and repairmen	4,900	3,700	75	5,500	4,400	79
Painters, construction and maintenance workers	5,200	3,100	73	4,800	3,500	72
Plasterers	5,100	3,600	72	6,400	*	*
Plumbers, pipefitters	5,600	4,000	71	6,400	4,500	71
Operatives, etc.						
Overall	$4,800	$3,600	75%	$5,400	$4,000	74%
Bus drivers	4,300	3,500	81	5,100	4,700	93
Mine operatives and laborers	4,300	3,500	80	5,400	3,800	70
Truck and tractor drivers	4,900	3,300	68	5,500	3,700	68
Other	4,800	3,800	80	5,400	4,100	77
Service workers (including private household)						
Overall	$3,900	$2,900	75%	$5,000	$3,300	66%
Barbers	4,500	2,800	62	4,900	3,500	72
Policemen and detectives	4,800	*	*	5,500	5,200	94

*Averages not computed for fewer than 1,000 persons.

U.S. *Census of Population: 1960*, Vol. II, Part 7B, *Occupation by Earnings and Education*.

laborers and service workers. This fact is clearly brought out in Table X-9, which shows the occupational distribution of white and nonwhite men by years of schooling.

A nonwhite man who has not gone beyond the eighth grade has very little chance of being anything more than a laborer, a porter, or a factory hand. Nearly eight out of every ten nonwhite men with only eight grades of schooling worked as laborers, service workers, or operatives at the time of the 1960 census. Among whites with the same amount of education only five out of ten worked at these low-paid jobs.

TABLE X-9

Education and Occupation, for White and Nonwhite Men Aged 18 to 64: 1960

Occupation group	White			Nonwhite		
	Elementary school graduate	High school graduate	College graduate	Elementary school graduate	High school graduate	College graduate
Number (thousands)	5,736	10,082	4,071	488	609	145
Professional and managerial workers	9%	21%	77%	3%	7%	72%
Farmers and farm managers	9	5	1	3	2	1
Clerical and sales workers	8	20	15	4	16	13
Craftsmen, foremen, etc.	28	25	4	13	15	4
Operatives, etc.	29	20	1	31	27	4
Service workers	6	5	1	17	18	5
Laborers	11	5	1	29	16	2

Note: Sums of tabulated figures in this chapter may not equal totals because of rounding.

U.S. Census of Population: 1960, Vol. II, Part 7B, *Occupation by Earnings and Education.*

The nonwhite high school graduate stands a somewhat better chance of getting a well-paid job, but even his chances are not very good. About six out of every ten nonwhite high school graduates were laborers, service workers, or operatives as compared with only three out of ten whites with the same amount of schooling.

Nonwhite college graduates seem to be able to find professional employment in relatively large numbers. About three out of every four were professional or managerial workers—nearly the same proportion as white college graduates. But there is one big difference. Nonwhites were concentrated in the lower-paid professions. One-third of the male nonwhite college graduates in professional employment were school-teachers as compared with only one-sixth of the whites. Moreover, earnings of nonwhites in the low-paid professions were considerably below those of whites. Relatively few nonwhites are in the higher paid professions. About 20 percent of the white male college graduates in professional employment were engineers as compared with only 8 percent of the nonwhites; 14 percent of the whites were lawyers or accountants, but only 6 percent of the nonwhites. There were proportionately as many nonwhite doctors as white, but the average earnings of the nonwhites were only half those received by the whites.

Table X-10 presents figures on the lifetime earnings of white and nonwhite men by years of school completed. The life tables for each color group were used to prepare the lifetime earnings. Since whites tend to live longer than nonwhites, on the average, their lifetime incomes will also tend to be greater, regardless of schooling; they simply enjoy more years of working life. The difference in life expectancy, however, accounts for only a small part of the difference in earnings and does not substantially change the conclusions. For example, on the basis of actual experience in 1959, nonwhite men could expect lifetime earnings of about $122,000 or about 51 percent of the white total. If nonwhites had the same life expectancy as whites, their expected lifetime earnings would be about $130,000 or 55 percent of the white total.

These figures show what a difference color makes! White high school graduates can expect $62,000 more than elementary school graduates over a lifetime; for nonwhites, the difference is less than half as much ($28,000). Similarly, the difference in lifetime earnings between white high school graduates and those with four years of college is $142,000; for nonwhites the difference is $34,000.

TABLE X-10

Education and Lifetime Earnings,
for White and Nonwhite Men Aged 18 to 64*

Schooling completed	White	Nonwhite	Ratio of nonwhite to white
Elementary school			
Less than 8 years	$157,000	$ 95,000	61%
8 years	191,000	123,000	64
High school			
1 to 3 years	$221,000	$132,000	60%
4 years	253,000	151,000	60
College			
1 to 3 years	$301,000	$162,000	54%
4 years	395,000	185,000	47
5 years or more	466,000	246,000	53

*Figures based on 1960 census.

U.S. Senate, 88th Congress, 1st Session, *Hearings Before the Committee on Labor and Public Welfare on Bills Relating to Equal Employment Opportunities,* July and August 1963.

The most disturbing fact shows up in the right-hand column of Table X-10. The income gap between white and nonwhite *widens* as education increases. The lifetime earnings of nonwhite elementary school graduates are 64 percent of those received by the whites. At the high school level this ratio drops to 60 percent and among college graduates it is only 47 percent. *The fact is that in 1959, the average non-white with four years of college could expect to earn less over a lifetime than the white who did not go beyond the eighth grade.* There are some regional differentials in these figures, but they are not as great as you might imagine. The nonwhite college graduate in the South might expect to earn about $154,000 in his lifetime. The southern white who only completed the eighth grade could expect to earn about 8 percent more ($167,000). In the northern and western states, where earnings

183

are considerably higher than in the South, the nonwhite with four years of college could expect to earn only slightly more in a lifetime ($209,000) than the white elementary school graduate ($198,000).

These findings support the belief that much of the gap between the earnings of whites and nonwhites is due to factors other than differences in training or ability. But the figures are far from conclusive in this respect. One need not be an apologist for discrimination to point out that the meaning of a year of school completed can be quite different for whites and nonwhites. In the first place, nonwhite children receive schooling of poorer quality. As a result, nonwhites who have completed the same number of years of school as whites will not be as well educated on the average.

This problem has received intensive study by Dr. Eli Ginzberg, director of the Conservation of Human Resources Project at Columbia University. He concludes that "schools in predominantly Negro neighborhoods are in serious disrepair, are staffed by inexperienced teachers and are unable to provide instruction geared to the widely different abilities of their students." Dr. Ginzberg cites many instances that attest to the lower quality of Negro schooling. He quotes a former speaker of the House of Representatives of Georgia as saying that "what the Negro child gets in the sixth grade, the white child gets in the third grade."[10]

James S. Coleman in his major study *Equality of Educational Opportunity* notes the relatively low achievement test scores of Negroes in elementary and high school as compared with the scores of whites, and the difficulty of the schools in overcoming the handicaps engendered by the environment of the children. He states that "schools bring little influence to bear on a child's achievement that is independent of his background and general social context; and . . . this very lack of an independent effect means that the inequalities imposed on children by their home, neighborhood, and peer environment are carried along to become the inequalities with which they confront adult life at the end of school."[11]

You must also remember that other factors—cultural, social, and economic conditions—affect the real education a student absorbs, even in a good school. And finally, performance on the job may have little to do with training or ability. Work habits and motivation may be just as closely related to earnings as education or training.

Statistics that take all of these factors into account have yet to be devised. But figures available from the 1960 census permit a closer examination of the problem than has heretofore been possible. Shown in Table X-11 are the expected lifetime earnings of white and nonwhite men with less than eight years of elementary school for three occupations—carpenters, truck drivers, and semiskilled factory workers. Since all of these men have very little schooling, the difference in formal education probably does not contribute significantly to the differential in earnings. Indeed, the low level of education for the entire group makes it likely that the great majority of these men, white and nonwhite alike, are below average in their ability to absorb formal education.

The jobs selected cover a range of skills. There are some who would argue that it is meaningless to lump all truck drivers together. The man

TABLE X-11

Lifetime Earnings* of Workers with Less than Eight Years of Schooling

Occupation	White	Nonwhite	Ratio of nonwhite to white
Carpenters			
Overall	$152,000	$91,000	60%
South	127,000	79,000	62
North and West	190,000	138,000	73
Truck drivers			
Overall	$162,000	$97,000	60%
South	132,000	86,000	65
North and West	189,000	140,000	74
Semiskilled factory workers			
Overall	$167,000	$120,000	72%
South	143,000	97,000	68
North and West	181,000	153,000	85

*From age 18 to 64 (based on 1960 census figures).

U.S. Senate, 88th Congress, 1st Session, *Hearings Before the Committee on Labor and Public Welfare on Bills Relating to Equal Employment Opportunities,* July and August 1963, p. 335.

who drives a huge diesel trailer requires entirely different skills from the deliveryman. The same argument can be made with some justification for carpenters; it cannot be validly made for semiskilled factory workers. These jobs are routine in nature and generally require little skill or experience.

The figures are shown separately for the South and for the rest of the country to take into account regional variations in earnings. The major control variables missing from the data are job performance and extent of employment. A quantitative measure of job performance cannot, of course, be obtained from census data. Figures on weeks worked were collected in the census, but were not tabulated for the groups shown in Table X-11. Even if the figures were available, it is doubtful that they would contribute much to an understanding of the situation. It is very likely that nonwhites have less regularity of employment than whites. But why is this so? How much of this unemployment is involuntary and the result of discrimination? This question cannot be answered by census data.

Despite the similarity of the occupations and schooling, sharp differences persist between the earnings of whites and nonwhites. In each of the three occupations, the earnings of nonwhites in the South averaged only about two-thirds that of the whites. In the North and West the differences were somewhat narrower; but even here nonwhite carpenters and truck drivers averaged only about three-fourths of the white total. Among semiskilled factory workers nonwhites averaged about 85 percent of the white total.

The analysis would indeed be incomplete if it were restricted to this one education group and only three occupations. The underlying census data contain similar information for about thirty different occupations. An analysis of these data produced findings very similar to those described in the table.

Education is not enough

Education is often prescribed as a remedy for the ills of the poor. School dropouts are urged to return. Unemployed workers are encouraged to enroll in occupational training programs. Even prisoners are given training in the hope that they can be rehabilitated. Is this prescription reasonable?

You have good reason to ask, why train the poor—particularly the nonwhite poor? The data above show how many people have struggled to get an education only to find their skills unrewarded. The clear meaning of these figures is that education alone is not enough. More harm than good may be done if people are trained and prevented from using their newly acquired skills. It will be to no avail to train Negroes as engineers, scientists, electricians, and plumbers if the only jobs they will get are carrying the mail or working on assembly lines.

Is it wrong, then, to urge the poor, particularly the nonwhites, to get more training? Obviously not. They may be lost with training, but they are surely lost without it. It is not the desire for education or the training programs which provide it that are wrong. The trouble lies with the discrimination. Efforts to improve the economic lot of the Negro must, therefore, be carried out simultaneously and with equal force on the two fronts—education and the elimination of barriers to employment. One without the other might do more harm than good.

In Chapter V it was demonstrated that in the 1960's the percentage of nonwhites in the highly skilled, well-paying jobs increased much more sharply than the percentage of white workers in these jobs. Between 1960 and 1969, the number of nonwhites employed as professional and technical workers increased by 109 percent, while the number of whites employed in these occupations increased by only 41 percent. The percentage increase in the number employed as managers, officials, and proprietors was more than three times as great for nonwhites as for whites. Also during this time period, the number of nonwhites employed in clerical occupations increased by 114 percent, while the number of whites in these occupations increased by only 33 percent. Combined with the increase in the number of nonwhites in these better jobs was a decline in the number employed in laboring and farm occupations. Real progress has been made, but much still remains to be done to further improve the economic condition of Negroes and other minority groups.

Who goes to college?

Since it seems clear that education is the surest road to financial success, we might take a good look at those lucky youths who get to college. Who are they? What kinds of families do they come from? How do they differ from high school graduates who don't go to college?

It has been said that in America nearly everyone goes to college. This, of course, is simply not true. It only seems that way when the United States is compared with European countries, where only a select few are permitted to get a higher education. At present, about 4 million American youngsters reach age 18 each year. About two-thirds of them graduate from high school and about one-half of the graduates enter college. Thus, we have a freshman class of about 1½ million students each year. If present trends continue, these first-year college enrollments will rise to about 2 million by 1975. Of course, not all the entering freshmen graduate—not by a long shot. In fact, about 25 percent drop out by the end of the freshman year and another 15 percent leave later. Only 60 percent of those who enter college leave with a sheepskin.

College students are drawn from all segments of American life. In 1966 about 14 percent of the students came from families with incomes under $5,000; 21 percent came from families in which incomes ranged from $5,000 to $7,500; about 20 percent came from families with incomes between $7,500 and $10,000; 28 percent came from families in which incomes ranged from $10,000 to $15,000, and 18 percent came from those with over $15,000.[12] It is clear that our colleges are not rich boys' clubs. Large numbers of low-income families are represented on the campuses.

The humble origins of many college students show up in other ways as well. Nearly 30 percent of the college students have fathers who never even graduated from high school, and the fathers of another third completed high school but had no college training. Thus six out of every ten college students in the United States were receiving higher education despite the fact that their fathers did not have this opportunity.[13]

This plebeian background is further reflected in the source of support for college attendance. In 1968 the average cost to an unmarried student for one year of college was about $1,100 at a public college and about $2,400 at a private college.[14] One out of every four college freshmen was paying the major part of his own way by his own work or savings. Only around half were paying the major part of their expenses through parental or family aid.[15]

Although college students are drawn from all walks of life, there can be little question that youths from higher income families are much more likely to attend college than are those brought up in families lower in the economic scale. The figures in Table X-12 show the income distribution of families with children of college age (18 to 24 years old). Among those families with a member attending college full time, 22 percent had incomes of over $15,000 as compared with only 9 percent of those who had no members attending college. Conversely, only 4 percent of those families with a full-time college student had incomes under $3,000 as compared with 13 percent of those families who had no child in college.

TABLE X-12

Families by Income and College Enrollment of Dependents*: October 1968

Family income	Families with dependents attending college full time	Families with dependents not attending college full time
Total	100%	100%
Under $3,000	4	13
$3,000 to $4,999	7	16
$5,000 to $7,499	15	21
$7,500 to $9,999	18	17
$10,000 to $14,999	27	18
$15,000 and over	22	9
Not reported	8	7

*Aged 18 to 24.

U.S. Bureau of the Census, "School Enrollment: October 1968 and 1967," *Current Population Reports*, Series P-20, No. 190, Table 13.

Not only is family income an important determinant of whether or not the children go to college, but the fathers' occupation and education are also important factors. In 1967 a national sample of persons who had been high school seniors in the fall of 1965 were asked about their college attendance after high school graduation. The findings in Table X-13 show that about 87 percent of those from families whose incomes

TABLE X-13

College Attendance of October 1965
High School Seniors: February 1967

	Number reporting (thousands)	Percentage attending college
Father's education		
Total	2,613	47%
Less than 8 years	249	22
8 years High school, 1 to 3 years	818	35
High school, 4 years	717	54
College, 1 to 3 years	295	63
College, 4 years or more	279	82
Not reported	255	33
*Occupation group of household head**		
Total	2,613	47%
Employed	2,370	48
White-collar worker	970	64
Manual or service worker	1,247	37
Farm worker	152	36
Unemployed or not in civilian labor force	210	31
Not reported	32	†
*Annual family income**		
Total	2,613	47%
Under $3,000	268	19
$3,000 to $3,999	167	32
$4,000 to $5,999	488	37
$6,000 to $7,499	367	41
$7,500 to $9,999	490	51
$10,000 to $14,999	477	61
$15,000 and over	160	87
Not reported	196	54

*As of October 1965.
†Base less than 150,000.

U.S. Bureau of the Census, "Factors Related to High School Graduation and College Attendance: 1967," *Current Population Reports*, Series P-20, No. 185, Tables 7 and 8.

were $15,000 or higher had gone on to college as compared with only 19 percent of those whose families' incomes were under $3,000. The likelihood of college attendance increased with each increase in family income. The importance of parental occupation in determining college attendance is shown by the fact that nearly two out of three of the high school graduates whose household head was a white-collar worker went on to college as compared with only about one in three of those whose household head was a manual, service, or farm worker. The influence of the fathers' education is shown by the fact that about 82 percent of the high school graduates whose father was a college graduate went on to college as contrasted with 54 percent of those whose father was a high school graduate, and only 22 percent of those whose father was not even an elementary school graduate.

The figures in Table X-14 show that the education of the father may be about as important as family income in influencing the decision of a youth to get higher education.

TABLE X-14

Percentage of Families with Children Attending College, by Education of Father and Family Income: 1960

All families	18%
Less than $5,000	9
Between $5,000 and $7,500	17
Between $7,500 and $10,000	32
$10,000 and over	44
Father not high school graduate	11
Less than $5,000	7
Between $5,000 and $7,500	14
Between $7,500 and $10,000	20
$10,000 and over	25
Father attended college	51
Less than $5,000	23
Between $5,000 and $7,500	37
Between $7,500 and $10,000	66
$10,000 and over	70

U.S. Bureau of the Census, *Current Population Reports—Population Characteristics*, Series P-20, No. 110, Table 10.

Overall, about 18 percent of the youths were enrolled in college in October 1960. The proportion varied considerably by income level, ranging from only one child out of ten for families with incomes under $5,000 to nearly five out of ten for families with incomes over $10,000. The important point to notice, however, is that children whose fathers attended college but had low incomes were just as likely to be enrolled on a college campus as those whose fathers had high incomes but considerably less schooling. The figures show that one-fourth of the children of college men with incomes under $5,000 were attending college. This was almost identical with the proportion for men with incomes over $10,000 who did not graduate from high school. Once a man has gone to college there is a very strong probability that his children will also go to college.

Family income is not only a key determinant of college attendance, but, as Table X-15 shows, it also has a significant influence on the type and quality of college a student attends. A comparison of college students from families with incomes of $15,000 or more with those from families with incomes of less than $3,000 shows that those at the upper income level are more likely than those at the lower income level to attend a four-year college rather than a two-year college, attend a private college rather than a public college, attend a large college rather than a small college, attend a high-tuition college rather than a low-tuition college, and attend a high-ranking college rather than a low-ranking college.

How "able" are American college students? Are there many bright youths who do not attend college? These questions are difficult to answer because there are no measures of innate intelligence. It is generally conceded that results on IQ or achievement tests are influenced by cultural and emotional factors and do not in any sense measure innate qualities. Despite their limitations, however, these measures have some utility as rough indicators of the relation between ability to perform and actual performance.

The Project TALENT longitudinal survey of high school students in the early 1960's provides information on the relationship of ability-achievement level, based on a battery of test scores, and the probability of entering college. Table X-16 shows that 79 percent of the high school graduates who are in the top fifth in ability enter college, as compared with only 20 percent of the graduates in the lowest fifth. Not only is there a very high correlation between ability and college attendance,

TABLE X-15

Family Income and Characteristics of College Attended*: October 1966

	Family income‡		
	Under $3,000	$7,500 to $9,999	$15,000 and over
Rank of college			
Low	25%	17%	10%
Medium	26	47	39
High	15	18	40
Not available	35	18	11
Type of college			
2-year	24%	23%	11%
4-year	76	77	89
Type of control:			
Public	58%	66%	46%
Private	33	30	50
Not available	10	4	4
Enrollment:			
10,000 or more	23%	43%	47%
2,500 to 9,999	29	36	24
Under 2,500†	48	21	29
Tuition and fees:			
Under $250	37%	28%	19%
$250 to $499	23	38	27
$500 to $999	18	13	15
$1,000 and over	13	17	34
Not available	11	4	4

*By dependent family members 14 to 34 years old.
†Includes colleges for which enrollment figures not available.
‡During preceding 12 months.

U.S. Bureau of the Census, "Characteristics of Students and Their Colleges, October 1966," *Current Population Reports*, Series P-20, No. 183, Tables 2, 4, and 9.

there is also a high correlation between socioeconomic status and college attendance. Classification of socioeconomic status is based on family income, father's educational attainment, and other factors. Among those in the highest socioeconomic status level, nearly 80 percent of the high school graduates entered college as compared with only 23 percent of those in the lowest socioeconomic status level.

However, it is significant that half of the brightest students who are in the lowest socioeconomic status level do not attend college as compared with only 5 percent of the brightest students from the highest socioeconomic status level. This loss is serious. The young people involved almost certainly lose future income. And the nation loses the best use of its most precious resource.

With the emphasis that is placed on graduate and professional training today, it is perhaps even more significant that five years after high school graduation those high school graduates in the top fifth by ability are *five times more likely to be in a graduate or professional school* if their parents were in the top socioeconomic quartile than if their parents were in the bottom socioeconomic quartile.[16]

TABLE X-16

Percentage of High School Graduates Entering College During the Five Years Following Graduation

Ability quintile	Socioeconomic status*				Total graduates
	1	2	3	4	
Top fifth	95%	79%	67%	50%	79%
Second fifth	84	63	52	36	60
Third fifth	69	46	34	24	41
Fourth fifth	56	34	27	17	28
Bottom fifth	40	28	19	15	20
Overall	79	53	39	23	54

*1 = highest status; 4 = lowest status.

Based on Project TALENT data, reported by Roger E. Bolton in "The Economics and Public Financing of Higher Education: An Overview," *The Economics and Financing of Higher Education in the United States*, Joint Economic Committee, Congress of the United States, 91st Congress, 1st Session, 1969.

XI

It's the Job That Counts

Work has always been something very special for man. In the past, it was something he had to do to survive physically, although the psychological benefits that were derived were probably just as important as the physical ones. It is little wonder that work was given an exalted position in the age of scarcity, when all of the major religions came into being. Man had to work to survive. The ancient Hebrews used the same word, *avodah*, for both work and worship. The Bhagavad-Gita cautioned that "without work, the world would perish." Under Christianity work became "a gateway to spirituality"; and the Protestant ethic required that man "use his gifts from God to multiply his rewards."[1] No doubt the wise men who founded and transmitted the moral code in each religion were as fully aware as we are of the importance of work as both a way of life and a way of making a living. Work has always provided a way of filling a large part of each day, an outlet for creativity and a way of socializing with other people, as well as a source of livelihood for the great mass of mankind.

With the industrial revolution work appeared to lose its spiritual and psychological meaning for many people. This trend has become even more pronounced with the advent of the electronic age. Dull men no doubt still find dull jobs as meaningful and challenging as ever. But when men of normal intelligence are required to do "idiot work" there is sure to be trouble. The feelings of many men about their jobs are well expressed in a song the Wobblies sang many years ago: "We go to work to get the dough to get the food to get the strength, to go to work to get the dough to get the food to get . . ."

The frequent complaint today that work has lost its meaning is not new. The diligent scholar could no doubt trace that feeling back to antiquity. Around the turn of the century that lovable Irishman Mr. Dooley, created by Finley Peter Dunne, expressed it very well on behalf of the Irish immigrants who toiled from morning till night helping to build this country:

> Yes, I know th' wur-ruk iv relief is goin' on, but what th' lads need is th' relief iv wur-ruk. . . . Manny a man doesn't know anny betther thin to think he's servin' Gawd best be poundin' slag fr'm day break to sunset an' thin goin' home too tired to stand or set or lay down. We've hammered it into their heads that they's some connection between a pickax an' a dish iv ham an' eggs an' bedad they can't be made to believe that wan ain't th' fruit iv the other. . . .[2]

Psychiatrist Erich Fromm believes that present-day industrialism is reducing modern man to "a well fed and well entertained automaton, who loses his individuality, his independence and his humanity."[3] This view presupposes that there was a time when the great mass of mankind derived individuality, independence, and humanity from his work. When? Where? Or is this merely an attempt to romanticize the past? If men are unhappy with their work today, it provides hope for the future to believe there was a time when this was not so. What folly makes us think that the peasant of normal intelligence found much meaning in fighting wars, digging ditches, or building castles so that his lord could live in luxury while he and his family barely kept body and soul together? It was something he had to do to survive. Lacking an alternative, he did it and rationalized his action. Every now and then men revolted, but for the most part they stayed in line until alternatives became possible. This is one of the major differences with respect to work between today and the past—alternatives are now possible for some people. There is enough of a surplus so that large numbers need not work in order to survive. To some extent, the turmoil on many college campuses today stems from the attempt to find meaning in a life where work is not necessary for survival.

Erich Fromm also argues that "we have witnessed a tremendous reduction of working hours within the last hundred years, and a working day of four, or even two hours does not seem to be a fantastic expectation for the future".[4] Perhaps this change will take place in some far distant future, but it does not seem to be a problem that need concern us much today. The average employee in manufacturing industries works the same number of hours today as he did forty years ago.[5] In a very interesting analysis of the use of leisure, Harold Wilensky points out that "the average man's gain in leisure with economic growth has been exaggerated. Estimates of annual and lifetime leisure suggest that the skilled urban worker may have gained the position of his 13th century counterpart. Upper strata here, in fact, lost out. Even though their worklives are shorter and vacations longer, these men work many steady hours week after week—sometimes reaching a truly startling lifetime total."[6] Men may not like their jobs today and they may not see much meaning in them, but a man's job is still probably the most important single influence on his life.

Thirty years ago, Dr. Alba Edwards, who was the Census Bureau's expert on occupational classification at the time, described the role of occupation in a man's life in the kind of language that rarely appears in government reports today. What he said then is still largely true today.

> The most nearly dominant single influence in a man's life is probably his occupation. More than anything else, perhaps, a man's occupation determines his course and his contribution in life. And when life's span is ended, quite likely there is no other single set of facts that will tell so well the kind of man he was and the part he played in life as will a detailed and chronological statement of the occupations he pursued. Indeed, there is no other single characteristic that tells so much about a man and his status—social, intellectual, and economic—as does his occupation.[7]

Since the job is so important to the individual, we might begin this examination of the relationship between occupation and earnings with an investigation of the relationship between a man's job and his family background, particularly his father's job. To do this, we will lean heavily on a study of occupational changes in a generation conducted by the Bureau of the Census in 1962 under the direction of two eminent sociologists, Professors Peter Blau and Otis Duncan.[8] In this study, a representative sample of American men were asked not only about their own first occupation, income, education, and the like, but also about their father's usual occupation. In a separate survey, a cross section of the American public were asked what degree of status they thought attached to each occupation, and these responses were used to derive a numerical

197

status "score" (ranging from 0 to 96) for each of 446 detailed census occupations.

As a result of these two surveys, it is possible to compare the occupational score of each man surveyed in 1962 with the score his father had, and thereby see how much influence the father's relative socioeconomic position had on the ranking of his son. Since the men surveyed were of different ages, it is also possible to get some impression about whether equality of opportunity has been increasing or decreasing by comparing the father-son status relationship of the older men with that of the younger.

Duncan and Blau found that "the occupational achievements of the sons were *not* in any large degree explained by the socioeconomic levels of their fathers. To be exact, only 16 percent of the variation in the occupational scores of the men surveyed in 1962 was explained by the father's occupational status."[9] On the basis of this and other evidence, they concluded that "there is a considerable degree of social mobility in America" and that "the degree of equality of opportunity has *not* been declining in recent decades."[10] One of the perennial questions that comes up is whether there is more or less equality of opportunity in the United States than in other countries. According to Duncan, occupational mobility is about the same in all industrialized countries, but "the ability to go from rags to riches in a single generation is greater in the United States than elsewhere."[11]

Negroes have far less occupational mobility than whites, although the picture may have changed somewhat since 1962. Negroes have shown much more rapid occupational advancement than whites since that time. Nevertheless, the basic relationships revealed by the survey of occupational changes in a generation are probably still valid.

Table XI-1 shows that in 1962 most Negro men worked at unskilled or semiskilled jobs, regardless of their fathers' occupations. Even if their fathers were in professional or managerial jobs, Negro men were usually operatives, service workers, or laborers. In contrast, the sons of white men showed considerable upgrading in their occupational status. For example, the sons of most white men who were in higher white-collar jobs ended up doing the same kind of work as their fathers, and nearly half of the sons of men in lower white-collar jobs upgraded themselves to higher status and better paid occupations. The sons of white men at each occupational level appear to be working at higher status jobs, on the average, than their fathers. Duncan summarizes the situation as fol-

TABLE XI-1

Mobility from Father's Occupation, by Race, for Civilian Men 25 to 64 Years Old: March 1962

Father's occupation*	Son's occupation*						Total workers (thousands)
	Higher white collar	Lower white collar	Higher manual	Lower manual	Farm	Not in experienced civilian labor force	
Negro							
Higher white collar	10.4%	9.7%	19.4%	53.0%	0.0%	7.5%	134
Lower white collar	14.5	9.1	6.0	69.1	0.0	7.3	55
Higher manual	8.8	6.8	11.2	64.1	2.8	6.4	251
Lower manual	8.0	7.0	11.5	63.2	1.8	8.4	973
Farm	3.1	3.0	6.4	59.8	16.2	11.6	1,389
Not reported	2.4	6.5	11.1	65.9	3.1	11.1	712
Overall	5.2	5.4	9.5	62.2	7.7	10.0	
Total (thousands)	182	190	334	2,184	272	352	3,514
Non-Negro							
Higher white collar	54.3%	15.3%	11.5%	11.9%	1.3%	5.6%	5,836
Lower white collar	45.1	18.3	13.5	14.6	1.5	7.1	2,652
Higher manual	28.1	11.8	27.9	24.0	1.0	7.3	6,512
Lower manual	21.3	11.5	22.5	36.0	1.7	6.9	8,798
Farm	16.5	7.0	19.8	28.8	20.4	7.5	9,991
Not reported	26.0	10.3	21.0	32.5	3.9	6.4	2,666
Overall	28.6	11.3	20.2	26.2	6.8	6.9	
Total (thousands)	10,414	4,130	7,359	9,560	2,475	2,517	36,455

*Combinations of census major occupation groups. *Higher white collar* = professional workers, etc., and managers, officials, and proprietors, except farm. *Lower white collar* = sales and clerical workers, etc. *Higher manual* = craftsmen, foremen, etc. *Lower manual* = operatives, etc., service workers, and laborers, except farm. *Farm* = farmers and farm managers, farm laborers, and foremen. Classification by "father's occupation" includes some men reporting on the occupation of a family head other than the father.

U.S. Department of Health, Education and Welfare, *Toward a Social Report*, Government Printing Office, 1969, p. 24.

lows: "The Negro man originating at the lower levels is likely to stay there, the white man to move up. The Negro originating at the higher levels is likely to move down; the white man seldom does. The contrast is stark."[12]

Stability of occupational rank

The study of occupations is full of surprises. One of the most surprising things of all is the stability of prestige ratings among occupations. In 1947 a survey conducted by the National Opinion Research Center asked a representative sample of the population to rank ninety occupations in terms of the prestige associated with each one. Each occupation was ranked as excellent, good, average, below average, and poor. On the basis of the ranks a composite score was assigned. This survey is known as the North-Hatt Study of occupational prestige. In 1963 this study was repeated using the same occupations and virtually identical procedures.[13] During the sixteen-year period that elapsed between the two studies, considerable changes took place in the quality and composition of the American labor force. One of the most significant changes was the attempt to upgrade the popular image of college professors and scientists. In the past they were not only relatively low-paid, but they were also often portrayed as absentminded, bumbling fools. Following the Russian success with Sputnik, a major attempt was made to improve the popular image of scientists and engineers, particularly those associated with space industries. There were many other changes as well. The long-term decline in the importance of agriculture and unskilled labor continued during this period as well as the increase in professional and white-collar employment. Despite these changes, however, the results of this study showed that the prestige ratings of the ninety occupations did not change much. The report states unequivocally that "a correlation of .99 between prestige scores derived from the 1947 North-Hatt NORC study of occupational prestige and a 1963 replication of it indicates that very few changes in occupational prestige ratings have occurred in the sixteen-year period."[14]

Despite this conclusion, the figures for selected occupations in Table XI-2 show some noteworthy changes. By and large, the effort to upgrade

TABLE XI-2

Selected Occupations Ranked by Prestige: 1947 and 1963

Occupation	1947	1963	Occupation	1947	1963
U.S. Supreme Court			Author of novels	31.5	34.5
Justice	1	1	Economist	34	34.5
Physician	2.5	2	Electrician	45	39
Nuclear physicist	18	3.5	Trained machinist	45	41.5
Scientist	8	3.5	Farm owner and		
State governor	2.5	5.5	operator	39	44
Cabinet member			Undertaker	47	44
(federal government)	4.5	8	Policeman	55	47
College professor	8	8	Bookkeeper	51.5	49.5
U.S. representative in			Insurance agent	51.5	51.5
Congress	8	8	Carpenter	58	53
Chemist	18	11	Manager of a small store		
Lawyer	18	11	in a city	49	54.5
Diplomat, U.S. foreign			Mail carrier	57	57
service	4.5	11	Plumber	59.5	59
Dentist	18	14	Barber	66	62.5
Architect	18	14	Machine operator in		
Psychologist	22	17.5	a factory	64.5	62.5
Minister	13	17.5	Corporal, U.S. Army	64.5	65.5
Member of the board			Garage mechanic	62	65.5
of directors of a large			Truck driver	71	67
corporation	18	17.5	Clerk in a store	68	70
Mayor of a large city	6	17.5	Restaurant cook	71	72.5
Priest	18	21.5	Singer in a nightclub	74.5	74
Civil engineer	23	21.5	Filling station		
Airline pilot	24.5	21.5	attendant	74.5	75
Banker	10.5	24.5	Coal miner	77.5	77.5
Sociologist	26.5	26	Restaurant waiter	79.5	80.5
Captain, U.S. Army	31.5	27.5	Taxi driver	77.5	80.5
Public-school teacher	36	29.5	Farmhand	76	83
Owner of a factory that			Janitor	85.5	83
employs about 100	26.5	31.5	Bartender	85.5	83
Building contractor	34	31.5	Soda fountain clerk	84	86
Artist (painter)	24.5	34.5	Garbage collector	88	88
Musician in a symphony			Shoe shiner	90	90
orchestra	29	34.5			

Derived from Robert Hodge, Paul Siegel, and Peter Rossi, "Occupational Prestige in the United States, 1925-63," *American Journal of Sociology,* November 1964.

the image of scientists appears to have been successful. Nuclear physicists jumped from a rank of 18 in 1947 to 3.5 in 1963, scientists rose in rank from 8 to 3.5, and chemists rose from 18 to 11. College professors, on the other hand, showed no change. They held the relatively high rank of 8 in both years. Ministers continued their long-term decline in prestige, dropping from a rank of 13 in 1947 to 17.5 in 1963. Government officials also experienced a major drop in prestige. Diplomats in the foreign service, for example, dropped from the exalted rank of 4.5 in 1947 to 11 in 1963. State governors dropped from a rank of 2.5 to 5.5 and members of the President's Cabinet dropped from 4.5 to 8. Contrary to widely held opinions, public-school teachers improved their image and increased from a rank of 36 in 1947 to 29.5 in 1963.

In general, the best paying jobs had the highest rank, but even in this respect there were some noteworthy exceptions. Economists, for example, are among the highest paid social scientists and yet they ranked far below psychologists and sociologists. Plumbers earn much more than carpenters, yet they rank lower on the prestige scale.

A ranking of occupations in terms of their average earnings shows the same kind of stability as the ranking in terms of prestige. In Table XI-3, 116 occupations were classified by wage levels in 1939, 1949, and 1959. This table was prepared by ranking all occupations from lowest to highest by median wage or salary income in each year. The occupations were then divided (approximately) into deciles based on number of workers, and the occupations included in each decile were identified. Messengers, for example, who were in the lowest decile in 1959, were also in the lowest decile in each of the two preceding censuses. This fact is indicated by the entry of "1" in the columns for 1939, 1949, and 1959, signifying the lowest decile in each year. Waiters, also, were in the lowest decile in 1959 but in the second decile in each of the preceding censuses.

Table XI-3 makes it quite clear that there is a high degree of stability in the structure of wages. Despite vastly different labor market conditions in 1939, 1949, and 1959, there were few marked changes in the relative income position of occupations. The greatest stability was found among the highest paid occupations. In the eighth, ninth, and tenth deciles in 1959, only one occupation—firemen—shifted rank by more than one decile during the twenty-year period. In every other case, these high-paying occupations were in the same or an adjacent decile in both 1939 and 1959. The stable composition of the very highest decile is not sur-

TABLE XI-3
Selected Occupations for Male Wage and Salary Workers, Ranked
by Median Wage or Salary Income: 1959, 1949, and 1939

Rank of occupation in 1959	Decile designation* for		Rank of occupation in 1959	Decile designation* for	
	1949	1939		1949	1939
Lowest tenth			Operatives (cont.)		
			Footwear	2	3
Messengers (except express)	1	1	Leather	3	5
Newsboys	1	1	Guards and watchmen	3	5
Shoemakers and repairers (except factory)	2	2	Barbers, beauticians, and manicurists	2	4
Attendants, auto service and parking	1	2	Cooks (except private household)	2	2
Private household workers	1	1	Elevator operators	2	5
Charmen, janitors, and porters	2	2	Laborers:		
			Food	2	3
Waiters, bartenders, and counter workers	2	2	Stone	3	2
			Machinery	3	4
Service workers (except private household)	1	1	Transportation equipment	3	3
Fishermen and oystermen	1	1	Construction	1	1
Lumbermen, raftsmen, and wood choppers	1	1	Transportation (except railway)	2	1
Laborers:			Telecommunications	2	5
Lumber	1	1	*Third tenth*		
Textile	2	1	Drivers, bus, taxi, and truck, and deliverymen	4	4
Trade	1	1	Operatives–food	5	5
Second tenth			Laborers:		
			Paper	3	3
Clergymen	3	7	Metal	3	4
Painters (construction), paperhangers, and glaziers	3	3	Railroad	3	2
Apprentices	2	1	*Fourth tenth*		
Operatives:			Musicians and music teachers	5	5
Knitting mill	5	4	Shipping and receiving clerks	5	5
Apparel	5	4	Stenographers, typists, and secretaries	8	8
Textile	2	2			
Lumber	1	2			

TABLE XI-3
Selected Occupations for Male Wage and Salary Workers, Ranked by Median Wage or Salary Income: 1959, 1949, and 1939—*Continued*

Rank of occupation in 1959	Decile designation* for 1949	1939	Rank of occupation in 1959	Decile designation* for 1949	1939
Fourth tenth (cont.)			Masons, tile setters, and stone cutters	6	5
Bakers	5	6	Motormen, railway, mine, factory, etc.	8	8
Carpenters	4	3	Operatives:		
Molders, metal	5	6	Paper	5	5
Plasterers and cement finishers	5	4	Rubber	7	7
Tailors and furriers	7	5	Transportation equipment	7	5
Mine operatives and laborers	3	3	*Seventh tenth*		
Painters (except construction and maintenance)	5	5	Sports instructors, athletes, and entertainers	7	6
Sailors and deckhands	3	2	Teachers	9	8
Operatives:			Salaried managers— personal services	8	9
Stone	5	5	Baggagemen, express messengers, and railway mail clerks	9	10
Metal	5	6	Bookkeepers, accountants, cashiers, and ticket agents	9	9
Longshoremen and stevedores	3	3	Mail carriers	9	10
Laborers:			Telegraph operators	9	9
Chemicals	5	3	Real estate agents and brokers	8	8
Motor vehicles	5	5	Boilermakers	9	8
Fifth tenth			Cabinetmakers and patternmakers	7	6
Mechanics and repairmen, and loom fixers	6	6	Inspectors	9	9
Stationary firemen	5	6	Rollers and rollhands, metal	7	8
Operatives—machinery	6	6	Roofers and sheet metal workers	7	6
Sixth tenth			Welders and flame cutters	8	8
Social, welfare, and recreation workers	8	9			
Salaried managers—eating and drinking places	7	7			
Salesmen and salesclerks	7	7			
Blacksmiths, forgemen, and hammermen	7	5			

TABLE XI-3

Selected Occupations for Male Wage and Salary Workers, Ranked by Median Wage or Salary Income: 1959, 1949, and 1939—*Continued*

Rank of occupation in 1959	Decile designation* for 1949	1939	Rank of occupation in 1959	Decile designation* for 1949	1939
Seventh tenth (cont.)			Electricians	9	9
			Foremen:		
Operatives—motor vehicles	8	7	Construction	9	8
			Manufacturing	10	9
Policemen, sheriffs, and marshals	8	10	Transportation, communications, and other public utilities	10	10
Eighth tenth			Linemen and servicemen, telegraphers, etc.	8	9
Salaried managers—retail trade (except eating and drinking)	10	9	Locomotive firemen	9	9
Compositors and typesetters	10	8	Printing craftsmen (except compositors and typesetters)	10	9
Machinists, millwrights, and toolmakers	8	8	*Highest tenth*		
Plumbers and pipe fitters	9	8	Authors, editors, and reporters	10	10
Stationary engineers, cranemen, and hoistmen	8	8	Chemists	10	10
Structural metal workers	9	7	College presidents, professors and instructors	10	10
Brakemen and switchmen, railroad	9	9	Engineers, civil	10	10
Operatives—chemicals	8	8	Engineers, electrical	10	10
Firemen, fire protection	8	10	Engineers, mechanical	10	10
Ninth tenth			Conductors, railroad	10	10
Artists and art teachers	9	9	Salaried managers:		
Designers and draftsmen	9	9	Manufacturing	10	10
Pharmacists	10	9	Finance	10	10
Postmasters and miscellaneous government officials	9	10	Business and repair services	10	10
			Transportation	10	10
Insurance agents and brokers	9	10	Trade	10	10
			Locomotive engineers	10	10

*Lowest tenth = 1; highest tenth = 10.

Herman P. Miller, *Income Distribution in the United States,* Government Printing Office, 1966, pp. 96-97.

prising since it largely includes professional workers, such as authors, chemists, college professors, engineers, and managers and officials of business establishments. Since most of these jobs require considerable skill, training, and long periods of education, it is to be expected that they will be among the highest paid from one period to the next. What is surprising is that two railroad jobs—locomotive engineers and conductors—have maintained their very high standing over two decades despite the decline in railroading as a major industry. The high standing of these occupations—along with locomotive firemen, who are in the ninth decile —may be due largely to the strength of their labor unions.

The ninth decile, in contrast to the very highest, contains more of a mixture of professional workers and craftsmen. In addition to artists, designers, pharmacists, and several other professional occupations, this decile includes foremen in construction and manufacturing, electricians, craftsmen in the printing trades, and linemen.

The eighth decile contains no professional occupations. Aside from firemen—the only service workers—it includes mainly craftsmen and operatives in chemical plants.

The seventh decile is interesting in that it contains a relatively large number of occupations that were in much higher relative positions in 1939 and 1949. Most of these are government jobs—schoolteachers, mail carriers, and policemen—which attained relatively high standing in the past because of regularity of employment. In recent years, however, pay raises in these occupations have not kept pace with raises in other jobs. Still other occupations that dropped from a higher decile to seventh place were bookkeepers and accountants, salaried managers of personal service establishments, baggagemen, telegraph operators, boilermakers, and inspectors.

The lowest decile, like the highest two, experienced practically no change in occupational composition during these twenty years, there being no occupation in this group that shifted rank by more than one decile. In general, stability in the lowest decile is largely due to the fact that most of the workers are unskilled, and there was little if any increase in the demand for their services.

The second decile showed several noteworthy changes. For example, clergymen, who as a group had been relatively highly paid in 1939, fell in the seventh decile in that year. By 1949 this occupation had fallen to the third decile, and by 1959, to the second. Despite a significant increase in church membership and organized religious activity since 1939,

the salaries paid to clergymen have lagged far behind the salaries received by most church members. Elevator operators, three groups of operatives, and one group of laborers who were in the fifth decile either in 1939 or 1949 dropped to the second decile in 1959. This drop was probably due mainly to the declining demand for operatives brought about by automation.

The professional elite

Professional work carries the highest status in America and brings in the most money. But, because it includes such economically disparate fields as medicine and the church, the nationwide average is quite low. In 1968 male professionals averaged $9,500 or just under $200 a week. The physician's traditional Cadillac accurately reflects his position at the top of the heap. In 1968 physicians and surgeons who were in independent practice averaged nearly $25,000; those who worked for someone else earned only half as much. Engineers did not do quite so well as the help-wanted ads indicate. They averaged only $12,000 during the year, about the same as most science fields. Teachers averaged only $8,200 and down near the bottom of the professional group were the clergy, who are in the lowest paid of all the professions. Many clergymen receive certain types of benefits, such as free living quarters, that are not reflected in their money income receipts, but even if rough allowance is made for this income received "in kind," it is very doubtful that the average earnings of clergymen even begin to approach those received in the other professions. Our spiritual leaders earn, on the average, less than truck drivers in large cities. For some representative science salaries, see Table XI-4.

The figures cited above are annual earnings. The total earned over a lifetime may be more informative because it eliminates the bias introduced by unusually high or low pay for beginners. You must remember that the numbers in Table XI-5 are averages—many men make more than that and many make less. Also, the figures represent *earnings* and not total income. The difference is important for the higher paid professionals, particularly those with independent practices, who often have income from investments, rental of property, annuities, and other sources.

Doctors, of course, are by far the highest paid professionals in our society. Their expected lifetime earnings are nearly three-quarters of a

---

TABLE XI-4

Median Salaries in Selected Science Fields: 1968

All fields	$13,200	Linguistics	$11,500
		Mathematics	13,000
Agricultural sciences	11,000	Atmospheric and space	
Anthropology	12,700	sciences	13,000
Biological sciences	13,000	Physics	14,000
Chemistry	13,500	Political science	12,000
Computer sciences	14,100	Psychology	13,200
Earth and marine sciences	12,900	Sociology	12,000
Economics	15,000	Statistics	14,900

Statistical Abstract of the United States, 1969, p. 528.

---

million dollars on the average, which means that many go well over the one-million mark. Dentists and lawyers rank next with about $600,000 each.

Below the medical and legal professions, the range of earnings is not very wide. Electrical and mechanical engineers are in the middle brackets of the engineering profession with a little over $350,000 each; aeronautical engineers are somewhat higher paid (nearly $400,000) and civil engineers are at the bottom of that profession (about $335,000). Despite the variation, the range of earnings in this profession is quite narrow.

Among natural scientists, geologists are at the top with about $450,000. One of the reasons for their high earnings is that many of these men work for the large oil companies. The discovery of valuable new oil wells is primarily dependent upon their brainpower. As a result, payment for their services is high. Biologists are at the bottom of this group with $310,000. Physicists earn a little less than geologists, and chemists are only slightly better off than biologists.

The level of earnings in the social sciences is not much different from that in the natural sciences, but the teaching profession is paid at a distinctly lower scale. College professors earn about as much as the lower paid engineers and scientists; high school and elementary school teachers earn very much less.

Clergymen, as noted before, are by far the lowest paid among the professions shown, with only $175,000. Since this profession includes itinerant preachers, self-appointed ministers of the gospel, and others who may have had little formal schooling or training, it is not entirely

TABLE XI-5

Lifetime* Earnings of Professional Men

Doctors	$717,000
Dentists	589,000
Lawyers	621,000
Engineers:	
Aeronautical	395,000
Electrical	372,000
Mechanical	360,000
Civil	335,000
Natural scientists:	
Geologists	446,000
Physicists	415,000
Chemists	327,000
Biologists	310,000
Social scientists:	
Economists	413,000
Psychologists	335,000
Statisticians	335,000
Teachers:	
Elementary school	232,000
High school	261,000
College	324,000
Accountants	313,000
Clergymen	175,000

*From age 18 to age 64 (based on 1960 census figures).

U.S. Senate, 88th Congress, 1st Session, *Hearings Before the Committee on Labor and Public Welfare on Bills Relating to Equal Employment Opportunities,* July and August 1963, Table 1.

valid to compare their earnings with those of more highly trained scientists or engineers. It is significant, however, that even those clergymen who have completed five or more years of college have expected lifetime earnings of only $184,000—considerably less than elementary school teachers and about the same as carpenters and truck drivers.

The range of earnings for professional women is much narrower than for men. For the country as a whole, professional women averaged about $4,800 in 1968 or about $90 a week. As in the case of men, the best paid jobs for women were in the medical and legal professions. Even in these occupations, however, the earnings were quite low relative to those of men.

Nurses and dietitians are two of the lowest paid groups of professionals among women. Both of these occupations are associated with hospitals, where wages tend to be quite low.

Salaried managers and proprietors

Managers and proprietors are America's second best-paid group. But because this classification, like the professions, includes such a miscellaneous mixture, the overall average income again is not impressive: about $9,300 in 1968. The managerial class takes in some of the wealthiest and most powerful men in our society—the top executives of large corporations. It also includes relatively low-paid officials in small firms. The diversity among proprietors is at least as great. Business firms run the whole gamut from the itinerant TV repairman to General Electric and from the corner fruit peddler to the United Fruit Company. There are millions of small companies that have little in the way of financial assets, employ an infinitesimal part of the labor force, and obtain an even smaller share of the total sales. At the top, of course, there are the industrial giants that own most of the capital wealth, employ most of the people, and sell most of the goods. The range is enormous and the differences in returns are equally great.

One additional fact must also be borne in mind in interpreting the earnings figures for these occupations. The distinction between the owner of a business and the manager is often just a legal fiction, particularly in the smaller firms. If a business is unincorporated, the owner-operator is classified as a proprietor. If the same business becomes a corporation, the owner-operator is called a salaried manager.

The owners and managers of manufacturing plants have higher incomes, on the average, than those in other industries. This is undoubtedly due to the fact that manufacturing firms tend to be larger and accordingly the returns are greater. The owners of wholesale businesses and managers of finance, insurance, and real estate businesses rank just below manufacturers. Lowest incomes, as might be expected, are received in restaurants and other retail stores, which are generally much smaller than the businesses mentioned above.

There are 14 million men in the United States who are employed as professional, technical, and managerial workers. In an effort to determine how many of these men are actually members of the managerial elite, the market research staff of *Fortune* magazine attempted to separate the wheat from the chaff. Using a special tabulation of Census Bureau data, they excluded all men with annual incomes under $25,000 and those who were employed as actors, athletes, clergymen, funeral directors, and in other occupations which do not involve business decision-making responsibility.[15] As a result of this analysis, *Fortune* concluded that about 300,000 men constitute the managerial elite in the American economy. About 250,000 are classified as managers and officials and 50,000 are scientists, engineers, and other professional and technical workers. The group is about equally divided between industry (which includes manufacturing, mining, construction, and transportation companies) and all other business activities, including financial institutions, wholesale and retail trade, and business and professional services.

Clerical and sales workers

The great majority of white-collar workers are salesmen or clerks. Increases in the size and complexity of businesses have strengthened the need for management services and other office functions. The administration of advertising, research, sales, personnel, and other activities requires bookkeepers, office machine operators, secretaries. Prosperity and the increase in leisure time have also heightened the need for sales workers. As a result there have been striking increases in employment in these kinds of jobs during the past decade.

The range of responsibility, and therefore earnings, is quite narrow in most clerical jobs. Sales personnel, however, range all the way from the girl who sells nylons at Macy's to the highly trained engineer who sells computers for IBM. The former needs little if any skill; the latter must have intimate familiarity with the technical aspects of the product. The differences in training and responsibility make the range of earnings far greater for salesmen than for clerks.

Salesmen and clerical workers averaged $6,500 in 1968. Retail store clerks averaged only $4,000, whereas other salesmen averaged $7,900. Among women, the range of salaries was even narrower. Salesladies in retail stores were at the bottom with only $1,300 in 1968; but, of course, most of these women worked only part of the year or at a part-time job throughout the year. Those who worked as salesladies full time throughout 1968 averaged $3,300. Secretaries and typists averaged $3,900 in 1968.

Craftsmen

One of the most durable of modern fallacies concerns the purportedly exorbitant wages paid craftsmen, particularly construction craftsmen. True, steamfitters in the Washington metropolitan area earn more than $7 an hour and they have a contract that will raise their rate to $9.30 an hour by 1971, but their work is intermittent (for weather and business reasons). What counts is their annual income—this is what they eat and pay the rent on. It is good but not fantastic. Other craftsmen do not do even as well as steamfitters.

Although craftsmen do not have as much formal schooling as clerical and sales workers, their incomes tend to be about the same or even somewhat higher. The national average for all men classified as craftsmen or foremen was $7,400 in 1968, or about $140 a week.

Foremen are still among the highest paid in the manual field, although there are some who believe that their position is not what it once was. Their average earnings in 1968 were $8,900.

The latest information available on the annual earnings of different types of craftsmen is from the 1960 census. At that time, the average earnings for the highest paid crafts in each of the trades shown in Table XI-6 centered around $6,000, or about $120 a week. The two top crafts in the building trades were electricians ($6,000) and plumbers ($5,600). In the printing trades, compositors made $5,800 and other craftsmen made $6,200. Airplane mechanics, who were the top group in their field, averaged $5,900; and tool and die makers and millwrights averaged $6,500 and $6,000 respectively.

Most craftsmen can expect lifetime earnings ranging from nearly $200,000 to about $250,000. The range is about $50,000 lower in the South than in the rest of the country.

TABLE XI-6

Median Earnings of Craftsmen: 1959

Overall	$5,200
Foremen	
Manufacturing of durable goods	7,300
Manufacturing of nondurable goods	6,400
Nonmanufacturing industries	6,100
Construction trades	
Electricians	6,000
Plumbers	5,600
Masons	4,800
Plasterers	4,600
Carpenters	4,200
Printing trades	
Compositors	5,800
Other	6,200
Mechanics	
Airplane	5,900
Automobile	4,300
Radio and TV	4,300
Metal trades	
Tool and die makers	6,500
Millwrights	6,000
Machinists	5,500
Structural metal workers	5,500
Boilermakers	5,500
Metal molders	4,800
Blacksmiths and forgemen	4,700

U.S. Census of Population: 1960, Detailed Characteristics, United States Summary, Table 208.

Electricians lead the field in the construction trades with a national average of about $250,000. They are followed closely by plumbers with about $240,000. Somewhat lower on the scale are masons and plasterers with about $210,000, and at the bottom are the carpenters with $185,000. Differences between the earnings of whites and nonwhites in these trades are much greater in the South than in the rest of the nation. The lifetime earnings of nonwhites in the South in these trades are about 50 to 60 percent of the white total. Even in the North nonwhites average only about 70 to 80 percent of the white total.

Airplane mechanics are about as well paid as electricians, with lifetime earnings of about $250,000. Automobile mechanics and TV repairmen, on the other hand, receive only as much as carpenters, who are among the lowest paid in the construction trades. (See Table XI-7.)

Union membership makes a difference. Table XI-8 shows that nearly half of all craftsmen were union members in 1966. They averaged $7,900 as compared with only $6,000 for those who were not members of a union, producing an earnings differential of nearly one-third in favor of the union members. Among year-round, full-time workers, the differential was only about one-fourth in favor of union members.

The earnings differential associated with union membership varies widely among different types of craftsmen. Among carpenters, for example, union members earned 74 percent more than men who were not union members. In the construction trades, the differential was 59 percent in favor of union members, among mechanics and repairmen it was 43 percent, and among metal craftsmen it was only 14 percent. In each case, the differential was narrowed somewhat when the comparison was restricted to men who worked full time throughout the year.

Semiskilled and service workers

Down near the bottom of the income pyramid are those men and women who perform the more routine tasks. They keep the assembly lines moving in our factories, haul the freight, bus us from one place to another, wait on us in restaurants, and perform the other services essential to urban living. For two of these service groups—policemen and firemen—earnings are on a par with those of the highest paid craftsmen. These jobs carry, of course, considerably more responsibility than most others in this category, and employment is usually obtained only after successful competition in mental and physical tests.

The other service trades for men—barbers, janitors, elevator operators, waiters, and the like—are relatively low-paying. Typical salaries range from about $60 to $80 a week (including tips). The national aver-

TABLE XI-7
Lifetime Earnings* of Craftsmen

Region and occupation	Earnings (thousands)			Ratio of nonwhite to white
	Overall	White	Nonwhite	
United States				
Construction trades				
Electricians	$251	$254	$189	74%
Plumbers	236	241	141	59
Masons	209	221	126	57
Plasterers	206	223	124	56
Carpenters	185	190	112	59
Mechanics				
Airplane	$248	$252	—	—
Automobile	187	192	$132	69%
Radio and TV	183	187	–	–
North and West				
Construction trades				
Electricians	$261	$264	—	—
Plumbers	252	255	$196	77%
Masons	229	235	163	69
Plasterers	223	232	–	–
Carpenters	209	211	164	78
Mechanics				
Airplane	$257	$261	—	—
Automobile	201	204	$164	80%
Radio and TV	194	197	–	–
South				
Construction trades				
Electricians	$223	$226	—	—
Plumbers	197	207	$103	50%
Masons	168	187	107	57
Plasterers	166	196	103	53
Carpenters	139	146	81	55
Mechanics				
Airplane	$231	$235	—	—
Automobile	153	161	$96	60%
Radio and TV	159	164	–	–

*From age 18 to age 64 (based on 1960 census figures).

U.S. Senate, 88th Congress, 1st Session, *Hearings Before the Committee on Labor and Public Welfare on Bills Relating to Equal Employment Opportunities*, July and August 1963, Table 1.

TABLE XI-8

Earnings of Union and Nonunion Craftsmen: 1966

	Overall	Car-penters	Other construc-tion crafts-men	Mechanics and repairmen	Other metal crafts-men
Number of workers					
Total (thousands)	8,552	765	1,656	2,118	1,295
Union members (thousands)	3,997	353	938	805	823
Percentage union	47%	46%	57%	38%	64%
Median earnings					
All workers:					
Union members	$7,863	$7,478	$7,962	$7,622	$7,922
Not union members	5,984	4,287	5,024	5,323	6,945
Differential:					
Amount	$1,779	$3,191	$2,938	$2,299	$977
Percentage	31%	74%	59%	43%	14%
Year-round, full-time workers:					
Union members	$8,288	$8,311	$8,701	$7,988	$8,273
Not union members	6,760	5,498	6,206	5,945	7,529
Differential:					
Amount	$1,528	$2,813	$2,495	$2,043	$744
Percentage	23%	51%	40%	34%	10%

U.S. Bureau of the Census.

age of earnings in 1968 was $5,900 for semiskilled workers and $3,700 for service workers. Bus drivers and truck drivers earn $100 to $120 a week, but taxicab drivers make considerably less.

Union membership makes a big difference in the earnings of semi-skilled workers, just as it does for craftsmen. In each occupation for which data are available the earnings of union men exceed those of men who do not belong to a union by a wide margin. Overall, about half of all semiskilled workers are union workers. In 1966 the earnings of union members exceeded those of men who did not belong to unions by about

$2,300 or 56 percent. Roughly the same differentials were found for drivers and deliverymen and for men employed in manufacturing industries. Union members doing semiskilled work in nonmanufacturing industries had somewhat higher incomes than those doing the same kind of work in manufacturing industries; however, men who were not union members in nonmanufacturing industries had incomes which were less than half those received by union men.

Although most women are employed in white-collar jobs, large numbers also work in factories and in the service trades. Earnings in these

TABLE XI-9

Median Earnings of Male Semiskilled and Service Workers: 1959

Semiskilled	
Overall	$4,300
Bus drivers	4,400
Truck drivers	4,200
Taxi drivers	3,300
Laundry and dry-cleaning workers	2,900
Factory workers:	
Chemicals	5,300
Automobiles	5,000
Paper	4,900
Machinery	4,800
Primary metals	4,800
Food	4,200
Apparel	3,800
Service	
Overall	3,300
Firemen	5,500
Policemen	5,200
Barbers	3,700
Elevator operators	3,400
Waiters	3,000
Janitors	2,800

See Table XI-6 for source.

jobs, as might be expected, are quite low. For the country as a whole, women who were semiskilled workers averaged only $2,300 in 1959, about half the amount earned by men doing the same kinds of work. The top-paying jobs were in the large manufacturing plants and the lowest paying ones were in laundry and dry-cleaning establishments. Service workers earned even less than semiskilled workers, and at the very bottom were domestics, who averaged only $700 in 1959. The national av-

TABLE XI-10

Earnings of Union and Nonunion Male Semiskilled Workers: 1966

| | Overall | Drivers and delivery- men | Manufacturing industries | | Nonmanu- facturing industries |
			Durable goods	Non- durable goods	
Number of workers					
Total (thousands)	9,832	2,228	3,014	1,775	1,588
Union members (thousands)	4,785	940	1,734	894	478
Percentage union	49%	42%	58%	50%	30%
Median earnings					
All workers:					
Union members	$6,379	$6,944	$6,373	$6,259	$6,496
Not union members	4,091	4,396	4,576	4,151	2,787
Differential:					
Amount	$2,288	$2,548	$1,797	$2,108	$3,709
Percentage	56%	58%	39%	51%	133%
Year-round, full-time workers:					
Union members	$6,917	$7,824	$6,800	$6,620	$7,290
Not union members	5,539	5,513	5,763	5,293	4,882
Differential:					
Amount	$1,378	$2,311	$1,037	$1,327	$2,408
Percentage	25%	42%	18%	25%	49%

U.S. Bureau of the Census.

erage in 1968 was $3,100 for semiskilled workers, $500 for private household workers, and $1,500 for other service workers.

TABLE XI-11

Median Earnings of Female Semiskilled and Service Workers: 1959

Semiskilled	
Overall	$2,300
Laundry and dry-cleaning workers	1,600
Factory workers:	
Durable goods	2,900
Nondurable goods	2,300
Service	
Overall*	1,400
Private household workers	700
Charwomen	1,300
Hairdressers	2,000
Practical nurses	1,800
Waitresses	1,100

*Except private household.

See Table XI-6 for source.

Unskilled workers

At the very bottom are those who earn their living literally by the sweat of their brows—the common laborers. These are the men who haul sticks and stones on construction projects, push things around in factories, grease cars and dent them on parking lots, and do anything that requires some brawn but little else. The low level of skill demanded is reflected in low earnings. The national average for unskilled workers in 1968 was $2,700.

Longshoremen are among the highest paid workers in the unskilled group, reflecting perhaps more the strength of their union than anything else.

TABLE XI-12

Median Earnings of Unskilled Men: 1959

Overall	$2,900
Longshoremen	4,700
Construction laborers	3,000
Factory laborers:	
Chemicals	4,000
Transportation equipment	4,200
Machinery	4,000
Primary metals	4,000
Food	3,400

See Table XI-6 for source.

XII

Why Don't You Work, like Other Wives Do?

Our affluent society would not be nearly so affluent if all married men had to support their families on what they alone make. Many people would be surprised at how far down the economic ladder single-income living would tumble them. The figures in Table XII-1 are most revealing.

The column to the left shows the number of families that would be at a given income level if the family were classified by the combined income of all its members—husband, wife, children, Aunt Sophie, etc. The column to the right shows how the same families would be distributed if you counted only the husband's income. Thus, for example, if a husband made $7,000 a year and the wife made $4,000, the family would be counted at the $10,000-to-$14,999 level in the column to the left and at the $7,000-to-$9,999 level in the column to the right. Only families having both a husband and a wife are included in these figures and each family is counted once in each column. The big difference between the two columns reveals a great deal about where the purchasing power in many of our middle-income families comes from.

Fifteen thousand dollars is not a very high income by any means. One family out of six received this much money in 1968. Yet if families were counted by the husband's income only, the number of families with incomes over $15,000 would be cut by one-half, from 7 million to 3½ million.

At the lower end of the distribution the change appears to be equally dramatic. An income of less than $3,000 a year to support two or more

TABLE XII-1

Family Incomes Compared with Husbands' Incomes: 1968

Income level	Number of families (millions)	
	By family income	By husband's income
Total	43.8	43.8
Under $3,000	3.3	6.1
$3,000 to $4,999	4.7	6.3
$5,000 to $6,999	6.1	8.5
$7,000 to $9,999	10.8	11.8
$10,000 to $14,999	11.8	7.8
$15,000 and over	7.1	3.5

U.S. Bureau of the Census, *Current Population Reports, Consumer Income,* Series P-60, No. 66, Tables 12 and 38.

people is low no matter how you slice it. Using the family income concept, there were only about 3 million such families in 1968. But if only the husband's income were counted that number would have been nearly doubled.

Evidently someone in the family is giving Dad a helping hand financially. Mother, of course. This does not mean that wives are the only family members who supplement the family incomes; but they account by far for the majority of this income. Figures for a recent year show that supplementary earners are almost equally divided between wives and other family members, largely sons and daughters. The wives, however, had significantly higher incomes than the other relatives, and a much larger share of it undoubtedly found its way into the family coffers.

Frederick Lewis Allen reported in *Only Yesterday* that in the early 1920's "no topic was so furiously discussed at luncheon tables from one end of the country to the other as the question whether the married woman should take a job and whether the mother had a right to."[1] This question has been resolved. Indeed, the tables have been turned and women who don't work, particularly if they have no small children at home are often called upon to account for their failure to earn an honest living.

223

WHY DON'T YOU WORK, LIKE OTHER WIVES DO?

The number of working women has been growing each year and the end is nowhere in sight. At the end of the second world war only about one-fifth of the married women were in the labor force; by the mid-sixties this proportion had risen to one-third, and by the end of the sixties it had risen still further to nearly two-fifths. There are many factors working in tandem to increase the number of working wives. For many years now, the American economy has been moving away from heavy industry jobs, which could be done only by men, to clerical, sales, and service jobs, which can be done by women as well as, or better than, by men. Since educational attainment has been increasing for young women as well as men, the supply has been growing of high school and college trained women to fill the needs of industry. Finally, labor-saving devices in the home and changing social attitudes have also increased the availability of married women for jobs. Several years ago a sample of husbands was asked the following question: "There are many wives who have jobs these days. Do you think it is a good thing for a wife to work, or a bad thing, or what?" About one-third gave a favorable reply, and 40 percent replied unfavorably. The others were either afraid to voice an opinion or they pretended that they had none. Most of the men who liked the idea of having their wives work had their eyes on the income; but there were others who were also concerned about their mates' welfare. They felt that if their wives stayed at home they might get bored or they would not have enough to do.[2]

TABLE XII-2

Percentage of Wives in the Labor Force: 1940 to 1968

1940	15%
1944	22
1947	20
1950	24
1955	28
1960	31
1965	35
1968	38

Statistical Abstract of the United States, 1969, p. 220.

You might think that the wives of the poorest paid men would be most likely to work because they are most in need of the money, but things don't quite work out that way. Only one-third of the men with earnings under $1,000 had working wives. One reason why so few of the women work at this income level is that they are older; about half of them are over 55 years of age. The proportion of working wives rises gradually with income until reaching a peak at the $5,000-to-$7,000 income level, where 47 percent of the wives were in the labor force in March 1969. Beyond this point on the income scale there is a gradual reduction in the worker rate among married women. The proportion of working wives dropped to 41 percent at the $8,000-to-$10,000 income level; 35 percent at the $10,000-to-$15,000 level; 26 percent at the $15,000-to-$25,000 level; and only 18 percent at the highest income level.

TABLE XII-3

Percentage of Wives in the Labor Force and Median Age of Wife, by Earnings of Husband: March 1969

Earnings of husband	Percentage of wives in labor force	Median age of wife
$1 to $999	33%	55
$1,000 to $1,999	38	50
$2,000 to $2,999	42	41
$3,000 to $3,999	44	39
$4,000 to $4,999	45	38
$5,000 to $5,999	47	39
$6,000 to $6,999	47	39
$7,000 to $7,999	45	39
$8,000 to $9,999	41	39
$10,000 to $14,999	35	40
$15,000 to $24,999	26	42
$25,000 and over	18	45

U.S. Bureau of the Census, *Current Population Reports,* Series P-60, No. 66, Tables 20 and 21.

Who minds the store?

The picture we get for a large proportion of the families, particularly those in the middle-income brackets, is that Mama works and Papa works. Who takes care of the home and the kids? How many children are being neglected because the mother is out working? The question is a good one, but the answer is far from simple. Some authors, Michael Harrington, for one, are anything but enthusiastic about the working mother. In *The Other America* he states that the "tremendous growth in the number of working wives is an expensive way to increase income. It will be paid for in terms of the impoverishment of home life, of children who receive less care, love, and supervision."[3] This view assumes that because Mama works she is neglecting the children. This is not necessarily the case. A very large proportion of women work only part of the year or they work at part-time jobs. This may still leave plenty of time for child care. But let us face the issue squarely and admit that many children have mothers who would rather work than stay home with them. Are we to assume that these children would necessarily be better off if their mothers stayed at home but were unhappy about it? The answer is at best debatable.

TABLE XII-4

Marital Status of Working Women*: March 1967

Marital status	All women (millions)	Working women (millions)	Percentage who are workers
Total	69.4	27.5	40%
Single	11.7	5.9	51
Married	46.2	17.5	38
Living with husband	43.2	15.9	37
Separated†	3.0	1.6	53
Widowed	9.2	2.5	27
Divorced	2.3	1.7	71

Note: Sums of tabulated figures in this chapter may not equal totals because of rounding.

*Age 16 and over.

†Includes women whose husbands were in the armed forces or who were not living in the same household for other reasons.

Elizabeth Waldman, "Marital and Family Characteristics of Workers, March 1967," *Monthly Labor Review,* December 1968, Table A.

Of course, not all working wives are mothers nor are all working women wives. The figures in Table XII-4 provide a good cross-section view of the characteristics of working women in 1967.

About 28 million women were in the labor force in March 1967; that is, they were either working or looking for work. Of these, about 16 million were married and living with their husbands. This group accounted for slightly more than half of all women workers. The remaining women workers were equally divided between those who were single and those who were widowed, divorced, or separated from their husbands.

Married women do not work as steadily as the other groups. The economic pressure for women living with their husbands is not quite as great in most cases as it is for other women. A little over one-third of the women living with their husbands were in the labor force in 1967. In contrast, nearly three out of every four divorcees were working or looking for work, as were half of the women who were separated from their husbands. In both of the latter situations, the high worker rates are primarily due to the fact that most of these women are in the prime working ages, 25 to 54 years old, and they are also largely dependent upon their own work for support. Worker rates are somewhat lower for single women, most of whom are under 20 years of age and still in school. Employment is much lower among widows, who tend to be older. Slightly more than half of all widows were over 65 years old in 1967.

Now that we know a little bit about working women, let's see what we can discover about the children they have left behind. The figures below summarize the situation.

The first thing that seems clear from these figures is that most married women who work do not have young children living with them. This was true for nearly half of the working wives and about 70 percent of the women who were widowed, divorced, or separated from their husbands. These ladies can hardly be accused of contributing to a social problem. Of course, many of the husbands may object to having their wives work, but it seems clear that their objections go unheeded.

There are about 13 million mothers who have school-age children at home. About 6½ million of these mothers were either working or looking for work. While there are many who feel that a large proportion of these mothers are creating social problems, there are equally strong feelings to the contrary. Most of the argument centers about the desirability of having the mother present when the child returns home from school

TABLE XII-5

Working Women* and Their Children: March 1967

Presence of children	Living with husbands (millions)		Widowed, divorced, or separated (millions)	
	All women	Workers	All women	Workers
Total	43.2	15.9	14.5	5.7
No children under 18 years old	18.4	7.2	11.7	3.9
Children 6 to 17 years old	11.7	5.3	1.6	1.2
Children 3 to 5 years old	5.0	1.6	0.6	0.3
Children under 3 years old	8.1	1.9	0.7	0.3

*Age 16 and over.

Elizabeth Waldman, "Marital and Family Characteristics of Workers, March 1967," *Monthly Labor Review*, December 1968, Table F.

in the afternoon. Those who object to the working mother lament the return of the child to an empty house. On the other hand, it must be recognized that a large proportion of working mothers have part-time jobs or intermittent employment and a good many of them are at home when the children return from school. But a case can even be made that the lack of a welcoming mother does not seriously deprive children. The former head of the Children's Bureau, Katherine Brownell Oettinger, puts the matter this way in *Work in the Lives of Married Women:*

> More and more of us are coming to believe it is not the amount of time spent with the child but what happens during that time that really matters, so far as parent-child relations are concerned. Children who have learned to count on mother being home to greet them after school and hear what happened may feel rejected if suddenly mother is not at home. Children whose companions have mothers waiting to greet them may also feel sad if they come home to an empty house. But children for whom adequate daytime provisions are made, and who are not geared to the expectation of a waiting mother at 3:00 p.m. may adjust to being greeted and listened to at five-thirty or six o'clock. The important thing is the quality of the greeting and listening, not whether it happens two hours earlier or later. . . .[4]

Next we come to the preschoolers between the ages of 3 and 5. Children in this age group don't quite need the constant attention that infants require. In many cases they are eligible for nursery school. There are 5½ million mothers of children aged 3 to 5 years. Only 2 million of these mothers worked; the others stayed at home. About half of the separated or divorced women were in the labor market as compared with only one-third of the wives. The great majority of the divorcees and separatees probably had to work by any objective standards. This judgment would probably also apply to most of the wives who worked.

Finally, we come to the mothers with children under 3 years of age. There are nearly 9 million such mothers, but only a little over 2 million were in the labor force. This is the age when children are most in need of a mother's care. It is quite clear that mothers of babies stay home. The great majority of those who go out to work do so out of economic necessity.

Who cares for the preschool youngsters whose parents both work? A report prepared by several University of Michigan professors in 1962 notes that about one-eighth of the families have a relative in the household who provides child care—generally an older brother or sister or a grandparent. In another one-sixth the children are placed in a nursery or a play school. The majority are cared for by a paid baby-sitter or by a relative who does not reside with the family. About half these spending units with children under 6 but with all adults working did not pay anything for child care.[5]

Why do they work?

It seems clear that at the lower income levels women work primarily for the money. About two-fifths of the men who averaged about $2,500 a year had working wives. These women averaged $1,900 a year. In other words, by working, these women could get their family incomes up to about $4,400 a year, which is above the poverty line if they had no more than three children. Similarly, nearly half of the men who earned $5,500 a year had working wives who averaged $2,700. These women added about 50 percent to their family income and brought the total above the $8,000 mark. The reason for the working wife seems rather clear at these lower income levels. It is not quite so easy to understand why one-quarter of the men who earn $20,000 a year have working wives. These women add only an average of $3,200 before taxes to the family income. The amount is considerably less on an after-tax basis.

TABLE XII-6

**Median Earnings of Wives,
by Earnings of Husbands: 1968**

Earnings of husband	Median earnings of wife	Ratio of wife's earnings to husband's
$1 to $999	$2,200	432%
$1,000 to $1,999	1,900	128
$2,000 to $2,999	1,900	74
$3,000 to $3,999	2,400	69
$4,000 to $4,999	2,700	59
$5,000 to $5,999	2,700	50
$6,000 to $6,999	3,000	46
$7,000 to $7,999	3,100	42
$8,000 to $9,999	3,000	34
$10,000 to $14,999	3,000	23
$15,000 to $24,999	3,200	17
$25,000 and over	3,900	11

U.S. Bureau of the Census.

Table XII-7 shows that about one-third of the wives of high-paid men have no children under 18 at home. It may be presumed that many of these women have limited household responsibilities. They are free to pursue a career or to find some other meaningful way to fill their time. Some develop hobbies, others work for charities, and still others work for money even though they may not need it. Another 17 percent of the women who have only one child under 18 at home may not be in too different a position from those women without children under 18 at home, if that child is in high school or college. This table also calls attention to the fact that about one-sixth of the high-paid men have one or more children away at college. Even a man who earns as much as $25,000 a year could use the financial help of a working wife if he is putting one or more children through a private college. Costs at these schools as high as $4,000 per year are not uncommon for tuition, room, and board. Clothes, trips home, and miscellaneous expenses bring the total even higher. It may be presumed, therefore, that many of the mothers in higher income families are willing to help put their sons and daughters through college.

The wives of high-paid men earn somewhat more than other wives, but the differences are not striking. In general, they make about $500 more per year than the wives of men earning between $7,000 and $15,000 a year. The biggest difference is among those with no children under 18. The wives of the high-paid men in this group earned $5,000 in 1967 as compared with an average of $4,300 for the wives of men with earnings between $7,000 and $15,000 a year. Presumably the reason for the difference is that the wives of the high-paid men are better educated than the other women and are more qualified for higher paid work. They may also have more contacts and the chance to be more selective in the jobs they take. In contrast, the earnings of women with two or more children at home did not vary according to the earnings of the husband. The wives in each of the earnings groups shown averaged around $2,700. The main reason for the lack of variation within this group is that a large proportion of these women were probably doing only part-time work. It is difficult to understand, on purely economic grounds, why a woman with two children under 18 would work if her husband made over $15,000 a year and all she made was $2,800. One can only surmise that these women were working mostly to get away from the house, or that they work just a few hours a day or a few months of the year. Surely after taxes, lunches, carfare, and other occupational expenses they were adding little to the family coffers.

Table XII-8 shows that career development may be an important reason why many of the wives of high-paid men work. Only one-fifth of the wives of men earning between $7,000 and $10,000 a year were in professional jobs. This proportion rose to nearly one-third for men in the next higher income bracket and it was nearly one-half for the high-paid men. Evidently a large proportion of the wives of high-paid men were trained for professional work. They quit working to raise a family and then return to the labor market to resume their careers or to develop new careers. But this accounts for only half of the working wives of high-paid men. Most of the others appear to be working at fairly routine clerical and sales jobs.

TABLE XII-7

**Working Status of Wives,
by Earnings of Husband: March 1968**

	Earnings of husband		
	$7,000 to $9,999	$10,000 to $14,999	$15,000 and over
Number of wives (millions)	10.9	5.9	2.6
Percent	100%	100%	100%
No children under 18	32	29	32
1 child under 18	20	19	17
2 or more children under 18	48	52	50
Percentage of wives in labor force:			
Total	39%	31%	23%
No children under 18	48	41	30
1 child under 18	40	34	27
2 or more children under 18	34	25	17
Median earnings of wives:			
Total	$3,400	$3,500	$4,000
No children under 18	4,200	4,400	5,000
1 child under 18	3,400	3,200	3,800
2 or more children under 18	2,600	2,700	2,800

U. S. Bureau of the Census.

TABLE XII-8

Occupations of Wives, by Earnings of Husband: March 1968

	Earnings of husband		
Occupation of wife	$7,000 to $9,999	$10,000 to $14,999	$15,000 and over
Professional or managerial	21%	31%	47%
Clerical or sales	48	49	44
Craftsmen or operatives	16	9	4
Service workers	15	11	5
Other	1	1	*

*Less than 0.5 percent.

U.S. Bureau of the Census.

XIII

A Glance into the Crystal Ball

Forecasters have never been liked. In ancient Rome the Emperor Constantius made a law forbidding "anyone to consult a soothsayer, a mathematician or a forecaster. . . . May curiosity to foretell the future be silenced forever." He prescribed the penalty of death for forecasting, but there is no evidence that even so severe a punishment could stop the practice.

In his *Inferno,* Dante reserved the Eighth Circle of Hell for forecasters, diviners, augurers, and sorcerers because they endeavored to foretell the future, which belongs to God alone. They were condemned to Hell, with their heads twisted completely around so that they were unable to see where they were going. Perhaps that is the reason forecasters to this day continue to have their heads screwed on backward. It is only by looking at the past that they can foretell the future.

What will be the level of income in 1985 and how will income be distributed among various segments of the population? No one really can answer these questions, of course, but if we assume that the long-run trends of the past continue into the future, it is possible to make some fairly reasonable guesses. In this chapter an attempt will be made to project income distribution into the future and, more importantly, to relate these findings to the twin problems of overpopulation and pollution. Concern about pollution in the United States today has led many people to believe that the chief way to fight pollution is by reducing the population growth rate to zero. At the heart of this argument is the assumption that the main cause of pollution is population growth: the fewer

234

the people, the less the pollution. An attempt will be made here to show that affluence is as much a danger to man's environment as population growth. There is a distinct danger that the growth in our private wealth will be matched only by our growing discomfort—unless we decide to spend our money more wisely in the future. The argument is presented in some detail in the pages that follow. Appendix C presents the underlying statistical support for the conclusions that are reached. This appendix contains projections to 1985 of births, deaths, marriages, households, families, income distribution by age, expenditure patterns, and a variety of other data that will interest those who enjoy trying to foresee the future. Although we start with a discussion of population problems, attention is soon directed to income distribution and the role it might play as both a creator of waste and a financial resource to improve comfort and the quality of life.

It is important to recognize at the outset that the conclusions presented here relate to the United States only and not to the rest of the world, particularly the underdeveloped part of it. Our fate may be tied to what happens in the rest of the world. We do, however, have population problems that are independent of the world problem. We can influence what the people do in Arkansas and Alabama; we have little, if any, influence over what the people do in Algeria and Afghanistan. We elect our own representatives who make our policies; we have no such control in foreign lands. We can and do supply other nations with financial and technical aid to help them control their population growth. In the end, however, we can serve only as interested bystanders in all countries except our own.

There are some who argue that we must reduce our population growth to zero to set an example for others. Paul Ehrlich is one such advocate. In *The Population Bomb* he states, "Our first step must be to immediately establish and advertise drastic policies designed to bring our own population size under control." This move would accomplish two things in his estimation: "It improves our chances of obtaining the kind of country and society we all want and it sets an example for the world."[1] Utter nonsense. It is time we stopped setting examples for others. We are not that virtuous or wise. Like any true believer, Mr. Ehrlich sees the light not only for himself but for the entire world and he is prepared to take drastic action on the basis of these beliefs. Here, for example, is how he would help India solve its population problem: "While we are working toward setting up a world program of the general sort outlined above, the United States could take effective unilateral action in many cases. . . . When [Chandrasekhar] suggested sterilizing all Indian males with three or more children, we should have applied pressure on the Indian government to go ahead with the plan. We should have volunteered logistic support in the form of helicopters, vehicles and surgical instruments. We should have sent doctors to aid in the program by setting up centers for training para-medical personnel to do vasectomies. Coercion? Perhaps, but coercion in a good cause."[2] Where have we heard that before?

To avoid the danger of misunderstanding, we might agree at the outset that it would be desirable for our population growth to slow down. It would be particularly advantageous to reduce the supply of unwanted children. Such children often become problems to themselves and to society. At some point we will undoubtedly have to stop growing. The only real questions are when, and should we be greatly concerned about that problem now.

The threat of overpopulation looms large in many American minds today. Articles appear almost daily in the press warning of the dire fate that awaits us unless we control our fertility. Some have even turned to "zero growth" as a panacea for many of our domestic ills. The fact is that many of our problems involving crime, pollution, and traffic jams may be aggravated by population growth, but neither their cause nor their solution is necessarily related to a change in the size of the population.

Before going any further, we might first examine the evidence regarding our future population. How much are we likely to grow by 1985 and what will be the distribution of the population by age, income, and other important characteristics? On the basis of this evidence, we might then try to develop some conclusions regarding the relative roles of population growth and affluence as contributors to public discomfort.

Projected population growth: 1970-1985

In 1967 the Bureau of the Census prepared four series of population projections which assumed that completed fertility would range from 3.35 children per woman (Series A) to 2.45 children (Series D). Mortality was assumed to decline slightly and net migration was assumed to continue at the 1970 level of about 400,000 per year.

Recent trends in fertility suggest that the higher figure is no longer a reasonable possibility for 1985. In 1970 the level of fertility is at Series D. Between 1940 and 1957, average age at marriage declined, the proportion of women who were married increased, intervals between births became shorter, and fertility rose sharply, especially during the postwar years. As a result, population growth between 1947 and 1957 averaged 1.7 percent per year, which is a very high rate for an industrial nation to sustain. Between 1957 and 1970, age at marriage and the spacing of births have increased slightly and fertility has dropped sharply. As a result, the growth rate dropped to 1.1 percent.

One of the main reasons for the drop in fertility in recent years is the fact that more young women are now having fewer children than women in the same age groups had during the 1950's. Since most of these women still profess a desire to have an average of three children, it is possible that they are merely postponing childbirth, just as their mothers accelerated their fertility immediately after World War II and then stopped having children relatively early in life. Many demographers, however, believe that this postponement will result in a reduction of completed fertility for these women. This uncertainty is one of the factors that complicates the problem of forecasting the population fifteen years hence. Another factor, which is even more important, is that many of the women who will begin to have children fifteen years from now are still playing with dolls. There is no way of knowing how many children they will decide to have; but they are likely to have better control over the number of children they bear than their mothers.

Since fertility in 1970 is at the Series D level and the outlook for the future is in the direction of still further reduction in fertility, it is likely that the population will be between 240 million and 250 million in 1985, representing an increase of 35 million to 45 million people over the 1970 level. The number of births should run between 4 million and 5 million per year and the rate of population increase should be between 1.0 and 1.5 percent per year. The growth rate will start at relatively low levels in the early seventies and rise for the next decade because the proportion of women in the childbearing ages will increase. In making this "prediction" we must bear in mind that population forecasters have a notorious record for inaccuracy. Even a brilliant man like J. M. Keynes, the father of modern economics, made the mistake of proclaiming in 1937: "We know much more securely than we know almost any other social or economic factor relating to the future that, in the place of the steady and indeed steeply rising level of population which we have experienced for a number of decades, we shall be faced in a very short time with a stationary or a declining level."[3] Within a decade, Keynes proved to be not only wrong but badly wrong. With the end of World War II most countries of the world embarked on an unparalleled increase in population growth.

Expected changes in age composition and household formation: 1970-1985

The only uncertainty about the age structure of the population in 1985 concerns the number and distribution of persons who will be under 15 at that time. Everyone else is now alive, and charting the flow of these people through the age structure is just a matter of simple arithmetic. The first of the postwar babies will be approaching his fortieth birthday in 1985, and the last of the great wave of births that began to subside in 1961 will be approaching 25. There will, therefore, be a very dramatic rise in the number of younger adults during this period. As a matter of fact, one-third of the expected population increase will be in the 25- to 34-year age group and an additional sixth will be in the 35- to 44-year group. Altogether, we might expect an additional 27 million people—more than half of the total expected increase—who will be in their twenties, thirties, and early forties. On the other hand, there will be virtually no change in the number who will be 45 to 64 years old in 1985 because this age group was born between 1921 and 1940, when the birthrate was low and the annual number of births was declining. Most of the remaining 20 million who are expected to be added to the population by 1985 will be preschoolers (9 million), school-age children 5 to 15 years old (5 million), and persons over 65 (5 million).

Perhaps the most significant fact about the expected change in age composition is the very sharp increase in the number of persons in their twenties and early thirties. Since this is the age at which most marriages take place, it is likely that between 1970 and 1985 the annual number of marriages will be relatively high. There is also likely to be a fairly rapid rate of household formation and also relatively large numbers of births. The 1970 level of about 2 million marriages annually is expected to rise gradually to a peak of about 2½ million by 1985. This rise in the number of marriages will increase the demand for housing. We will need about 2 million new dwelling units per year to accommodate the new families that will be formed and to replace the units that are wearing out. Any appreciable increase in housing standards or an increase in the tendency for youngsters to move out on their own at an early age would increase the demand for housing even more. Since the number of younger households will be rising rapidly between 1970 and 1985, it is likely that much of the demand will be for apartments rather than for private homes because that is the kind of housing newlyweds generally prefer. We can already see tendencies in this direction in many suburban areas. As a result of the rapid rise in land values and the increase in the cost of constructing one-family homes, many new high-rise apartment buildings are springing up just outside the city limits. These apartments are generally close to nearby shopping areas and public transportation facilities. If this trend should continue it could result in a radical change in present land use and life-styles.

The expected trends in age distribution are also likely to have an important impact on future school enrollments. The number of elementary school pupils will probably drop slightly during the next few years, return to its present level by 1980, and then rise somewhat by 1985. High school enrollment is expected to change relatively little before 1985. This breathing spell should make it possible to divert some of the funds that were going for classroom construction to much-needed improvements and experimentation in education, particularly in slum areas. The number of college students, however, is expected to rise by over 50 percent from its present level of 7½ million to about 11½ million in 1985. About half of the expected rise in college enrollment is due to population increase, and an equal amount to a rise in the proportion of young people attending college. Breakthroughs are badly needed in our ability to handle the large number of young people who are entering college today and are often inadequately prepared for higher education. This problem may get worse in the future as larger proportions of graduating classes seek admission to colleges and universities.

The rapid growth in the number of young adults between 20 and 34 years of age and the lack of growth in the 45- to 64-year age group may have particularly significant implications for the structure of executive management and political leadership in the future. For one thing, it may mean that there will be a shortage of experienced older men available for positions of leadership in politics, industrial management, and government. Those who will be available will be much in demand and there may be some pressure for them to postpone retirement. At the same time, a large reservoir of young, well-educated men with great expectations will be available to fill these jobs. As a result, by 1985 we might expect to see more young leaders in politics, private industry, and the upper echelons of government service than is the case today.

The shortage of mature men for positions of leadership may also provide greater opportunities for women. Although a very large proportion of married women now work, relatively few attain responsible positions. Many are not trained for such jobs and others with training have family responsibilities which prevent them from capitalizing fully on that training. Young women coming into the labor force today, however, will be far better trained, on the average, than their mothers were and they will have much better control over the number and spacing of their children. Moreover, the crucial baby-sitting problem may be eased for many with the advent of Head Start programs, day-care centers, and general acceptance of the idea that many 3- and 4-year-olds are better off in school than they are at home. As a result of these developments it may be possible for more young women to pursue their careers almost as seriously as men and to be available for responsible jobs when they are needed.

Expected changes in income distribution: 1970-1985

Barring any major catastrophe, American families will have far higher incomes in 1985 than they have today. A reasonable indication of just how much richer we will be is provided by the projected income distribution shown in Table XIII-1. This distribution is based on the assumption that during the years ahead the Lorenz Curve (that is, the cumulative percentage distribution of families and of income) will be constant for each age group and that the level of income will continue to rise at the same rate as it has risen during recent years. Overall, this growth rate has been a little over 3 percent per year. The rate was somewhat higher for the younger age groups and lower for the older ones. The figures are all in dollars of 1968 purchasing power and represent amounts before the deduction of taxes. The assumption is that taxes are just one of the ways in which we spend our money.

TABLE XIII-1

Distribution of Families and Unrelated Individuals and Aggregate Income, by Income Level: 1968 and 1985

Income levels*	Families		Families and individuals	
	1968	1985	1968	1985
Number (millions)	50.5	66.7	64.3	85.9
Percent	100%	100%	100%	100%
Under $3,000	10	4	19	9
$3,000 to $4,999	12	6	14	8
$5,000 to $9,999	38	18	34	19
$10,000 to $14,999	25	23	21	21
$15,000 to $24,999	12	33	10	29
$25,000 and over	3	16	2	15
Aggregate income (billions)	$486	$1,074	$544	$1,277
Percent	100%	100%	100%	100%
Under $3,000	2	1	4	1
$3,000 to $4,999	5	1	6	2
$5,000 to $9,999	29	8	30	9
$10,000 to $14,999	31	18	30	17
$15,000 to $24,999	23	37	21	35
$25,000 and over	10	35	9	36
Mean income	$9,600	$16,100	$8,500	$14,900
Median income	$8,600	$14,700	$7,400	$13,500

Note: Sums of tabulated figures in this chapter may not equal totals because of rounding.

*In 1968 dollars.

Herman P. Miller, "Tomorrow's Consumer," paper prepared for National Industrial Conference Board, Conference on the Consumer Market, New York, March 24, 1970.

On the basis of these assumptions, real incomes will double by 1985. In 1968, family money incomes totaled less than $500 billion. This aggregate is expected to exceed $1 trillion by 1985. Median family

Distribution of Aggregate Income Among Families and Unrelated Individuals by Age of Head and Income Level: 1968 and 1985*

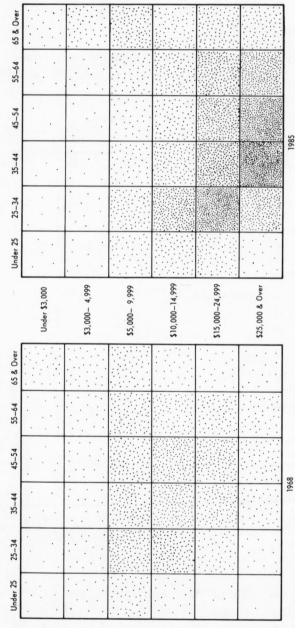

*Each dot represents $300,000 of family money income, in 1968 dollars.

See Table XIII-1 for source.

income is expected to rise from $8,600 today to $14,700 in 1985, measured in dollars of constant purchasing power. In 1968, about one-third of total income was received by families with incomes over $15,000. By 1985 families at this income level will receive nearly three-fourths of the aggregate income. Moreover, because of the combined impact of both income and population growth, the number of dollars (in constant purchasing power) at this upper income level will be about five times as great as today.

The configuration of purchasing power in 1968 and in 1985 in terms of age groups and income levels is shown in the accompanying chart, where each dot represents $300 million of family money income in 1968 dollars. Because of the expected growth in income there are more than twice as many dots in the chart for 1985 as for 1968. This chart shows very clearly that most of the added purchasing power will occur in the 25- to 44-year age group and among the higher income groups. In 1968 about 42 percent of all the purchasing power was in the 25- to 44-year age category. In 1985 this age group will account for about half of the purchasing power.

Conclusions

1. Today our population is growing at the rate of 1.1 percent (roughly 2½ million) per year, and it has been growing at that rate for nearly a decade. According to the judgment of many eminent demographers, in the absence of a major disaster or drastic changes in social and economic conditions, this rate may rise during the seventies and early eighties as the proportion of women in the childbearing years increases, but it should then recede to its present level or perhaps even go below it. A slower rate of growth would be desirable. It would make it easier to cope with the many domestic problems we now have, which are caused by a variety of factors in addition to population growth. At the same time, however, the expected rate of population growth during the coming years should not present insurmountable problems. We have had far higher growth rates in the past with no demonstrable harmful effects.

We must also remember that a stationary population will have problems of its own which may be as serious as those we face today with moderate growth. It was only a little over thirty years ago that the specter of economic stagnation haunted many industrialized Western countries and caused a brilliant economist like Keynes to write about the economic consequences of a declining population. Before embracing the concept of a stationary population too warmly, we had better face up to the fact that such a population would be much older than the present one. It would have an equal number of people under 15 and over 60, and the average age would be 37 as compared with 30 at present. An affluent society with a stationary population would probably be more resistant to change than our present society, because wealth and conservatism tend to increase with age. If the present establishment seems intolerable to the youth of America, imagine how it might be under a stationary population, where rich old men would be even more likely to be running things.

2. We do have serious population problems today and they are likely to intensify in the near future. These problems relate to the geographic distribution and to the values of our people rather than to their numbers and rates of growth. The continued loss of population in the central cities of most large metropolitan areas is making it extremely difficult to provide adequate services for those who continue to live there. The growing concentration of affluent whites in the suburbs and of Negroes in the central cities has increased the polarization of our society. The increase in residential segregation within cities and the deterioration of conditions in our worst slums tend to increase racial tensions. Although one-half of our counties have lost population during the past decade, the crowded metropolitan areas keep gaining people, thereby placing a further strain on the resources in those places. These are some of the population problems that are threatening to tear us apart as a society.

The recent report of the National Commission on the Causes and Prevention of Violence, issued in November 1969, contains a description of the American city of the future which is both realistic and terrifying. The report notes that unless effective action is taken soon to improve conditions in our cities, within a few years

> central business districts . . . will be largely deserted except for police patrols during night-time hours. High-rise apartment buildings and residential compounds protected by private guards and security devices will be fortified cells . . . ownership of guns will be almost universal in the suburbs, homes will be fortified by an array of devices from window grills to electronic surveillance equipment, armed citizen volunteers in cars will supplement inadequate police

patrols in neighborhoods closer to the central city . . . private automobiles, taxicabs and commercial vehicles will be routinely equipped with unbreakable glass, light armor and other security features . . . streets and residential neighborhoods in the central cities will be places of terror with widespread crime, perhaps entirely out of police control during night-time hours."[4]

In light of this prospect, it seems unreasonable to make no distinction between population problems associated with growth and those associated with distribution. There is no question that we can manage very well between now and 1985 with a 1 percent rate of growth in population. There is some question whether we can survive as a free society if the tensions we have experienced during the past few years continue or multiply.

3. There is some connection between pollution, high crime rates, transportation problems, and other social ills and the rate of population growth. These problems, however, are more directly related to other factors, such as the geographic distribution of people, the customs and morals of the people, the underlying social and economic conditions, and the intensity of the effort that is made to cope directly with our social maladies. No one really knows what share of the trouble is due to population growth and what share to these other factors. The latter are probably more important. Professor Ansley Coale, in his presidential address to the Population Association of America, pointed out in 1968 that Sydney, Australia, has traffic jams and pollution even though it is situated in a country which is nearly as large as the United States but has only 12 million people.[5] Pollution, traffic jams, delinquency, and crime are no worse in France, England, and Holland than in the United States, although population densities in those countries are between five and thirty times as great as here. It seems that trying to deal with the social problems we now have by persuading women not to have babies is like treating cancer with a sedative. It may relieve the pain, but it won't make the problem go away. If we attack our social ills directly during the seventies the way we attacked outer space during the sixties, we may begin to see results. One big difference, of course, is that it cost only $5 billion per year to get to the moon whereas it would cost at least $20 billion per year to clean up some of the mess we have created.

4. If real incomes grow during the near future at the same rate as during the recent past—and many eminent economists think they will— we will have resources which may be used either to intensify or to alleviate many of the problems associated with population distribution. The

richer we get the more we increase our demands for privacy, more spacious living quarters, recreational facilities, automobiles, roads, and other material goods. Jean Mayer has pointed out that "rich people occupy much more space, consume more of each natural resource, disturb the ecology more, and create more land, air, water, chemical, thermal, and radioactive pollution than poor people."[6] From this he concludes that it is "more urgent to control the numbers of the rich than it is to control the numbers of the poor."[7] A better solution would be for the rich to control their spending better than they do and for the poor to control their fertility better than they do. Unless we learn to spend our money in less destructive ways, it is likely that the growth in our affluence will exacerbate many of the problems we now have.

APPENDIX A

The Validity of
Income Statistics

Most of the income figures in this book come from either the decennial census or the annual sample surveys of income conducted by the Bureau of the Census. In order to appraise these figures, it is necessary to understand how censuses and sample surveys are conducted.

The principal source of population data in the United States is the Decennial Census of Population, a house-to-house enumeration made every ten years. The first census was taken in 1790 in accordance with a constitutional provision for a population count every decade. The primary purpose of the Census of Population, as set forth in the Constitution, is to provide a basis for the apportionment of members of the House of Representatives among the several states. It was very soon recognized that much more information than a simple count of persons by age and sex was needed and that it could be obtained by enumerators while they were in the household. So additional questions were added to the census schedule very early in our history.

In 1940 income questions were asked in response to demands for data that might throw light on the causes and impact of the depression of the thirties. Despite the long experience with the collection of financial data, some objections were anticipated. For this reason, the questions were kept simple. Each person was asked to report only the amount of wages or salaries received during 1939 and whether he received $50 or more of nonwage income. Specific questions about the amount of nonwage income received were not asked for fear of antagonizing some respondents. To further minimize resistance, respondents were not asked to report the exact amount of wage income if it was above $5,000, and confidential forms were provided for those respondents who did not wish to report their information to local enumerators (who might also be neighbors).

The cooperation of the public was excellent. Only 2 percent of the wage and salary workers failed to report their income and only 200,000 people bothered to use the confidential forms (15 million forms had been printed). An appraisal of these data that was published by the National Bureau of Economic Research stated that although "the amount of wages and salaries was somewhat underreported ... the 1939 statistics were reasonably accurate and they provided a wealth of data on income."[1]

Following the success of the 1940 census and the widespread use made of the income data that were collected, there were strong demands for the inclusion of income questions in the 1950 census. These demands came from many different sources: business groups, labor unions, government agencies, research organizations, universities, and many others. The demand this time was for total income and not just wages, partly because the wage data were unduly restrictive, but also because it had been demonstrated in numerous sample surveys that respondents would willingly provide detailed information on sources of income.

Income questions included in the 1950 census were quite different from those used in 1940. In the first place, the scope was expanded to include all types of income and not just wages and salaries. A second change involved the movement of the income questions from a 100 percent basis to a 20 percent sample. Every fifth line on the 1950 census questionnaire was marked "sample line." The person enumerated on that line was asked a special set of sample questions. In the case of income he was asked to report the amount received during 1949 from wages and salaries, self-employment, and income other than earnings. If the sample person was a family head, the same questions were repeated for other family members as a group. The enumerator had no control in the selection of the "sample lines" because persons had to be listed in a prescribed order on the census questionnaire.

The shift in the income questions to a sample basis did not represent a downgrading in the importance of this item nor did it reduce the quality of the statistics. On the contrary, the income questions were considered very important and it was felt that the shift to a sample might improve the accuracy of the data because the money saved by reducing the cost of enumeration could be used to provide better training for the enumerators. The reasoning behind the change of the income questions to a sample basis in 1950 has been explained as follows: "The income questions were moved from 100 percent to 20 percent coverage . . . as a part of the historical development of census taking. The uses of the statistics for these items did not require 100 percent enumeration, and money and time were saved by putting the items on a sample basis. The sample was still a very large one compared to those used to collect annual data and it provided usable income information for relatively small areas."[2]

Public cooperation in the 1950 census was, once again, very good. Complete income information was obtained from 93 percent of the persons of whom the questions were asked. A special study that was made of nonrespondents showed that their incomes did not differ appreciably from those incomes reported.[3]

In 1960 the sample was expanded to 25 percent. The same income questions were used as in 1950, but there were some important changes in procedures. In the first place, the sample was changed to a household basis instead of a line basis. This change had important implications for the quality of the income data. It meant that in 1960 every fourth household, selected at random, was in the sample and income questions were asked individually for each member of the household. In 1950 every fifth *person* was in the sample, and if he was a household head income questions were asked for him and for all his relatives in the household *as a group*. The use of separate income questions for each family member in 1960 considerably improved the quality of the family income statistics.

Another important change introduced in 1960 was the advance distribution of forms and the use of self-enumeration. The 1960 census was the first in which self-enumeration was used. A questionnaire, entitled "Advance Census Report," was mailed to every household in the country. This questionnaire contained the complete-count (100 percent) information collected in the census: name, address, age, sex, color, marital status, and household relationship. The instructions on the ACR requested that one or more members enter on the form the answers to all questions for each person in the household. The enumerator was instructed to correct omissions and obviously wrong entries by asking the necessary questions. In sparsely populated areas (with 65 percent of the

THE VALIDITY OF INCOME STATISTICS

land area and 18 percent of the population), the enumerator collected the complete-count information and also asked the sample questions at the time of his visit. In the rest of the United States, where most of the population lives, the enumerator collected the complete-count information and also left with each sample household a Household Questionnaire, containing the sample questions to be answered. Income was one of these sample items. The respondents were requested to complete these questionnaires and mail them to the local census offices. Where this was not done, or where the schedules were incomplete, follow-up visits were made to collect the missing information.

The Current Population Survey

The income data from the decennial censuses are primarily designed to provide figures for geographic areas like cities, towns, and census tracts or for small groups in the population for which data cannot be obtained from other sources. For example, if you wanted to know how much carpenters make a year in Pittsburgh or how many elderly couples with incomes under $1,000 were living in substandard housing in Chicago, you almost certainly would have to take a census or a very large sample. Although sampling was used to collect the census income data, the samples were very large and they provide figures that vary only slightly from the information that would be obtained from a complete count. Of course, even a 25 percent sample would be too small to produce reliable figures for individual city blocks or for other very small areas, but for most purposes it is more than adequate.

Conducting a census is a very expensive undertaking and it is done only once every ten years. Between censuses there is need for nationwide information to show major trends and to help formulate national policy. For example, we might want to know each year how many elderly couples in the country as a whole live in substandard housing, or we might want to know how the composition of the bottom or top income groups has changed. This type of information does not require a census. It can be obtained from a relatively small sample survey. That is the function of the Current Population Survey (CPS) conducted by the Bureau of the Census. The size and design of CPS have been changed several times during the twenty years it has been in operation. The following is a description of the survey in mid-1963.

CPS is a nationwide survey, covering about 50,000 interviewed households widely distributed throughout the fifty states and the District of Columbia. It provides monthly data on employment and unemployment. Once each year, in March, information on annual income is also collected.

The CPS is a scientifically designed, carefully controlled sample. A complete description of the procedures used to design the sample and insure the accuracy of the results appears in the Census Bureau reports *The Current Population Survey: A Report on Methodology*, Technical Paper No. 7; and *Concepts and Methods Used in Manpower Statistics from the Current Population Survey*, June 1967, Series P-23, No. 22.

The Washington office staff directly concerned with CPS is relatively small, consisting of about ten statisticians and a clerical force of about fifteen people; others are added at peak periods each month to meet a rapid time schedule. The statisticians are assisted by specialists from other parts of the Census Bureau and from other federal agencies. They are responsible for the definitions used, the preparation of questionnaires and instructions, determination of sample design and estimation techniques, the planning of processing and tabulation procedures, and the review and analysis of the results.

The field work is conducted through twelve regional offices. Each office is directed by a regional supervisor who has several assistants. They supervise a total of about 950 part-time enumerators and are responsible for their selection and training, review of their work each month, and periodic field checks and direct observation. Detailed instructions are provided by the Washington staff on selection of sample areas, training procedures, and review of work. The enumerators are mostly women who work part time. All of them must pass written tests of their ability to read maps and to absorb written instructions.

The heart of CPS is, of course, the sample. If that is wrong, nothing else can be right except by chance. The number of areas covered and the number of interviews conducted in each area depends primarily on the size of the sampling error that can be tolerated and the total amount of money available for the survey. One of the key determinants of the nature and design of the CPS sample is the fact that Congress authorizes an annual budget of about $4.5 million for the survey. The second major determinant is the fact that the survey is intended to measure an unemployment level of 2,500,000 with a standard error of 75,000. This means that the sample must be designed in such a way that when unemployment is 2,500,000 the chances should be nineteen out of twenty that a full census would not produce results outside of the range 2,350,000 and 2,650,000, i.e., within a band of two standard errors above and below the figure provided by the sample. Given the cost and the desired level of reliability, it was determined that about 50,000 households could be interviewed in 449 primary sampling units.

The actual mechanics for the selection of the sample are described in the Census Bureau's Technical Paper No. 7. The basic procedure involves the grouping of the 3,103 counties and independent cities of the United States into about 1,900 primary sampling units (PSU) consisting usually of a county or a group of contiguous counties. The 107 largest standard metropolitan statistical areas are automatically included in the sample as are five other special cases. All of the other PSU's are classified into 245 groups, and one or two PSU's are selected in a random manner to represent each group.

The selection of individual households within each PSU for enumeration each month is made in the following way. The PSU is divided into enumeration districts, each containing about 800 people. (These same enumeration districts were assignments for individual enumerators in the 1960 census.) A sample of enumeration districts is then selected with probability proportionate to its population size in 1960. The selected districts are then divided into segments or clusters which contain an average of about six dwelling units or other living quarters. For the nation as a whole, about 6,000 segments are in the sample in any given month. The enumerators visit these segments and interview the people living there.

Reliability of the figures—
sampling error

Since the income figures collected by the Bureau of the Census are based on samples, they differ somewhat from the figures that would have been obtained from a complete census using the same questionnaires, instructions, and enumerators. The measure of the variation due to sampling is called the standard error. It shows the variations that occur *by chance* because a sample rather than the entire population is used. Table A-1 shows the standard errors for selected characteristics

based on the 25 percent sample used in the 1960 census and the Current
Population Survey. The chances are two out of three that an estimate

TABLE A-1

Standard Error of Median Income,
for Census and Current Population Survey

	1960 census		March 1960 CPS	
	Median income	Standard error	Median income	Standard error
Families				
Overall	$5,660	$0	$5,417	$38
White	5,893	0	5,643	24
Nonwhite	3,161	0	2,917	95
Unattached individuals				
Overall	1,596	0	1,556	55
White	1,654	0	1,663	70
Nonwhite	1,217	0	1,075	116
Male professional workers				
United States	6,619	0	6,725	122
Chicago Metropolitan Area	7,385	40	–	–
Male managerial workers				
United States	6,664	0	6,315	130
Chicago Metropolitan Area	8,474	58	–	–
Male nonfarm laborers				
United States	2,948	0	3,150	107
Chicago Metropolitan Area	4,259	65	–	–
Female professional workers				
United States	3,625	0	3,603	127
Chicago Metropolitan Area	4,153	85	–	–

Computed from figures shown in *U.S. Census of Population: 1960, General
Social and Economic Characteristics, United States Summary*; and *Current Population Reports—Consumer Income*, Series P-60, No. 35.

from the sample would differ from a complete census figure by less than the standard error.

As you can see from the figures in the table, the sampling variability of the 1960 census figures is so small that it can be ignored for large areas or for major groups. This is because of the very large size of the sample. The CPS figures are subject to much wider sampling variations because this is a sample of 1 in about 1,500 as compared with 1 in 4 used in the census. But even the variations for CPS are relatively small for those characteristics that are based on a large number of persons or families. For example, the average (median) income of all families in the March 1960 CPS was $5,417. The standard error of this estimate was only $38. This means that, had a complete census been taken using the questionnaire, training, and enumerators used in CPS, the chances are two out of three that the median would have been within the range $5,379–$5,455. For other characteristics, like the median income for nonwhite individuals, the relative sampling error is considerably larger; but even here it is small enough to provide usable figures for many characteristics at the national level.

Errors in response and nonreporting are potentially more serious than sampling errors. In fact, these are the kinds of errors most people have in mind when they speak of the shortcomings of census income data. They are discussed in some detail below.

Accuracy of the figures

Sampling errors in census income statistics can virtually be ignored when major national totals are being considered. The same generalization cannot be made with respect to the *accuracy* of the figures, because major errors can and do arise from nonresponse and poor reporting. Unlike sampling errors, which are computed according to standard and generally accepted statistical procedures, there are no such procedures for measuring the accuracy of a survey. Evaluations must be prepared separately for each type of statistic, and their acceptance depends largely on judgments regarding the reliability of the figures used as benchmarks.

One of the outstanding innovations introduced in the 1950 Census of Population and Housing was an intensive effort to evaluate the statistics that were collected. A carefully designed Reinterview Survey was conducted, record checks were made, and numerous other studies were undertaken for the purpose of measuring the quality of the data and discovering methods of improving future censuses and household surveys. These studies led to major changes in the methods used in the 1960 censuses and there is general agreement that for most subjects, including income, the 1960 data are more accurate than those collected ten years earlier. The evaluation effort, started in 1950, was intensified in 1960. The following are brief descriptions of the major sources of data that were used to evaluate the income statistics.

a. *Office of Business Economics (OBE) estimates.* The Office of Business Economics of the Department of Commerce prepares annual estimates of gross national product, national income, and other related measures that comprise the national income accounts. Primary emphasis in this series is placed on aggregates, which have been published annually since the early forties and are generally ranked among the most important and most accurate of all statistical series prepared by the federal government.

Most projects in the census evaluation program in 1950 and 1960 required the collection of additional data with which the original census results could be compared or which would in other ways throw light on possible biases or other shortcomings in the data. The OBE estimates, however, provided an excellent benchmark against which the census results could be compared. At relatively little expense, the published figures were recast by OBE on a directly comparable basis with the census figures.

b. *Current Population Survey (CPS).* In 1950 and 1960 persons who were asked about income in the March CPS were also asked to report income information in April in the decennial census. Comparisons of the answers, called a CPS-census matching study, provide two different measures of income for the same year for each person, collected on the average about one month apart.

c. *Reinterview Surveys.* Several months after the completion of the field work in the 1950 and 1960 censuses, households that had been asked about income were reinterviewed. The purpose of the reinterview survey was to provide a quality check of the information originally obtained in the censuses. Therefore, the enumerators were specially selected, paid premium rates, and given intensive training by members of the Washington staff in the use of a very detailed questionnaire.

d. *Tax returns.* In 1950 and 1960 an attempt was made to compare the income data obtained in the census for given individuals with comparable information available on tax returns of the Internal Revenue Service. In 1950 a sample of census returns was selected and an attempt was then made to locate the records for that sample in the files of IRS. A relatively large proportion of the records could not be found. In 1960 the procedure was reversed and a sample of tax returns was first selected and then matched with census returns.

Comparison of census and OBE aggregates

The aggregate income estimates published by the Office of Business Economics of the Department of Commerce are the most comprehensive income figures published by the federal government. They are based largely on data derived from business and governmental sources, including industrial and population censuses, employees' wage reports under the social security program, and records of disbursements to individuals by governmental agencies. Because of the great care and effort that goes into the compilation of these data, they hold a unique position as a cornerstone of the statistical program of the federal government. These data provide an excellent benchmark for the evaluation of the income figures collected in the decennial censuses and the annual household surveys.

The census and OBE aggregates are not directly comparable in the form in which they are published. The census figures represent total money income, which is defined as the sum of money wages and salaries, net income from self-employment, and income other than earnings. More detailed classifications within each of these types of income were not collected in the decennial censuses. The "unearned" income category includes social security, veterans' payments, and other government or private pensions; interest, dividends, and income from annuities, estates, or trusts; net income from boarders or lodgers or from renting property to others; and other types of income including unemployment or sickness benefits, public assistance, alimony, military dependency allotments, and other periodic income other than earnings. The OBE estimates of personal income are prepared in great detail with respect to income classification and they can be adjusted by adding and subtracting components so as to be made conceptually comparable with the money income figures described above.

A comparison of census and OBE estimates of aggregate income by type of income is shown for 1949 and 1959 in Table A-2. CPS data for the same years are also shown in this table to provide a general background against which the overall census results may be compared.

In 1949 the census aggregates represented 91 percent of the OBE estimate and in 1959 this proportion was increased to 94 percent. In both years CPS obtained a smaller percentage of the aggregate, 84 percent in 1949 and 87 percent in 1959.

A comparison of the census and OBE estimates by type of income

TABLE A-2

Comparison of Three Types of Aggregate Income Estimates: 1949 and 1959

Type of income	Income estimate (billions)			Ratio of census to OBE figures	Ratio of CPS to OBE figures
	OBE	Census	CPS		
1949					
Overall	$191.0	$173.2	$159.8	91%	84%
Wages and salaries	128.8	124.3	120.0	97	93
Self-employment	31.3	31.1	26.5	99	85
Other	30.9	16.6	13.3	54	43
1959					
Overall	$351.4	$331.7	$306.7	94%	87%
Wages and salaries	249.1	246.5	233.5	99	94
Self-employment	42.2	47.9	38.3	114	91
Other	60.1	37.3	32.7	62	54

Herman P. Miller, *Income Distribution in the United States*, Government Printing Office, 1966, p. 173.

TABLE A-3

Comparison of CPS and OBE Estimates of Total Money Income
for Families and Unattached Individuals: 1944 to 1968

| Year | Income estimate (billions) | | Ratio of Census Bureau to OBE figures |
	CPS	OBE	
1968	$544	$624	87%
1967	497	572	87
1966*	449	531	85
1966	455	531	86
1965	420	487	86
1964	393	453	87
1963	369	428	86
1962	354	405	87
1961	339	381	89
1960	320	368	87
1959	332†⎱ 303 ⎰	352	94 86
1958	280	328	85
1957	265	321	83
1956	257	305	84
1955	235	284	83
1954	218	263	83
1953	216	263	82
1952	203	245	83
1951	189	231	82
1950	171	208	82
1949	157†⎱ 156 ⎰	190	83 82
1948	157	191	82
1947	148	180	82
1946	130	166	78
1945	114	154	74
1944	111	140	79

*Based on revised methodology.
†Based on decennial census rather than on CPS.

For 1944 to 1962 figures: Herman P. Miller, *Income Distribution in the United States*, Government Printing Office, 1966, Table I-4, p. 11; OBE figures for 1963 to 1968 estimated by Census Bureau.

shows that in 1949 and 1959 there was very close agreement for wages and salaries but evidence of substantial underreporting of income other than earnings in the census. The census wage and salary aggregate amounted to 99 percent of the OBE estimate in 1959 and 97 percent in 1949. The census estimate of income other than earnings, on the other hand, amounted to only 62 percent of the OBE estimate in 1959 and 54 percent in 1949. In each case the census estimate was in closer agreement with OBE than were the CPS figures. There was also substantial reduction in underreporting from one census to the next.

An annual comparison of CPS and OBE data for 1944–1968 is presented in Table A-3. This table shows that there has been a gradual improvement in the quality of CPS income data over the years. Prior to 1950, the CPS income surveys obtained about 80 percent of the comparable OBE aggregates. During the fifties, the coverage improved gradually from a low of 82 percent at the beginning of the decade to a high of 86 percent at the end of the decade. During the sixties, the coverage was 86 percent or better in most years.

Comparison of CPS and census

Essentially two types of comparisons can be made between the income data collected in CPS and in the census: (a) distributions or averages can be compared for many different characteristics, such as age, sex, color, education, etc., and (b) tabulations can be made for an identical sample of persons who provided information in both surveys.

Overall comparisons of distributions and averages reveal net differences between the two surveys but they provide little insight into the reasons for these differences. Moreover, comparisons of this type do not provide a validation of either set of statistics since neither one can be regarded as a suitable benchmark. Despite these limitations, there is understandable interest in comparing the results of these two surveys since they both attempt to measure the same thing. In addition, the CPS income surveys have provided meaningful and useful income statistics for nearly twenty years, and to this extent, at least, they provide a reasonable base against which the census results can be compared.

The second type of comparison, generally referred to as a CPS-census match, involves the analysis of reports obtained for an identical sample of persons who were included in both CPS and the census. Persons who were interviewed in the CPS in March 1960 were also included in the decennial sample and were asked to provide income information. A similar study was made in 1950. As might be expected, a large proportion of the respondents did not report the same figures in both surveys. The CPS-census match provides a vehicle for measuring the extent of response variation and its likely impact on selected cross-classifications of income and other variables. This study provides a basis for getting behind the net errors detected in overall distributions and discovering some of the reasons for the differences. To the extent that non-respondents in one survey were interviewed in the other, the CPS-census match also sheds light on possible biases introduced into each set of data due to nonresponse.

In 1949 and 1959 the census estimates tended to exceed CPS. For all males and for white males the differences amounted to about $100 in both years; for nonwhites the absolute and relative differences were considerably greater, amounting to $150 in 1949 and $300 in 1959. The latter figure represents a 15 percent differential between the two estimates. For females, both white and nonwhite, the census estimates tended to exceed CPS by about $100 in 1949 and 1959.

The estimates cited above are for the country as a whole. For male and female nonfarm residents the differences in both years were so small as to be insignificant. In contrast, the census medians for male farm residents in both years were about one-fourth higher than CPS, and for females the 1959 median was also substantially higher than CPS. It is possible that the farm income figures are overstated in the census because of a tendency to report gross income from farm operations rather than net income.

About one-fourth of the persons who were in the March 1960 income supplement to CPS were asked to report income information in the 1960 census. Similarly, about one-fifth of the persons in the March 1950 income supplement were asked to report on income in the 1950 census. Upon completion of each census, an attempt was made to match the reports obtained for identical persons in CPS and the census, using name, address, age, sex, color, and other means of identification. In 1960, census records were found for about 93 percent of the persons who were in the CPS income sample. After the records were matched a comparison was made of the amount of income reported in each survey. The results of such a comparison with respect to total money income are summarized in Table A-4. The income concept and period covered by both surveys were the same. Therefore, variations in the responses are not due to conceptual differences but rather to a variety of other factors. In 1950 these included differences in the quality of the enumerators, and variability of response due to such things as the memory factor and change in respondents. In addition to the factors noted above, differences for 1960 could be due to the use of self-enumeration in the census as compared with direct enumeration in CPS.

Table A-4 shows that there are considerable variations in the reports received for identical persons in each survey; however, these variations

TABLE A-4

Consistency of Income Reporting
in Current Population Survey and Census: 1950 and 1960

	Male		Female	
Comparison of CPS and census	1950	1960	1950	1960
Percentage in same income class in CPS and census	62%	56%	77%	73%
Percentage in a higher income class in CPS	21%	20%	13%	14%
Percentage in a higher income class in census	18%	24%	11%	13%
Percentage with income in census reporting no income in CPS	43%	26%	12%	12%
Percentage with income in CPS reporting no income in census	38%	34%	14%	14%
Median income:				
CPS	$2,514	$4,327	$1,152	$1,508
Census	2,444	4,406	1,163	1,524
Nonrespondents in CPS:				
Percentage reporting in census	75%	90%	85%	92%
Median income in census	$3,095	$4,862	$1,000	$2,491
Nonrespondents in census:				
Percentage reporting in CPS	88%	88%	92%	94%
Median income in CPS	$2,373	$3,216	$1,000	$1,093

Herman P. Miller, *Income Distribution in the United States*, Government Printing Office, 1966, p. 206.

tended to cancel each other, leaving the overall distributions unchanged. This was true for both males and females in both censuses. This table shows no significant differences in the medians, the distributions by income levels, or the proportions of income recipients.

Comparison of census and Reinterview Survey results

Upon completion of the field work in the 1950 and 1960 censuses, intensive Reinterview Surveys (RES) were conducted to detect possible biases in the census results. In 1950 about 25,000 households were reinterviewed but income information was obtained only for about 5,000 households that were in the 20 percent sample. In 1960 the RES sample consisted of about 3,400 households that were included in the 25 percent census sample.

The RES is intended to serve as a benchmark against which the census results can be compared. For this reason, the special measures described below were incorporated in RES to insure that the most accurate results were obtained. Partly because of these measures, field cost per person in the 1950 RES was about twenty times that in the census.

1. The income information was obtained whenever possible from the person himself (in the census, information for all household members was obtained from any responsible member of the household).
2. RES used detailed "probing" questions in contrast to the more general questions used in the census.
3. Superior interviewers were selected and given more intensive training and closer supervision than was possible in the census.
4. The RES and census information was compared case by case and attempts were made to reconcile discrepancies in the field.

Despite these efforts to obtain the most accurate answers, the RES results have several shortcomings. In the first place, the accuracy of the information depends on how well the interviewers did their job, on the adequacy of the information provided by the respondents, and on their willingness to cooperate. In addition, the effectiveness of RES as an evaluation of the censuses is reduced by the length of the interval between the two surveys. In 1950 most of the field work was not done until August or September, or about four or five months after the completion of the census and eight or nine months after the end of the calendar year to which the income data pertained. In 1960, 1,400 households in RES were interviewed in July, but the remaining 2,000 were not interviewed until October.

In general, the 1950 data suggest that the major difference between RES and the census was that RES found a relatively large number of persons with small amounts of income who reported no income in the census. For persons who reported $1 or more of income in both surveys, the overall results were very similar despite considerable variability of response.

Table A-5 shows that about 25 percent of the men without income in RES reported income in the census, but proportionately nearly twice

TABLE A-5

Consistency of Income Reporting in Reinterview Survey and Census: 1960

Comparison of RES and census	Male	Female
Percentage in same income class in RES and census	60%	71%
Percentage in a higher income class in RES	24%	20%
Percentage in a higher income class in census	16%	10%
Percentage with income in census reporting no income in RES	25%	9%
Percentage with income in RES reporting no income in census	41%	20%
Median income:		
RES	$4,501	$1,578
Census	$4,507	$1,501

Herman P. Miller, *Income Distribution in the United States*, Government Printing Office, 1966, p. 211.

as many who reported no income in the census were found to have income in RES. This difference is considerably greater than that noted earlier for the CPS-census matching study and is probably due to the more intensive questioning used in RES. For men who reported income in both surveys, however, the medians were about $4,500 in each survey and the differences by income level were very small. In the aggregate, therefore, the RES results do not differ substantially from those obtained in the census.

Table A-5 also shows that variability of response in the 1960 RES-census matching study was very similar to that obtained in the CPS-census matching study. About 60 percent of the men were in the same income interval in RES and the census, 24 percent were in a higher RES interval, and 16 percent were in a higher census interval.

APPENDIX B

Tools of Income Distribution Analysis

Distribution of consumer units by income levels

Our story begins with the distribution of families and unrelated individuals by income levels. Let us assume that we have conducted a survey of 1,000 families of two or more persons and 200 unrelated individuals (persons who live alone or with nonrelatives). Assume further that each of these units has answered the questions asked regarding their incomes. By ranking them from lowest to highest and dividing them into class intervals we would obtain the distributions shown in Table B-1, columns 2 and 3. The first column is simply a summation of columns 2 and 3, and in columns 4, 5, and 6 the absolute numbers have been converted into percentages. On this basis we could say that 2.6 percent of the families (column 5) in our hypothetical survey have incomes over $25,000 or that 10.3 percent have incomes under $3,000.

The median income shown in Table B-1 is the income of the middle family or unrelated individual in our distribution. It is the dollar value associated with the 50 percent point in the distribution.

Conversion of frequencies to aggregates

Aggregates are obtained by multiplying the number of families or

TABLE B-1

Distribution of Families and Unrelated Individuals by Money Income Level

Annual income	Number of units			Percentage distribution		
	Overall (1)	Families (2)	Unrelated individuals (3)	Overall (4)	Families (5)	Unrelated individuals (6)
Total	1,200	1,000	200	100.0%	100.0%	100.0%
Under $1,000	48	18	30	4.0	1.8	15.0
$1,000 to $1,999	82	34	48	6.8	3.4	24.0
$2,000 to $2,999	76	51	25	6.3	5.1	12.5
$3,000 to $3,999	83	61	22	6.9	6.1	11.0
$4,000 to $4,999	76	60	16	6.3	6.0	8.0
$5,000 to $5,999	82	69	13	6.8	6.9	6.5
$6,000 to $6,999	87	76	11	7.2	7.6	5.5
$7,000 to $7,999	92	82	10	7.7	8.2	5.0
$8,000 to $8,999	85	79	6	7.1	7.9	3.0
$9,000 to $9,999	78	73	5	6.5	7.3	2.5
$10,000 to $11,999	131	125	6	10.9	12.5	3.0
$12,000 to $14,999	129	125	4	10.7	12.5	2.0
$15,000 to $24,999	124	121	3	10.3	12.1	1.5
$25,000 and over	27	26	1	2.2	2.6	0.5
Median income	$7,717	$8,620	$2,880	—	—	—

unrelated individuals at each income level by the average income for that level. For most purposes it can be assumed that the midpoint of each income level is the average (e.g., $5,500 is the average for the $5,000 to $5,999 income level). The value for the open-end interval is estimated by fitting a Pareto Curve to the data. The mechanics for this computation are shown in Table B-2. The logic underlying this practice is discussed later in this appendix, when the Pareto Curve is examined in some detail. The average (or mean) income is obtained by dividing the aggregate income by the number of families and individuals.

Conversion to income shares (Lorenz Curve)

For many purposes we want to know the share of income received by different segments of the population. A question that often comes up is what share of the income is received by the poorest fifth of the families, or by the top 5 percent. Table B-3 and the graph for the Lorenz Curve show the ingredients for making such a computation. The figures in Table B-3 were copied from Tables B-1 and B-2. This table shows the cumulative percentage distribution of families and of aggregate income received by families by income levels. These numbers are shown on the Lorenz Curve, which is obtained by plotting the cumulative percentage of families on the X axis against the cumulative percentage of aggregate income received by these families on the Y axis. If all units had approximately the same incomes, the Lorenz Curve would be represented by the diagonal shown in the diagram. Curves drawn to actual data invariably fall below this line, and the greater the degree of inequality in the distribution of income, the greater the area between the diagonal line and the Lorenz Curve.

Alternative method of obtaining income shares

Table B-4 presents a more precise method for computing income shares. In this table the computation is shown for each fifth of the

TABLE B-2
Aggregate Income of Families and Unrelated Individuals by Income Level

Annual income	Income midpoint	Number of units			Aggregate income (thousands)		
		Overall (1)	Families (2)	Unrelated individuals (3)	Overall (4)	Families (5)	Unrelated individuals (6)
Total	—	1,200	1,000	200	$10,761,823	$9,931,274	$830,549
Under $1,000	$500	48	18	30	24,000	9,000	15,000
$1,000 to $1,999	1,500	82	34	48	123,000	51,000	72,000
$2,000 to $2,999	2,500	76	51	25	190,000	127,500	62,500
$3,000 to $3,999	3,500	83	61	22	290,500	213,500	77,000
$4,000 to $4,999	4,500	76	60	16	342,000	270,000	72,000
$5,000 to $5,999	5,500	82	69	13	451,000	379,500	71,500
$6,000 to $6,999	6,500	87	76	11	565,500	494,000	71,500
$7,000 to $7,999	7,500	92	82	10	690,000	615,000	75,000
$8,000 to $8,999	8,500	85	79	6	722,500	671,500	51,000
$9,000 to $9,999	9,500	78	73	5	741,000	693,500	47,500
$10,000 to $11,999	11,000	131	125	6	1,441,000	1,375,000	66,000
$12,000 to $14,999	13,500	129	125	4	1,741,500	1,687,500	54,000
$15,000 to $24,999	20,000	124	121	3	2,480,000	2,420,000	60,000
$25,000 and over*	35,549	27	26	1	959,823	924,274	35,549
Mean income	—	—	—	—	$8,968	$9,931	$4,153

*Pareto Curve:

$$\bar{X} = X\left(\frac{V}{V-1}\right)$$

	Number	Logarithm
$c = 151$ (124 + 27)		2.178977
$d = 27$		1.431364
$a = \$15,000$		4.176091
$b = \$25,000$		4.397940

$$\frac{2.178977 - 1.431364}{4.397940 - 4.176091} = \frac{.747613}{.221849} = 3.369918 = V$$

$$\frac{V}{V-1} = \frac{3.369918}{2.369918} = 1.421956$$

1.421956 times $25,000 = \$35,549
= average for $25,000-and-over interval

where $V = \dfrac{c-d}{b-a}$

$\bar{X}$ = estimated mean of open-end interval
X = lower limit of open-end interval
a = logarithm of lower limit of interval preceding open-end interval
b = logarithm of lower limit of open-end interval
c = logarithm of the sum of frequencies in open-end interval and preceding interval
d = logarithm of frequency in open-end interval

269

Lorenz Curve Showing Percentage Distribution of Families and Family Aggregate Income

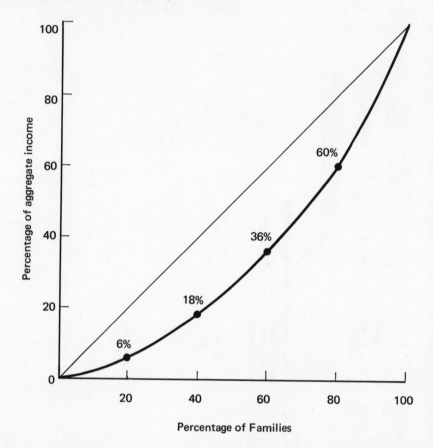

families and for the top 5 percent. Since there are a total of 1,000 families, the lowest fifth contains 200, the lowest 40 percent contains 400, etc. The number of families at each income level is shown in column 3 and the cumulative number is shown in column 4. From column 4 we can ascertain that the 164th family is in the $3,000–$3,999 income class and that the 200th family, which is the one we are looking for to establish the bottom quintile, is in the $4,000–$4,999 income class. Since there are a total of 60 families in this class and we want the 36th family, in order to obtain a total of 200 (164 + 36) we split the aggre-

TABLE B-3

Percentage Distribution of Family Aggregate Income by Income Level

Annual income	Simple distribution		Cumulative distribution	
	1,000 families	$9,931,274 aggregate income	1,000 families	$9,931,274 aggregate income
Under $1,000	1.8%	0.1%	1.8%	0.1%
$1,000 to $1,999	3.4	0.5	5.2	0.6
$2,000 to $2,999	5.1	1.3	10.3	1.9
$3,000 to $3,999	6.1	2.1	16.4	4.0
$4,000 to $4,999	6.0	2.7	22.4	6.7
$5,000 to $5,999	6.9	3.8	29.3	10.5
$6,000 to $6,999	7.6	5.0	36.9	15.5
$7,000 to $7,999	8.2	6.2	45.1	21.7
$8,000 to $8,999	7.9	6.8	53.0	28.5
$9,000 to $9,999	7.3	7.0	60.3	35.5
$10,000 to $11,999	12.5	13.8	72.8	49.3
$12,000 to $14,999	12.5	17.0	85.3	66.3
$15,000 to $24,999	12.1	24.4	97.4	90.7
$25,000 and over	2.6	9.3	100.0	100.0

TABLE B-4

Aggregate Income for Each Fifth of Families by Income Level

Annual income	Number of families in each quintile (1)	Income midpoint (2)	Number of families (3)	Cumulative number of families (4)	Total aggregate income (5)
All levels		–	1,000	–	$9,931,274
Under $1,000		$500	18	18	9,000
$1,000 to $1,999		1,500	34	52	51,000
$2,000 to $2,999		2,500	51	103	127,500
$3,000 to $3,999		3,500	61	164	213,500
$4,000 to $4,999	200	4,500	60	224	270,000
$5,000 to $5,999		5,500	69	293	379,500
$6,000 to $6,999		6,500	76	369	494,000
$7,000 to $7,999	400	7,500	82	451	615,000
$8,000 to $8,999		8,500	79	530	671,500
$9,000 to $9,999	600	9,500	73	603	693,500
$10,000 to $11,999		11,000	125	728	1,375,000
$12,000 to $14,999	800	13,500	125	853	1,687,500
$15,000 to $24,999	950	20,000	121	974	2,420,000
$25,000 and over		35,549	26	1,000	924,274
Top 5 percent	950				

TABLE B-4

Aggregate Income for Each Fifth of Families
by Income Level—*Continued*

Annual income	Split of fifths of families (6)	Split of aggregate income (7)	Aggregate of income fifths (8)	Percentage distribution of aggregate income (9)	Quintile
All levels			$9,931,274		
Under $1,000					
$1,000 to $1,999					
$2,000 to $2,999			$563,000	5.7%	Lowest fifth
$3,000 to $3,999					
$4,000 to $4,999	36 .60000	$162,000			
	24 .40000	$108,000			
$5,000 to $5,999					
$6,000 to $6,999			$1,214,001	12.2%	Second fifth
$7,000 to to $7,999	31 .37805	$232,501			
	51 .62195	$382,499			
$8,000 to $8,999			$1,718,996	17.3%	Middle fifth
$9,000 to $9,999	70 .95890	$664,997			
	3 .04110	$28,503			
$10,000 to $11,999			$2,375,503	23.9%	Fourth fifth
$12,000 to $14,999	72 .57600	$972,000			
$15,000 to $24,999	53 .42400	$715,500			
	97 .80165		$4,059,774	40.9%	Highest fifth
$25,000 and over	24 .19835				
Top 5 percent		$480,007	$1,404,281	14.1%	

gate at this level by giving 60 percent to the bottom fifth and 40 percent to the next fifth. This computation is shown in columns 6 and 7. In column 8, the aggregate for the bottom fifth is summed and we can see from column 9 that it represents 5.7 percent of the aggregate income. A similar computation is performed for each fifth and for the top 5 percent.

Gini Index

The Gini Index is a measure of income concentration which ranges from 0 to 1. The smaller the index, the less the amount of concentration.

The Gini Index is defined as the proportion of the total area under the diagonal that is between the diagonal and the Lorenz Curve. The relationship can be expressed as follows (using the notation in the accompanying figure):

$$L = \frac{A}{A+B} = \frac{\text{area between curve and diagonal}}{\text{area under diagonal}}$$

Since the cumulative percentages on each axis add to 100, the area in the entire square is 1 and the area under the diagonal is 1/2. Therefore the expression above can be rewritten as follows:

$$L = \frac{1/2 - \text{area under curve}}{1/2} = 1 - 2 \text{ (area under curve)}$$

If we assume that the curve between any two points is approximated by a straight line, the area for any segment of the curve can be expressed as follows:

$$(f_{i+1} - f_i)\frac{(y_i + y_{i+1})}{2}$$

When summed over all intervals, the area under the curve is

$$\sum_{f=1}^{n} (f_{i+1} - f_i)\frac{(y_i + y_{i+1})}{2}$$

Computation of Gini Index of Concentration

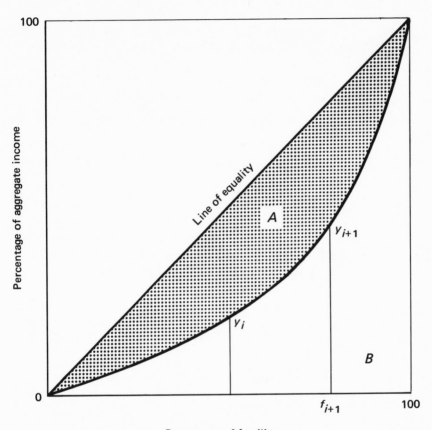

Percentage of families

Substituting in the expression for L (page 274) yields the formula that was used in computing the Gini Index:

$$L = 1 - 2 \sum_{i=1}^{n} (f_{i+1} - f_i) \frac{(y_i + y_{i+1})}{2}$$

$$L = 1 - \sum_{i=1}^{n} (f_{i+1} - f_i)(y_i + y_{i+1})$$

275

$$L = 1 - \sum_{i=1}^{n} f_{i+1}y_{i+1} - f_iy_i + f_{i+1}y_i - f_iy_{i+1}$$

Where f_iy_i ranges from 0 to 100, the expression $f_{i+1}y_{i+1} - f_iy_i = 1$. This can be shown as follows:

$$f_1y_1 - f_0y_0$$
$$f_2y_2 - f_1y_1$$
$$f_3y_3 - f_2y_2$$
$$f_4y_4 - f_3y_3$$
$$f_ny_n$$

Since $f_ny_n = 100\%$ in this case, the net result is that $f_ny_n - f_0y_0 = 1$. Therefore, the computation of the Gini Index can be made by inserting the proper values in the expression $f_{i+1}y_i - f_iy_{i+1}$. This calculation is shown in Table B-5, where

$$f_1 = 1.8 \qquad y_1 = 0.1$$
$$f_2 = 5.2 \qquad y_2 = 0.6$$
$$f_3 = 10.3 \qquad y_3 = 1.9$$
$$f_{14} = 100.0 \qquad y_{14} = 100.0$$

Pareto Curve

Vilfredo Pareto was an Italian economist who conducted some of the earliest empirical studies of income distribution. After studying the income tax return statistics for several European countries during the latter part of the last century, he concluded that they could all be characterized by the single function $Y = AX^{-V}$, where Y is the number of incomes exceeding a given income level X and where A and V are

TABLE B-5

Computation of Gini Index for Families

Annual income	Percentage distribution		Cumulative percentage distribution		Gini Index	
	Number	Aggregate income	Number	Aggregate income		
Under $1,000	1.8%	0.1%	1.8%	0.1%	–	–
$1,000 to $1,999	3.4	0.5	5.2	0.6	1.08	0.52
$2,000 to $2,999	5.1	1.3	10.3	1.9	9.88	6.18
$3,000 to $3,999	6.1	2.1	16.4	4.0	41.20	31.16
$4,000 to $4,999	6.0	2.7	22.4	6.7	109.88	89.60
$5,000 to $5,999	6.9	3.8	29.3	10.5	235.20	196.31
$6,000 to $6,999	7.6	5.0	36.9	15.5	454.15	387.45
$7,000 to $7,999	8.2	6.2	45.1	21.7	800.73	699.05
$8,000 to $8,999	7.9	6.8	53.0	28.5	1,285.35	1,150.10
$9,000 to $9,999	7.3	7.0	60.3	35.5	1,881.50	1,718.55
$10,000 to $11,999	12.5	13.8	72.8	49.3	2,972.79	2,584.40
$12,000 to $14,999	12.5	17.0	85.3	66.3	4,826.64	4,205.29
$15,000 to $24,999	12.1	24.4	97.4	90.7	7,736.71	6,457.62
$25,000 and over	2.6	9.3	100.0	100.0	9,740.00	9,070.00
Total	100.0	100.0	–	–	30,095.11	26,596.23

$$
\begin{array}{r}
30,095.11 \\
-26,596.23 \\
\hline
3,498.88
\end{array}
$$

Gini Index = .350

constants. The logarithmic form of this curve ($\log Y = \log A - V \log X$) is, of course, a straight line. That is, if the logarithms of the income sizes are charted on a vertical scale, the resulting points will fall on a straight line. Graphically, the curve would appear as shown in the accompanying diagram.

Pareto Curve Showing Distribution of Families by Income Level

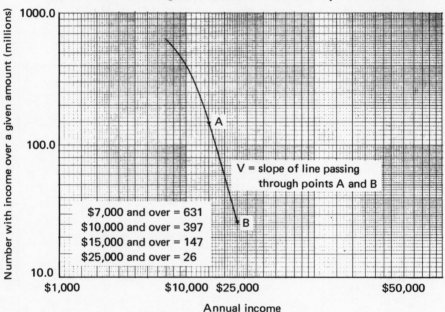

Pareto believed that the term V in his equation was very stable and generally had a value of about 1.5. Even his own data, however, showed that V ranged from 1.24 to 1.89, and more recent findings also cast great doubt on the constancy of V. However, it is generally recognized that the Pareto Curve does adequately describe the tail of many different types of income distribution. It is in that connection—principally in estimating the mean of the open end of a distribution—that Pareto's work continues to be used as a tool in income analysis.

The mean for the tail of a distribution (e.g., $25,000 and over) can be estimated from the following expression, where X is the amount of income and Y is the number of families having that income:

$$\overline{X} = \frac{\int_{25,000}^{\infty} XY \, dx}{\int_{25,000}^{\infty} Y \, dx}$$

A value for Y can be substituted in the above equation from the Pareto Curve. Since the Pareto Curve is normally expressed in its cumulative form ($Y = AX^{-V}$, where Y is the number of families having an income of X *or greater*), we must use the first derivative in order to obtain the noncumulative value of Y that is required in the above expression:

$$Y = -\frac{AV}{X^{V+1}}$$

Substituting this expression in the equation above, we have:

$$\overline{X} = \frac{\int_{25,000}^{\infty} X \left(-\frac{AV}{X^{V+1}} \right) dx}{\int_{25,000}^{\infty} -\frac{AV}{X^{V+1}} \, dx} = \frac{\int \frac{dx}{X^{V}}}{\int \frac{dx}{X^{V+1}}}$$

$$= \frac{\frac{X^{-(V-1)}}{V-1}}{\frac{X^{-V}}{V}} = X \left(\frac{V}{V-1} \right)$$

Projections of income distribution

Since the shape of the Lorenz Curve has been fairly constant over a long period of time, it is possible to use a simple method to prepare reasonable projections of family income distributions. It must be recognized, of course, that any projection—no matter how complex the method—is only as good as the assumptions that are made. In the case of income distribution, there are two basic assumptions: the growth rate and the stability of income shares. If the assumptions regarding the growth rate are incorrect, the income level that is projected will be either too low or too high; and if there is a major change in the distribution of income, then the resulting projection of families at any given income level will be incorrect.

Assume that we want to prepare a family income distribution for 1985 expressed in 1968 dollars. That is, we want to see how the projected distribution for 1985 compares with the distribution in 1968. We would first have to assume a growth rate for this period. Since incomes in the past twenty years have grown at the rate of 3 percent per year compounded, we could assume that incomes during the 1968–1985 period would continue to grow at the rate of 3 percent per year. On this basis (see Table B-6) we would multiply each of the dollar amounts in the 1968 distribution (column 1) by 1.65283, since that is the value of $1 compounded for seventeen years at 3 percent per year. This operation would produce an income distribution with the dollar values shown in column 2. In other words, in 1985, 1.8 percent of the families would have incomes under $1,653. By simple interpolation, we can obtain the data in column 5 which show the number of families in 1985 with incomes under $1,000. In other words, on the basis of column 5 we can say that in 1985, 0.8 percent of the families will have incomes under $1,000; 2.5 percent will have incomes under $2,000, etc.

If these results are plotted on logarithmic normal paper, as in the accompanying diagram, any point in the 1985 income distribution can be estimated graphically.

Percentage Distribution of Families in 1968 and 1985 (Projected), by Total Money Income

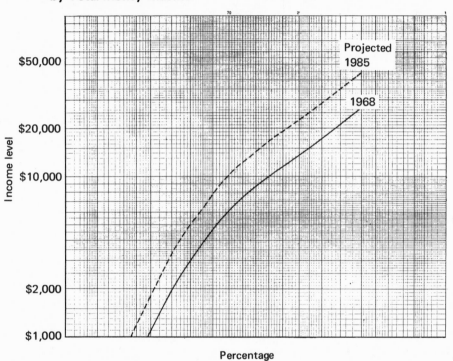

TABLE B-6

Projection to 1985 of Income Distribution for Families

Annual income			1968		1985	
Original (1)	Projected* (2)	Simple distribution (3)	Cumulative distribution (4)	Simple distribution (5)	Cumulative distribution (6)
Under $1,000	Under $1,653	1.8%	1.8%	0.8%	0.8%
$1,000 to $1,999	$1,654 to $3,306	3.4	5.2	1.7	2.5
$2,000 to $2,999	$3,307 to $4,958	5.1	10.3	2.0	4.5
$3,000 to $3,999	$4,959 to $6,611	6.1	16.4	3.0	7.5
$4,000 to $4,999	$6,612 to $8,264	6.0	22.4	2.5	10.0
$5,000 to $5,999	$8,265 to $9,917	6.9	29.3	4.0	14.0
$6,000 to $6,999	$9,918 to $11,570	7.6	36.9	3.5	17.5
$7,000 to $7,999	$11,571 to $13,223	8.2	45.1	3.0	20.5
$8,000 to $8,999	$13,224 to $14,875	7.9	53.0	4.5	25.0
$9,000 to $9,999	$14,876 to $16,528	7.3	60.3	4.0	29.0
$10,000 to $11,999	$16,529 to $19,834	12.5	72.8	10.5	39.5
$12,000 to $14,999	$19,835 to $24,792	12.5	85.3	13.5	53.0
$15,000 to $24,999	$24,793 to $41,321	12.1	97.4	32.0	85.0
$25,000 and over	$41,322 and over	2.6	100.0	15.0	100.0
Median income		$8,620		$14,247	

*1985 income intervals, based on an assumed 3 percent growth rate for seventeen years. Factor = 1.65283.

APPENDIX C

Projections of Selected Characteristics to 1985

TABLE C-1

Projections of Population to 1985*

Estimates (millions)

1955	165.9
1960	180.7
1965	194.6
1970	206.0

	Series B	Series C	Series D
Projections (millions)			
1975	223.8	219.4	215.4
1980	243.3	235.2	227.7
1985	264.6	252.9	241.7

Assumptions for completed fertility	
Series B	3.10 children per woman
Series C	2.78 children per woman
Series D	2.45 children per woman

*As of July 1. Includes armed forces overseas.

Derived from U.S. Bureau of the Census, *Current Population Reports—Population Estimates,* Series P-25, No. 388, Table 1.

TABLE C-2
Projections of Components of Population Change to 1985*

Period	Population at beginning of period (millions)	Average annual number (millions)		
		Net change	Births	Deaths
Estimates				
1955-60	165.9	3.0	4.3	1.6
1960-65	180.7	2.8	4.2	1.8
1965-70	194.6	2.3	3.8	1.9
Projections				
1970-75	206.0	2.7	4.3	2.1
1975-80	219.4	3.2	4.9	2.2
1980-85	235.2	3.5	5.4	2.3

*Series C.

Derived from U.S. Bureau of the Census, *Current Population Reports—Population Characteristics,* Series P-25, No. 388, Table 1.

TABLE C-3
Projection of Rates of Population Change to 1985*

Period	Average annual change in population	Average annual birthrate* (per 1,000 people)	Average annual deathrate* (per 1,000 people)
Estimates			
1955-60	1.7%	24.7	9.4
1960-65	1.5	22.2	9.4
1965-70	1.1	18.1	9.6
Projections			
1970-75	1.3%	20.3	9.7
1975-80	1.4	21.8	9.6
1980-85	1.5	22.2	9.4

*Series C.

Derived from U.S. Bureau of the Census, *Current Population Reports—Population Estimates,* Series P-25, No. 388, Table 1.

TABLE C-4

Projected Growth, Within and Outside Standard Metropolitan Statistical Areas, to 1985

Area	Population (millions)		Net change		Percentage distribution	
	1970	1985	Number (millions)	Percentage	1970	1985
Total	205.1	252.2	47.1	23.0%	100%	100%
Within SMSA's	140.0	178.1	38.1	27.2	68	71
Central cities	59.8	65.6	5.8	9.7	29	26
Ring areas	80.2	112.6	32.4	40.4	39	45
Outside SMSA's	65.2	74.0	8.8	13.5	32	29

Projections from National Commission on Urban Problems, *Challenge of America's Metropolitan Population Outlook—1960 to 1985;* 1970 figures prepared from consistent data for recent years.

TABLE C-5

Projected Growth, Standard Metropolitan Statistical Areas, by Color to 1985

Area	Population (millions)		Net change		Percentage distribution	
	1970	1985	Number (millions)	Percentage	1970	1985
White	121.3	151.2	29.9	24.6%	100%	100%
Central cities	44.9	45.4	0.6	1.3	37	30
Ring areas	76.4	105.7	29.2	38.2	63	70
Nonwhite	18.6	27.0	8.4	45.2	100	100
Central cities	14.9	20.1	5.1	34.0	81	75
Ring areas	3.8	6.8	3.1	8.4	20	25

Projections from National Commission on Urban Problems, *Challenge of America's Metropolitan Population Outlook—1960 to 1985;* 1970 figures prepared from consistent data for recent years.

TABLE C-6

Projections of Population by Age to 1985*

Age	Population (millions)		Net change 1970 to 1985		Net change 1955 to 1970	
	1970	1985	Number (millions)	Percent-age	Number (millions)	Percent-age
All ages	206.0	252.9	46.8	22.7%	40.1	24.2%
Under 5 years	18.7	26.6	7.9	42.2	0.2	0.9
5 to 9 years	20.6	24.4	3.9	18.7	3.8	22.9
10 to 14 years	20.7	21.5	0.8	4.1	7.0	51.6
15 to 19 years	19.1	19.2	0.1	0.5	8.1	73.0
20 to 24 years	17.3	21.1	3.8	22.1	6.5	61.1
25 to 34 years	25.3	40.7	15.4	60.8	1.0	4.3
35 to 44 years	23.0	31.4	8.4	36.7	0.1	0.2
45 to 54 years	23.3	21.7	−1.6	−7.0	4.4	23.5
55 to 64 years	18.5	21.2	2.7	14.8	3.9	26.5
65 years and over	19.6	25.0	5.4	27.5	5.1	34.8

*Series C.
Derived from U.S. Bureau of the Census, *Current Population Reports—Population Characteristics*, Series P-25, No. 388, Table 2.

TABLE C-7

Projections of Households, Families, and Marriages to 1985

Period	Number at beginning of period		Average annual change		Average annual number of marriages
	House-holds	Families	House-holds	Families	
Estimates (millions)					
1960–65	52.8	45.1	0.9	0.5	1.6
1965–70	57.3	47.8	1.2	0.9	1.8
1970–75	63.3	52.2	1.3	1.0	2.1
Projections (millions)					
1975–80	70.0	57.1	1.5	1.1	2.3
1980–85	77.3	62.7	1.4	1.1	2.5

Derived from U.S. Bureau of the Census, *Current Population Reports—Population Estimates*, Series P-25, No. 388, Tables 10 and 12.

TABLE C-8

Projections of Households by Age of Head to 1985*

Age of head	Number of households (millions)		Net change	
	1970	1985	Number (millions)	Percentage
Primary families				
All ages	52.1	68.2	16.1	31.0%
Under 25 years	4.0	5.1	1.2	29.0
25 to 34 years	10.8	18.5	7.7	71.1
35 to 44 years	11.0	15.8	4.8	43.9
45 to 54 years	10.7	10.1	−0.7	−6.1
55 to 64 years	8.2	9.5	1.2	15.0
65 years and over	7.3	9.2	1.9	25.8
Primary individuals				
All ages	11.2	16.2	5.0	44.4%
Under 25 years	0.8	1.4	0.6	73.8
25 to 34 years	1.0	2.2	1.3	129.6
35 to 44 years	0.7	1.2	0.5	62.0
45 to 54 years	1.4	1.2	−0.2	−16.1
55 to 64 years	2.4	2.7	0.3	12.8
65 years and over	5.0	7.6	2.6	52.8

*Series 1.

Derived from U.S. Bureau of the Census, *Current Population Reports—Population Characteristics,* Series P-25, No. 388, Table 13.

TABLE C-9

Projections of Fall School Enrollment to 1985*

Year	Overall	Elementary school	High school	College
Estimates (millions)				
1955	37.5	27.1	8.0	2.4
1960	46.3	32.4	10.2	3.6
1965	53.8	35.1	13.0	5.7
1970	58.9	36.5	15.0	7.4
Projections (millions)				
1975	60.4	34.7	16.3	9.5
1980	63.0	36.2	15.6	11.2
1985	68.7	41.5	15.6	11.7

*Series C-1.

Derived from U.S. Bureau of the Census, *Current Population Reports—Population Estimates,* Series P-25, No. 388, Table 8.

TABLE C-10

Projections of Current Expenditures
for All Families and Unrelated Individuals, to 1985

Expenditure	1968 outlay (billions)	1985 outlay* (billions)	Percentage increase
Total aggregate income	$544	$1,277	135%
Taxes	64	195	205
Savings	55	132	140
Expenditures for current consumption	425	950	124
Food, beverages, tobacco	97	188	94
Housing	61	150	146
Household operation and furnishings	63	133	111
Clothing and clothing materials	39	77	97
Personal and medical care	46	139	202
Transportation	60	120	100
Recreation, education, contributions, other	59	143	142

*In 1968 dollars.

Herman P. Miller, "Tomorrow's Consumer," paper prepared for National Industrial Conference Board, Conference on the Consumer Market, New York, March 24, 1970.

NOTES

Chapter I

[1] *Washington Post,* January 5, 1969.

[2] Message from President Richard M. Nixon to the Congress of the United States, "The Public Welfare System," *Congressional Record,* August 11, 1969, pp. 9582-5.

[3] *Hearings Before a Subcommittee of the Committee on Government Operations,* House of Representatives, 91st Congress, 1st Session, September 15 and 16, 1969, p. 10.

[4] *Ibid.*

[5] *Ibid.,* p. 25.

[6] "Lord Carlisle's Lecture at Leeds," *Littell's Living Age,* XXVIII (1851), pp. 197, 203. Quoted in John Braemen, Robert Bremner, and Everett Walters, *Change and Continuity in Twentieth Century America.* Columbus, Ohio, Ohio State University Press, 1964, p. 263.

[7] *Washington Post,* February 19, 1970.

[8] Survey Research Center, University of Michigan, *Attitudes Toward Inflation: Supplement to the Outlook for Consumer Demand,* November 1969, Table 7.

[9] Quoted in November 1969 issue of the monthly survey published by Morgan Guaranty Trust Company of New York.

Chapter II

[1] Robin Barlow, Harvey Brazer, and James Morgan, *Economic Behavior of the Affluent.* Washington, D.C., The Brookings Institution, 1966, p. 150.

[2] Paul R. Ehrlich, *The Population Bomb.* New York, Ballantine Books, 1968, p. 186.

290

[3] Paul A. Samuelson, *Economics: An Introductory Analysis,* 5th ed. New York, McGraw-Hill Book Co., Inc., 1961, p. 113.

[4] William C. Mitchell, "The American Polity and the Redistribution of Income," *American Behavioral Scientist,* Vol. 13, No. 2 (November/December 1969), p. 204.

[5] Article by W. Irwin Gillespie, "Effect of Public Expenditures on the Distribution of Income" in Richard A. Musgrave, *Essays in Fiscal Federalism.* Washington, D.C., The Brookings Institution, 1965.

[6] *Ibid.,* pp. 133-4.

[7] Charles Péguy, *Basic Verities.* New York, Pantheon Books, 1943, p. 61.

[8] Lincoln's statement was a reply to the New York Workingmen's Democratic Republican Association, March 21, 1864. It is quoted in *The Collected Works of Abraham Lincoln,* Vol. 7, ed. by Roy P. Basler. New Brunswick, N.J., Rutgers University Press, 1953, p. 259.

[9] R. H. Tawney, *Equality.* New York, G. P. Putnam's Sons (Capricorn Books), 1961, p. 40.

[10] Aldous Huxley, *Ends and Means.* New York, Harper & Row, Publishers, 1937, p. 187.

[11] For Max Eastman's ideas, see the above source.

[12] United Nations Economic and Social Council, *Statistics of Income Distribution,* E/CN.3/184, January 1954, p. 6.

[13] Simon Kuznets, "Quantitative Aspects of the Economic Growth of Nations," *Economic Development and Cultural Change,* Vol. XI, No. 2 (January 1963), p. 12.

Chapter III

[1] Clarence B. Randall, *The Folklore of Management.* Boston, Little, Brown and Co., 1961 (New York, New American Library, Mentor Books, 1962, p. 54).

[2] *U.S. Census of Population: 1960, General Social and Economic Characteristics, United States Summary,* Table C-2.

[3] *Hearings Before a Subcommittee of the Committee on Commerce on S. Res. 231,* 76th Congress, 3rd Session, February 1940, p. 63.

[4] *The New York Times,* December 7, 1949.

[5] U.S. Bureau of the Census, *Evaluation and Research Program of the U.S. Census of Population and Housing,* Series ER-60, No. 8.

Chapter IV

[1] Committee for Economic Development, *Economic Growth in the United States,* 1969, p. 13.

NOTES

[2] *Ibid.*, p. 14 (comment by S. Bayard Colgate).

[3] *Ibid.*

[4] *Washington Post,* February 8, 1970.

[5] Robert L. Heilbroner, *The Future as History.* New York, Harper & Row, Publishers, 1960 (New York, Grove Press, Evergreen Books, 1961, p. 119).

[6] U.S. Bureau of the Census, *Historical Statistics of the United States, Colonial Times to 1957,* Series S 70-80.

[7] *U.S. Census of Housing: 1940,* Vol. II, *General Characteristics,* Table 6B.

[8] Sumner H. Slichter, *Economic Growth in the United States.* Baton Rouge, La., Louisiana State University Press, 1961 (New York, The Crowell-Collier Publishing Co., Collier Books, 1963, p. 19).

[9] Arthur F. Burns, *Looking Forward,* 31st Annual Report of the National Bureau of Economic Research, p. 4.

[10] Paul A. Samuelson, *Economics: An Introductory Analysis,* 5th ed. New York, McGraw-Hill Book Co., Inc., 1961, p. 114.

[11] Editors of Fortune, *The Changing American Market.* New York, Garden City Books (Hanover House), 1955, p. 52.

[12] Sumner H. Slichter, *op. cit.,* pp. 29-30.

[13] Arnold J. Toynbee, *Civilization on Trial.* New York, Oxford University Press, 1948, p. 25.

[14] Thorstein Veblen, *The Theory of the Leisure Class.* New York, Modern Library, 1934, pp. 102-114.

[15] Gabriel Kolko, *Wealth and Power in America.* New York, Frederick A. Praeger, Inc., 1962.

[16] *Ibid.*, p. 13.

[17] *Ibid.*, p. 14.

[18] Selma Goldsmith and others, "Size Distribution of Income Since the Mid-Thirties," *Review of Economics and Statistics,* February 1954, p. 20.

[19] M. Liebenberg and J. M. Fitzwilliams, "Size Distribution of Personal Income, 1957-60," *Survey of Current Business,* May 1961, p. 14.

Chapter V

[1] Elliot Liebow, *Talley's Corner.* Boston, Little, Brown and Co., 1967, p. 4.

[2] James Farmer, "Employment Opportunity and the Negro," *Economic and Business Bulletin,* Temple University, September 1967, p. 21.

[3] *Life,* January 9, 1970, p. 104.

[4] Gabriel Kolko, *Wealth and Power in America.* New York, Frederick A. Praeger, Inc., 1962, p. 93.

[5] Jessie Bernard, *Marriage and Family Among Negroes.* Englewood, N.J., Prentice-Hall, Inc., 1966, p. 6.

[6] *Ibid.*

[7] Hertha Riese, *Heal the Hurt Child.* Chicago, University of Chicago Press, 1962, p. 125.

[8] *Ibid.*, p. 126.

[9] Kenneth B. Clark, "Explosion in the Ghetto," *Psychology Today*, September 1967, p. 38.

[10] Patricia Schiller, "Sex Attitudes in the Ghetto," *Sexology*, January 1969.

[11] Health and Welfare Council of the National Capital Area, *Poverty's Children*, March 1966, p. 26.

[12] *Ibid.*, p. 27.

[13] Reynolds Farley, "The Urbanization of Negroes in the United States," *Journal of Social History*, Spring 1968, p. 253.

[14] Kenneth B. Clark, "The Negro and the Urban Crisis" in Kermit Gordon, ed., *Agenda for the Nation.* Washington, D.C., The Brookings Institution, 1968, p. 135.

[15] *The New York Times*, February 25, 1970.

[16] U.S. Department of Labor, Office of Policy Planning and Research, *The Negro Family: The Case for National Action*, March 1965.

[17] *Ibid.*, preface.

[18] *Ibid.*, p. 5.

[19] Clark, "The Negro and the Urban Crisis," *op. cit.*, p. 131.

[20] *Ibid.*, p. 131.

Chapter VI

[1] Helen H. Lamale and Margaret S. Stotz, "The Interim City Worker's Family Budget," *Monthly Labor Review*, August 1960, Table 3.

[2] *U.S. Census of Housing: 1960, Metropolitan Housing*, Table A-16.

[3] A. J. Jaffe, ed., "Demographic and Labor Force Characteristics of the New York City Puerto Rican Population," *Puerto Rican Population of New York City*, a series of papers delivered before the New York area chapter of American Statistical Association, October 21, 1953. New York, Columbia University, Bureau of Applied Social Research, January 1954, p. 24.

[4] Christopher Rand, *The Puerto Ricans.* New York, Oxford University Press, 1958, p. 52.

[5] *Ibid.*, p. 44.

[6] The figures in the section on Spanish-Americans are for those who are white. The comparison throughout, therefore, is between white Spanish-Americans and other whites.

[7] Quoted in Carey McWilliams, *Brothers Under the Skin*. Boston, Little, Brown and Company, 1951, p. 131.

[8] *Ibid.*, p. 79.

[9] Derived from U.S. Bureau of the Census, *Current Population Reports*, Series P-23, No. 18.

[10] Will Herberg, *Protestant-Catholic-Jew.* New York, Doubleday & Company, Inc., 1955 (Anchor Books, 1960, p. 9).

NOTES

Chapter VII

[1] Sar A. Levitan,.*Programs in Aid of the Poor for the 1970's*. Baltimore, Johns Hopkins Press, 1970, p. 13

[2] Robert H. Bremner, *From the Depths*. New York, New York University Press, 1956, p. 6.

[3] *Ibid.*, p. 10.

[4] Sar A. Levitan, *Programs in Aid of the Poor*. Kalamazoo, Mich., The Upjohn Institute, 1965, p. 3.

[5] Arthur F. Burns, "The Control of Government Expenditures," address delivered at 32nd Annual Dinner Meeting of Tax Foundation, Plaza Hotel, New York, December 2, 1969.

[6] M. Elaine Burgess and Daniel O. Price, *An American Dependency Challenge*. Chicago, American Public Welfare Association, 1963, p. 179.

[7] *Ibid.*, p. 109.

[8] Bayard Rustin, "From Protest to Politics," *Commentary*, February, 1965, p. 27.

[9] Statement made in 1909, quoted in *Encyclopedia Britannica* (1950 ed.), Vol. 18, p. 220.

[10] Herbert Hoover, *Memoirs of Herbert Hoover: The Cabinet and the Presidency, 1920-1933*. New York, The Macmillan Company, 1952, Vol. II, pp. 195-196.

[11] *Economic Report of the President*, 1965, p. 169.

[12] U.S. Department of Agriculture, *Food Consumption and Dietary Levels of Households in the United States*, ARS 626, August 1957.

[13] Victor Fuchs, "Toward a Theory of Poverty," in U.S. Chamber of Commerce, *The Concept of Poverty*. Washington, D.C., 1965, p. 74.

[14] *Ibid.*, p. 75.

[15] Health and Welfare Council of the National Capital Area, *Poverty's Children*, March 1966, pp. 11, 12, 18, 19.

[16] Levitan, *Programs in Aid of the Poor for the 1970's. Ibid.*, p. 6.

Chapter VIII

[1] Charles E. Silberman, *Crisis in Black and White*. New York, Random House, Inc., 1964, p. 309.

[2] Sar A. Levitan, *Programs in Aid of the Poor for the 1970's*. Baltimore, Johns Hopkins Press, 1970, p. 13.

[3] *Ibid.*, p. 51.

[4] Message from President Nixon to the Congress of the United States, "The Public Welfare System," *Congressional Record*, August 11, 1969, pp. 9582-85.

[5] *Washington Post*, January 5, 1969.

[6] Article by William Raspberry, *Washington Post*, February 25, 1970.

[7] Sar A. Levitan, "Manpower Programs and the New Federalism," *The Conference Board Record*, March 1970.

[8]Office of Economic Opportunity, *Preliminary Results of the New Jersey Graduated Work Incentive Experiment,* February 18, 1970, p. 11.

[9]*Ibid.,* p. 3.

[10]*Ibid.*

Chapter IX

[1]*Economic Report of the President,* January 1962, pp. 9-10.

[2]Ferdinand Lundberg, *The Rich and the Super-Rich.* New York, Lyle Stuart, Inc., 1968 (Bantam Books, 1969, p. 29).

[3]This description is based on an interview with Mr. Singer which appeared in *The New York Times* on January 6, 1970.

[4]Board of Governors of the Federal Reserve System, *Survey of Financial Characteristics of Consumers,* August 1966, p. 1.

[5]Robin Barlow, Harvey Brazer, and James Morgan, *Economic Behavior of the Affluent.* Washington, D.C., The Brookings Institution, 1966, p. 134.

[6]*Ibid.,* p. 135.

[7]Lundberg, *op. cit.,* p. 55.

[8]Morris R. Cohen, *American Thought.* New York, The Free Press of Glencoe, 1954 (New York, The Crowell-Collier Publishing Co., Collier Books, 1962, p. 48).

[9]Quoted in Frederick Lewis Allen, *The Big Change.* New York, Harper & Row, Publishers, 1952 (New York, Bantam Books, Inc., 1961, p. 215).

[10]Frederick Lewis Allen's statement is from the above source, p. 216.

[11]Independent confirmation of this finding is reported in Barlow, Brazer, and Morgan, *op. cit.* This report notes that "less than one-tenth of the high income groups reported that more than half of their total wealth was from inheritances; three-fifths reported no inheritance at all, and another fifth said that inheritances amounted to less than 15 percent of their total assets. Among those with largest portfolios ($500,000 or more), however, nearly one-fourth reported that more than half of their current total assets resulted from inheritances" (p. 92).

[12]Lundberg, *op. cit.,* p. 24.

[13]Robert J. Lampman, *The Share of Top Wealth-Holders in National Wealth, 1922-56.* Princeton, N.J., Princeton University Press, 1962, p. 52.

[14]Internal Revenue Service, *Personal Wealth: Supplemental Report to Statistics of Income, 1962,* p. 16.

[15]*U.S. News and World Report,* December 15, 1969.

[16]*The Saturday Evening Post,* July 31, 1965.

[17]Charles Sopkin, *Money Talks.* New York, Random House, Inc., 1964, p. ix.

Chapter X

[1]Christopher Rand, *The Puerto Ricans.* New York, Oxford University Press, 1958, p. 73.

NOTES

[2] James Baldwin, *Nobody Knows My Name*. New York, The Dial Press, Inc., 1961 (Dell Publishing Co., Inc., 1962, p. 106).

[3] Seymour E. Harris, *The Market for College Graduates and Related Aspects of Education and Income*. Cambridge, Mass., Harvard University Press, 1949, p. 64.

[4] C. Wright Mills, *White Collar*. New York, Oxford University Press, 1951, p. 270.

[5] Andrew F. Brimmer, "The Black Revolution and the Economic Future of Negroes in the United States," commencement address delivered at Tennessee Agricultural and Industrial State University, June 8, 1969.

[6] The share of income received by the top 5 percent of the nonwhite families fluctuated between 15 percent and 17 percent in each year since 1947, without any evidence of a trend. See U.S. Bureau of the Census, *Current Population Reports*, Series P-60, No. 66, p. 22.

[7] Henry Owen, *Washington Post*, February 12, 1970.

[8] James N. Morgan and others, *Income and Welfare in the United States*. New York, McGraw-Hill Book Company, Inc., 1962, p. 51.

[9] Quoted in Harry Kursh, *Apprenticeships in America*. New York, W. W. Norton & Company, Inc., 1958, p. 65.

[10] Eli Ginsberg, *The Negro Potential*. New York, Columbia University Press, 1956, pp. 53, 58.

[11] James S. Coleman, *Equality of Educational Opportunity*. Government Printing Office, Washington, D.C., 1966, p. 325.

[12] U.S. Bureau of the Census, *Current Population Reports*, Series P-20, No. 183, Table D.

[13] *Ibid.*, Table B.

[14] Unpublished data of the U.S. Office of Education.

[15] American Council on Education, *National Norms for Entering College Freshmen, Fall 1968*, A.C.E. Research Report, Vol. 3, No. 1.

[16] Department of Health, Education and Welfare, *Toward a Social Report*, Government Printing Office, Washington, D.C., 1969, p. 20.

Chapter XI

[1] Aaron Levenstein, *Why People Work*. New York, The Crowell-Collier Publishing Co., 1962, p. 173.

[2] Louis Filler, ed., *The World of Mr. Dooley*. New York, The Crowell-Collier Publishing Co., 1962, p. 38.

[3] Levenstein, *op. cit.*, p. 152.

[4] Erich Fromm, *The Sane Society*. New York, Fawcett World Library, 1955, p. 251.

[5] *Economic Report of the President*, February 1970, p. 210.

[6] Harold I. Wilensky, "The Uneven Distribution of Leisure," *Social Problems*, Summer 1961, p. 55.

[7] Alba M. Edwards, *Comparative Occupation Statistics for the United States, 1870 to 1940*. Government Printing Office, Washington, D.C., 1943, p. xi.

[8]Peter M. Blau and Otis D. Duncan, *The American Occupational Structure.* New York, John Wiley and Sons, 1967. Some of the more important findings of this study were summarized by Duncan in U.S. Department of Health, Education and Welfare, *Toward a Social Report.* Government Printing Office, Washington, D.C., 1969.

[9]*Toward a Social Report. Ibid.,* p. 17.

[10]*Ibid.,* p. 18.

[11]*Ibid.*

[12]*Ibid.,* p. 24.

[13]Robert Hodge, Paul Siegel, and Peter Rossi, "Occupational Prestige in the United States, 1925-63," *American Journal of Sociology,* November 1964.

[14]*Ibid.,* p. 286.

[15]A complete listing of the jobs which qualify for the managerial elite is included in the *Fortune* report "A Study of the Management Universe Based on Special Tabulations of the U.S. Bureau of the Census," Time Inc., 1969.

Chapter XII

[1]Frederick Lewis Allen, *Only Yesterday.* New York, Harper & Row, Publishers (Bantam Books, Inc., 1959, p. 68).

[2]James N. Morgan and others, *Income and Welfare in the United States.* New York, McGraw-Hill Book Company, Inc., 1962, p. 112.

[3]Michael Harrington, *The Other America.* New York, The Macmillan Company, 1962, p. 179.

[4]Katherine B. Oettinger, "Maternal Employment and Children," in National Manpower Council, *Work in the Lives of Married Women.* New York, Columbia University Press, 1958, p. 143.

[5]Morgan and others, *op. cit.,* p. 111.

Chapter XIII

[1]Paul R. Ehrlich, *The Population Bomb.* New York, Ballantine Books, 1968, p. 135.

[2]*Ibid.,* p. 165.

[3]J. M. Keynes, "Some Economic Consequences of a Declining Population," *The Eugenics Review,* April 1937, p. 13.

[4]National Commission on the Causes and Prevention of Violence, *Commission Statement on Violent Crime,* November 1969, p. 16.

[5]Ansley J. Coale, "Should the United States Start a Campaign for Fewer Births?" *Population Index,* October-December 1968, p. 470.

[6]Jean Mayer, "Toward a Non-Malthusian Population Policy," *Columbia Forum,* Summer 1969, p. 5.

[7]*Ibid.*

Appendix A

[1] Edwin D. Goldfield, "Decennial Census and Current Population Survey Data on Income," in *Studies in Income and Wealth,* Vol. 23. Princeton, N.J., Princeton University Press, 1958, p. 43. This volume was based on a conference sponsored by the National Bureau of Economic Research.
[2] *Ibid.,* p. 56.
[3] *Ibid.,* pp. 211-12.

Index

Population growth (cont.)
 rate of, 124, 243
 and rising aggregate income (compared), 4-6
Poverty, 105-46
 anti-poverty programs, 106-10, 112-13
 defined, 110-12, 117-23
  incidence of poverty under alternative definitions (table), 121
 elimination of, 114-17
 as handed down, 112
 of immigrants, 111; see also Immigration
 as major issue, 2
 tables
  family food plan, 119
  income threshold, 118
  persons below poverty level by color, 122
  persons by poverty status, 125
  persons in families by poverty status, 128-29
 See also Income maintenance; Poor, the
Production workers, see Workers
Productivity, growing, 116
Professionals, 208-11
 earnings of (tables), 209, 210
Proprietors, salaries, 211-12
Protestants
 education of, 103-4; table, 104
 income of (table), 102
 in population, 101
Puerto Ricans, 88-94
 education of, 89, 167
 housing for, 89-91, 92; tables, 90, 92, 94
 immigration of, 91-94
 income of, 88-89, 92; tables, 89, 93
 in population, 88

Rand, Christopher, 91-93, 167
Randall, Clarence, 27
Real estate, wealth in, 162
Reinterview Surveys (RES), 255-56
 and census statistics (compared), 262-64; table, 264
Religion, 101-4
 educational status and, table, 103-4
 family income and, table, 102

Religion (cont.)
 occupational status and, 103-4; table, 104
RES, see Reinterview Surveys
Revelle, Roger, 3
Rich, the, 147-65; tables, 151, 158
 defined, 148-50
 distribution of wealth and, 156-58; table, 157
 employment of, 152-55; table, 153
 Lundberg on, 148, 152, 157-58
 See also Millionaires; Well-to-do
Riese, Hertha, 60
Riots
 conditions for, 86
 unemployment and Watts, 70
Roosevelt, Franklin D., 45, 107
Rustin, Bayard, 70, 113

Sample surveys, 30, 87; see also Current Population Survey
Samuelson, Paul, 45
Sandburg, Carl, 1-2
Saunders, Lyle, 98
Schiller, Patricia, 61
Semiskilled workers, incomes of, 215, 217; tables, 218-20
Service workers, incomes of, 215, 217-20; tables, 218, 220
Sex and ignorance, 61-62
Singer, Isaac Bashevis, 149
Slichter, Sumner, 46
Slums, 84-86, 107; tables, 85, 86; see also Housing; Immigration
Social security, 109
 for the poor, 130, 134-36
Sokolsky, George, 29
Sopkin, Charles, 164
Spanish-Americans, 95-101
 education of, 97-98; table, 97
 housing for, 99-101; table, 100
 income of, 96-99, 100-1; table, 96
 origins of, 95-96
 in population, 95
 See also Puerto Ricans
Statistics
 reliability of, 27-35
 validity of, 247-64
Stocks, wealth in, 162, 163
Students, see College students
Suburbs, growth of, 65-67; see also Cities